A SENSE OF ASIA

SOL SANDERS

A SENSE OF
ASIA

New York ✠ CHARLES SCRIBNER'S SONS

✤ ✤ *To that fraternity of "old hands"*
some in Asia and some in the West
some mentioned in these pages
some martyred for what they believed
who all have dreamed of a world
where differences of skin and culture
would be celebrated ✤

PREFACE ❈

Why another journalist's book on Asia?

One morning in the fall of 1947 I received a telephone call from Steve Siteman, assistant to the American Socialist leader, Norman Thomas. Steve told me he had had a visit from a young Asian student from Indochina. He had arrived in New York from Tokyo—like hundreds of other Asians through the years—with a letter of introduction to the veteran American radical. Thomas was well known throughout Asia, among the young nationalist intellectuals, as the foremost American friend of the independence movements.

As a young "yipsel"—a member of the Socialist Party's youth organization—I had concerned myself with Indonesia and its then current claim at the United Nations in New York for recognition. Steve had called me, he explained, because I "knew" about Indochina. But the young student insisted that he was a Vietnamese—whatever that was. Steve said he thought: Indonesia, Indochina, well. . . .

I "explained" to Steve that Vietnamese was the new name for Annamese, the principal racial group of French Indochina; that they had an independence movement; that while Ho Chi Minh, their leader, was a Communist, "we" had great hopes for their being weaned away.

Let me hasten to say that I was only twenty-one. I had spent a few months during World War II in India as an ambulance driver and, therefore, thought I knew everything about Asia as only a young self-styled radical could.

Twenty years later, a large part of which I have spent somewhere in Asia, that young Vietnamese is a veteran of many Saigon political skirmishes. Steve, like the rest of us, has learned in a bitter fashion where Vietnam is, why Indochina and Indonesia are not to be confused.

vii

PREFACE

And I? Well, I no longer have all the answers for what is happening in Asia.

This book was undertaken in the midst of the great debate over Vietnam. I returned to the United States on a sabbatical, to find a tremendous clash of opinion over what the U.S. was doing in Asia, whether it was doing it correctly, and, to many, whether we should be involved at all.

Leaving aside the exaggerations of those who seem to forget that all great decisions facing the United States have involved intellectual convulsions, it is clear that the "Asian question" will continue to divide our society for a long time.

I found it difficult to discuss the issues with Americans who had not lived and worked in Asia. And even among old friends who had shared some of these experiences, there was sometimes little common ground. It was this feeling of helplessness in putting forth my position in the debate that was the motivation for this book.

What I am trying to do here is, then, to give a set of premises, a list of basic assumptions, about what I think is going on in Asia. Out of these arise my answers, or at least my approaches, to the more particular problems of American foreign policy.

It is not meant to be a "tort" of the academic kind. No footnotes; only a few statistics. As the reader will soon find, I am a partisan of that hoary school of historians who believe that truth lies in a kind of intuitive judgment based on as much detail as an individual can acquire. I am not only intellectually opposed to the new computer approach to the social sciences, but I am frightened by what I believe are its implication for our thought processes.

If the reader discovers a welter of contradictions, I can only point to the infinite complications of life itself. Have we, particularly we Americans, not had enough of simplistic "golden key" formulas to domestic as well as foreign problems?

All I can do is say that this is what I saw, what I felt, what I experienced in much of the past two decades of working and living in Asia. I offer it only as a speculative framework for a discussion that will go on, hopefully, more productively with my friends.

CONTENTS ❋

PREFACE   *vii*

PART ONE ✤ THE ASIANS

1. A Geographical Expression   *3*

2. Countries, Not Nations   *28*

3. The Brown Sahibs   *48*

4. Autocrats in Search of Machines   *72*

PART TWO ✤ THE AMERICANS

5. The Establishment for Export   *103*

6. "Beautiful India, Beautiful America"   *132*

7. Pseudo-Sciences and the Professors   *165*

8. Asian Standard Time   *187*

PART THREE ✤ THE FUTURE

9. Twenty Lost Years   *205*

10. The Onrushing Catastrophe   *228*

ix

CONTENTS

11. No Escape from Commitment   *252*

12. The American As a Revolutionary   *277*

13. The Job   *298*

POSTSCRIPT: Articles of Faith   *314*

BIBLIOGRAPHY   *321*

INDEX   *331*

x

A SENSE OF ASIA

PART ONE ✽

THE
ASIANS

1 ✢

A Geographical Expression

TAKE a small airplane, as I did a few years ago, and fly at dawn from the old British Royal Air Force island base of Labuan in the South China Seas toward the mainland of Borneo.

Below you lies the sea and beyond the Borneo coast falls away —hundreds of thousands of square miles of virtually uninhabited virgin jungle, swamp, savannas, and towering in the background the thirteen-thousand-foot peak of Mt. Kinabulu in Sabah. On the horizon a tropical, molten sun quickly rises, pushing through layers of cloud and fog.

It is a sight of breath-taking beauty. One could imagine that this must have been what the world was like at some prehistoric beginning. Somewhere down below one could picture the dinosaurs just climbing out of the swamps. And some pre-human species might have been bounding along through the jungle.

The overwhelming impression of the vastness of nature, our tiny plane, my scheduled reporting pursuits against the background of the timelessness of Borneo, all inspired awe.

In trying to draw for a reader who has not been there a picture of what Asia is, it is one of the memories that come flooding back. But the jungles of Borneo are not typical of Asia. Nor, for that matter, are a thousand other landscapes I have seen and could describe. For there is no common climate, no common setting, no common civilization, and no common race in Asia.

Although the geographers may say differently, there are really no well-defined limits to the continent. Does Asia stop at Sinai— as the maps say in the West? Why? Certainly the Arab East, as the pan-Arab nationalists are wont to call it, is bound to the Maghreb and the Arabs who live in Africa—the same language, the same desert, the same modes of life. Or when you cross the Karakorams from India onto the Tibetan plateau in Ladakh, you have left the world of heat and teeming humanity behind for another world of the windswept, solitary plateaus of central Asia. Or looking across a river or a man-made barrier into China—as I have on so many occasions from India, from Vietnam, from the Hong Kong New Territories—you wonder if that vast expanse of China is not really another world totally unto itself.

General de Gaulle has talked of Europe from the Atlantic to the Urals. But the steppe culture does not halt on Asia's side of the Urals. Nor would the Soviet Union accept a definition of their nation that omits the three-fourths of its area and one-quarter of its population which is, formally, in Asia. To the south, Australia and New Zealand are increasingly becoming a part of Asia. The Australians used to joke when they spoke of "the Near North," substituting this phrase for the West's "Far East," when under Soekarno's dictatorship it looked like Indonesia was shaping up into a potential enemy. Now the phrase is common parlance "Down Under."

The truth is simple, of course. There is no Asia except as a rough geographic concept.

The very immensity of the continent precludes homogeneity. The land mass of Asia is four times that of Europe, including the European regions of the Soviet Union. It is more than twice the size of North America. Even including the vastness of the Canadian North and the Brazilian Amazonia, it is still larger than the whole land mass of the Western Hemisphere.

Distances in Asia usually catch the new arrival unawares. A Tokyo to Singapore jet trip, for example, is the equivalent of New York to Lisbon. Or the same distance from London east would put you down in the Persian Gulf outside the bounds of Europe, or south would take you below the Sahara to the heart of central Africa. From Tehran to Manila is as far as from San Francisco to

4

Honolulu and return. And the Indo-Pakistan "subcontinent" is just that, for Karachi to Madras is about the same distance as Paris to Kiev. Even with the speed of jet aircraft today, the Tokyo-Beirut trip across the belly of Asia is an in-flight journey of eighteen hours.

Asia's population, growing at a rate that can only be guessed at, is three times Europe's (including European Russia) and nearly nine times North America's. Today the majority of human beings are Asians—and increasingly that will be so. By 2000, two out of every three people on the planet will likely live somewhere in Asia.

If you think in terms of nation-states, of the seven largest countries by population in the world, only two—the U.S. and the Soviet Union—are outside Asia (and that is, of course, ignoring the fact that the Soviets are also Asian).

You get some feeling of the enormity of Asian populations from a little exercise which I did some years ago at the United Nations when the annual question of Chinese representation came before the General Assembly. The argument runs, of course, that the Chinese Nationalist regime in Taiwan (Formosa) does not represent China. In fact, it is asserted that it represents nothing and should be replaced by the Chinese Communists in Peking assuming China's seat both in the Assembly and as one of the five permanent members in the Security Council.

Whatever the merits of the debate, there is one interesting sidelight: Although Taiwan (if you omit all Chinese Nationalist pretensions to representing the people on the Mainland) is one of the smallest nations in East Asia—only Singapore, Laos, Cambodia, Malaysia, and Nepal have smaller populations—its thirteen million make it a fairly big state in the United Nations list. In the U.N. Taiwan ranks thirty-fourth, with nearly three-quarters of the United Nations members smaller than it.

But this vastness of Asia's geography and its peoples is only one aspect of its variety. The average Occidental appears to think in clichéd terms about Asia, attributing to all of it his acquaintance with one particular part. Neither palm trees nor terraced rice fields nor steppes predominate. China's Manchuria, like Russia's Siberia farther north, is among the coldest places in

5

the world in winter. Winter temperatures range from —17°F to 30°F. In the Indo-Pakistan Punjab plain, summer heat is excruciating. One of the hottest places in the world is in the western (Pakistan) Punjab where temperatures above 120°F have been recorded for long periods.

One of the world's largest deserts is the Gobi in Mongolia (six times as big as New York State). It is perhaps the driest place on earth, but only a few hundred miles south across the Himalayas in India's Assam state is one of the wettest places in the world— Cherrapunji, where an average of more than 450 inches of rain falls annually.

The Himalayas, the roof of the world, contain twenty-three peaks over 20,000 feet, including twelve of the thirteen highest mountains of the world. But directly below them and paralleling them for some two thousand miles across northern India is the Indo-Gangetic plain—one of the flattest parts of the world with a fall less than one thousand feet from the Indo-Pakistan border to the mouth of the Ganges-Brahmaputra in Bengal.

The jungles of the Sundarbans in East Pakistan are as dense and full of wild animals as any African gameland. Borneo abounds in wilderness, much of it still largely unexplored. But the plain of the Yellow River in North China may have been under cultivation longer than any other place in the world. And the recent discoveries of Mohenjo-Daro, a highly developed, urban civilization, in present-day Pakistan reveal that man lived and prospered in the valley of the Sind over four thousand years ago.

The varieties of physical environment are matched by the vast heterogeneity of Asian peoples. There is no common Asian physiological appearance, no common cultural pattern.

Take color. A Punjabi from the northwestern regions of the Indian subcontinent could easily pass as a Mediterranean European (many Punjabis are doing just that in Britain and West Germany today). In fact, Pathans, the Persian-speaking tribes of the Northwest Frontier of Pakistan and Afghanistan, are often blond or redheaded. Japanese from the northern areas of Honshu Island, the main island of the archipelago, are often lighter-skinned than Americans of Italian or Mexican ancestry.

Although the epicanthic fold of the eyelid—what makes some

Oriental people look like they have "slanted" eyes—is considered a standard characteristic of Japanese and Chinese by most Westerners, it is not necessarily true. In China this characteristic appears at most among half the population, sometimes in some areas in only one out of five persons.

Most peasants in the southern Indian state of Tamiland are a gray-black, darker than many American Negroes. But they do not have the flaring nostrils and other characteristics of most African black-skinned peoples. Yet the Malay peoples of Southeast Asia often have just these characteristics but are much lighter-skinned than most black Africans.

Many years ago I was touring Indonesia in the party of President Soekarno. We were being entertained by a military pipe band from the island of Ambon in east Indonesia. I had a strong sense of having heard and seen the whole performance and situation before.

And then I remembered that it reminded me very strongly of a Mexican troupe I had seen. One of the accompanying cabinet ministers, Dr. Johannes Leimena, himself an Ambonese, pointed out that many parts of east Indonesia were heavily influenced by the Portuguese. It was one of the places the incredible Jesuit, Francis Xavier, visited on his missionary travels in East Asia. There was a certain amount of miscegenation at a time when the population was only a fraction of what it is today. An Indonesian anthropologist has estimated that one in ten Indonesians has European blood—given the huge expansion of population (more than thirty-five times in Java alone) since Dutch influence began. So the similarity to a mestizo group in Mexico was probably more real than imagined.

INDIANS VIS-À-VIS CHINESE

If Asians do not resemble each other physically, the cultural dissimilarities are equally strong. Nowhere is the contrast so strong as between the Indians and the Chinese—the two largest bodies of people on the continent.

The Indian lives in the present. He expresses himself well verbally, and volubly. He is tolerant to the point of indifference

7

about his neighbors and his environment. He has a vast ability to see problems from a number of perspectives—it is no accident that modern European philosophies of relativism trace their ancestry, in part, to the eighteenth- and nineteenth-century interest of the German philosophers in philology, Sanskrit, and Indian philosophy.

The Chinese is pragmatic, highly motivated toward concrete accomplishments. He is literal, and visually oriented, conceptualizes in writing if literate. It is not uncommon to see two educated Chinese explaining themselves, one to the other, by "writing" imaginary Chinese ideographs in the palms of their hands in order to distinguish homonyms. There is not much interest or tolerance of anything but the generally accepted orthodoxy of the moment. There is an admiration for accomplishment. And interest in speculative thinking is only toward some formula which may work out problems on a grand scale—a kind of magic key to life. The Chinese has a profound sense of history, a chronology that precedes him and moves into the future through his children.

Is it not significant that the Indians burn their dead, throw their ashes into the rivers, while the Chinese have always made the tomb and the records of the dead the center of their whole culture?

Contrast the fact that some South Indian cultures have left enormous physical ruins, but almost no literary record of their regimes. Chinese dynasties, on the other hand, kept elaborate journals—sometimes counterfeiting what went before in order to make a point but nevertheless with a deep sense of record-keeping.

One of the great mysteries of civilization is the difference between Indian and Chinese absorption of the stranger. Today in India, you can find two families living side by side with no apparent physiological differences. Yet one will claim that because his ancestors in perhaps some mythical past came from some other area of the subcontinent, or perhaps crossed from beyond the Himalayas, he is apart. He worships different gods, eats different foods, puts on different dress than his neighbor.

In China, by contrast, there is a vast range of physiological types who have been assimilated. People who only a few generations ago—in the long history of this part of the world—were members of tribal societies have taken on the Han culture, Chinese written language, the Confucian ethic, and so forth.

There were remnant Jewish communities in South India when Israel was created in 1948, most of whom emigrated to the Zionist state. Only graves remained to mark the lost identity—lost through assimilation—of the once large and prosperous Jewish colony which existed from the second century B.C. to as late as the eighteenth century in northern China.

An Indian diplomat once remarked to me on this basic difference between the two cultures and told his own story: As a young man in Bengal, he had studied Chinese history and language at Rabindranath Tagore's university. Just before the outbreak of the Japanese war in China in 1937, he went to Nationalist China to study and teach in a university.

Later, as the Chinese Nationalist regime had to retreat before the Japanese advance, he moved with one of the "refugee" universities into southwestern China. It was a remote area far from other foreigners.

"I ate Chinese food all the time," my friend said. "I spoke Chinese; I wore a Chinese robe. Despite my dark skin and my obvious foreign physical characteristics, my Chinese colleagues and my students accepted me as one of them. And I felt my own identity slipping away from me. Had I not left, surely I would have become Chinese."

In India today one has just the opposite sense of this Chinese process of homogenization. The peculiar system of caste and subcaste appears to grow, not to amalgamate, or to be dynamited even by the impact of modern technology and the demands of modern industrial organization.

In fact, one sees the possibility of new subcaste groups being created almost before your eyes. Just as today you have caste groups who derive their identity from their occupations in a relatively remote past—the *Kaistes,* for example, who were Hindu bureaucrats under the Moslem Moghul rule—one might guess that such new groups are forming.

The great majority of secretaries of a particular sort—that is, secretary in the American sense of an employee who is stenog-

9

rapher, typist, appointments secretary, and *chef de cabinet*—in the modernized offices of Bombay, New Delhi, and increasingly in Calcutta, are an example. They are recruited almost exclusively from Indian Christians of the Portuguese East Indian and Goan communities.

There are very few Indians of other caste groups entering this "profession." It remains to be seen, of course, whether these new occupational groups, drawn from older caste roles, will remain as rigidly apart as groupings have been in the past.

My own feeling is that they will. Caste newspapers, increased communication among members of a group, the electoral system in independent India which has resulted in caste-bloc voting, and an increasingly competitive political and economic system appear to some Indian and foreign sociologists to have reinforced rather than undermined the structure of caste.

JAPANESE PEOPLE

But if Indians and Chinese have their peculiar cultural identities, hard to define but so different from one another, so do the Japanese.

John Donne could not have written his "Devotions XVII" had he been a Japanese poet. For the Japanese are, each, "an island unto himself." There are no more solitary individuals on the face of the earth; unable to communicate except in either clichés or bursts of emotion among themselves, much less with the outsider. The average Japanese is "a loner" in modern American parlance.

No one since the Greeks has cherished tragedy like the modern Japanese. The standard Japanese contemporary movie plot usually involves a love affair that is doomed from the beginning, a suicide or two, catastrophe following catastrophe. But it is not American soap opera; there is no real hope that in some fashion or another everything will come out all right.

The Japanese "know" that it doesn't. The mood of love affairs is "fall" not "spring" as in Western popular literature. And a tragic ending to a film or popular love story in the magazines is as clichéd in Japan as "the happy ending" with "boy gets girl" in the West.

One of the prices the Japanese have paid for the modernization of their country in less than a hundred years is widespread great feelings of social insecurity. In the effort to make life livable, to cover up for this insecurity in social situations, the Japanese try to channel behavior in totally formal and predictable patterns. Almost any act becomes ceremonial—at least in the eyes of a Westerner.

A few years ago a journalist friend and his wife, both Americans, moved into a new neighborhood in Japan. The wife had grown up in Honolulu. Her family had had a Japanese servant when she was young, and as a child she spoke the language with some facility. One of the rituals which she was expected to perform in the new Tokyo neighborhood was a call on a neighbor.

The neighbor was an elderly *grande dame* of the old regime, a member of the imperial court in the prewar period. My friend's wife knew that it was to be a formal interview.

She consulted her Japanese women friends and they, in turn calling on their mothers, told her of what the interview would consist. The group then proceeded to literally script the whole conversation. My friend's wife, at her cosmetic table in the mornings during the next month, memorized what she was to say to the former peeress and what the old lady would say in return.

When she actually made the call, the old lady, after two or three salutations and replies, took a deep breath through her teeth in the Japanese manner, knowing that she was dealing with a "pro," someone who knew the ritual. The ceremony came off without a hitch. And the old lady later told a mutual acquaintance that my friend's wife "was a young lady properly brought up."

In a minor way, I often have had the same experience in Tokyo. I speak rather rudimentary Japanese, but I can make myself understood to taxi drivers. When I enter the cab and give the address to which I am going, a conversation usually ensues. And I can predict, almost without exception, what the first five or ten minutes of that conversation will be. The questions are always the same, and my replies are standard for those foreigners who have lived for some time in Japan.

Like most residents in Japan, I have spent many hours in Tokyo's 15,000 bars. The enormous number is often explained in sociological terms as simply the retreat of men from the fantastically crowded (by Western standards) aspects of Japanese family life. Most foreigners also assume a great deal of sexual promiscuity in Japanese life, with the bars serving as rendezvous places.

Yet I think this explanation is not the correct one. A Japanese man retreats to the bar after his work day in a crowded and frenzied office for the same reason that an American—or a European —often finds it so much easier, in an emotional crisis, to "pour out his heart" to a stranger.

The average Japanese bar girl is far more of a "soft shoulder to cry on" than she is a bewitching sex symbol. I am convinced that far less often than it is assumed, the relations of the bar girl and customer are asexual.

In fact, she plays the role of the historic *geisha*, but to a much wider segment of the society because of the rising standard of living which permits bar expenditures for even a "salary man" (white collar worker) today. This is one of confidante, counselor, innocent playmate, but rarely sex partner.

My point is that because of his isolation, the average Japanese male has this need for a friendly ear far more often than does his Western (or other Asian) counterpart.

There is another current which marks Japanese personality and life and sets it apart from other Asians and to a considerable extent from the other industrialized societies. It is the Japanese feeling for beauty. I know of no other society where it is so strong, with perhaps the exception of the island of Bali in Indonesia.

You find even the most mundane Japanese businessman, the most brutalized manual laborer, or isolated farmer has a strong empathy for artistic expression. And I believe that by any objective standards their artistic values are sensitive and intelligent.

It arises out of an unspoken but profoundly felt Japanese animism which has continued almost unmodified into the twentieth century. It continues despite the imposition of Buddhism and other religious influences from China on this earlier Japanese cultural concept. And it has survived the introduction of Western science and technology. It is amoral.

One example that comes to mind is a Japanese restaurant I used to visit in the Shinjuku area of Tokyo—a kind of combination of

Greenwich Village of other years, Chelsea in London, and South Chicago. This particular restaurant had one specialty of the house. There was a large tank containing live river carp. They were served on a dish surrounded by seaweed and sprays of other greenery.

But the fish was served alive. Its flanks were filleted by strokes of the knife and chunks of flesh were made convenient to be detached with chopsticks. The fish was arranged in a dramatic pose, "stood" on his tail by being impaled on a chopstick. It very much resembled the idealized trout "in flight" caught by a fisherman that decorates the covers of an American sports magazine.

The fish was very much alive. And, sometimes, while I and my friends were removing the pieces of flesh, eating them raw, the fish would flip off the dish into the air. When we had had enough of the raw fish, the carcass, including the head—revered in Japan and China as it is in Central Europe as the best part of the fish and the delicacy reserved for the head of the family—was sent back to the kitchen to be made into a delicious soup which was served as the second course.

This method of serving fish is traditional in Japan, although discouraged these days because of the widespread presence of a liver fluke, a very insidious parasite, in some Japanese rivers.

My point, though, is that none of my Japanese friends ever considered the question of "cruelty" to the fish. Nor did the idea occur to them that the whole episode might be considered a revolting spectacle. The standard—and I believe heartfelt expression—when the fish was brought to us was: "Beautiful, isn't it?" And, indeed, by a standard of aesthetics which I grew accustomed to, it was a glorious sight.

Or take the case of a Japanese novelty which has become almost a standard item in the shops in the U.S. selling knickknacks: It is a group of real butterflies, encased in a sheet of plastic film to be used as a place setting for a dining table. It is an idea that would have occurred to no one else, perhaps, but the Japanese.

The very concept of the Japanese garden is another facet of the very special character of this original people. While the Italians and the French formalize their settings with gravel paths, marble statues, and geometric designs, and the English, however neat the arrangements, like a riot of different flowers growing as spectacularly as nature will permit in their miserable climate, the Japanese attempt something else.

A Japanese garden is nature recreated in microcosm. There is logic in this because of the extremely limited space—only 15 per cent of the total area of Japan is arable. But it is a nature in which beauty is a result of the most brutal processes. Trees are purposely miniaturized, limbs are broken and twisted to achieve a sense of time and struggle (in part patterned on the legendary landscapes of the western China river gorges).

Nothing is allowed to grow "free" and "naturally." Miracles are accomplished with care that defies all comparison with the attention which even the most assiduous English gardener lavishes on his lawns. What Westerner has not marveled, the first time he has seen a Tokyo garden literally wrapped up for the winter?

I do not minimize the achievement. Tokyo is the only large city in the world where you can turn the corner from the worst chaos of the modern industrial society and see a tiny oasis of "nature."

When I moved into a paper and plywood Japanese house in the heart of Tokyo, the gardener of an American friend within a matter of hours turned my rubbish-ridden backyard of only fifteen or twenty square feet into a marvelous miniature garden that shut out the world (except for the rumble of the streetcar out front that shook my fragile little house constantly).

It was replete with twelve- to fifteen-foot tall evergreen trees, a traditional stone lamp, and a tiny fountain—all this only a few feet from the "concrete and neon jungle" that characterizes much of Tokyo.

Paralleling this special Japanese sense of beauty is a basic animistic concept that all things have life and being, perhaps equally shared among things we term animate and inanimate. It accounts for the Japanese love and attractive use of stones in gardens.

But it has other fascinating facets:

One day I left my office with my very intelligent and very "Westernized" young Japanese secretary. She had been educated in part in the United States, spoke English very well. And she had an enormous capacity not only for detail in our office, but also for larger concepts ranging from economics to being a very shrewd judge of personalities.

As we approached my automobile, I remarked that there was a short in its electrical system. I said the proof was that my tail brake lights were burning, even though the brake was not on (we were approaching the car from the rear).

Her answer was rather startling: "But the lights wouldn't go on in the daytime." I puzzled over that one for a second, and I soon realized that there was no confusion of language. Rather, until I joked her out of it, my young friend's subconscious assumption was that the car, itself, had a "mind" of its own, a will, and responded to daylight in an "intelligent" fashion.

More than anything else, perhaps, the Japanese set themselves apart by their whole concept of work. Nowhere in the world—not even in Germany—do work and activity for their own sake play the role they do in Japanese life and personality.

I have teased some of my Japanese friends for years that their frenzied activity is sometimes self-defeating. One of my favorite examples is what happens on the typical Japanese airliner, as distinguished from the typical American commercial plane:

If you ring the button on one of the European or American carriers for service, the result is either a measured response; that is members of the crew had decided at an earlier time which one is to serve you, or there is a small "debate" as to who is going to handle it at the service center. But in a Japanese plane, the normal reaction is for all those crew members not otherwise engaged momentarily to fall over one another descending on your seat to see what must be done.

In a sense, economic development on the grand scale follows this pattern in the Japanese economy. Japanese steel companies, which expanded production capacity by 30 per cent in one year in 1967, grow not in relation to market estimates or sales developments, but rather in a kind of competitive race for maintaining or pushing their position among the ranks of the Japanese steel producers.

This growth is rationalized by the economists in terms of Japan's very real need to expand her markets, particularly her overseas markets, to pay for the overwhelming proportion of the raw materials she must import from abroad to keep going. Virtually the only thing the Japanese have to sell is their own labor, and, obviously, the more they can put into a product—with any amount of efficiency—the more they can "earn" for their own consumption at home. So increased activity conforms with the whole pattern of increasing the size of the economy in order to raise living standards. But underlying all this is the Japanese need to keep moving, to work hard, to maintain frenzied activity for its own sake.

This also results in the famous and enormous Japanese capacity for detail. Sometimes the larger picture of what is happening in their own society and the world is lost by this concentration on detail. An American or another foreigner (and it is also significant that the word for foreigner in Japanese is literally "outside person") often becomes immediately an oracle in Japan, no matter his qualifications, if he is able to generalize on issues, especially on those concerning the Japanese themselves. They will accept generalizations from a foreigner, often based on less information than they themselves have, mostly because few Japanese have the "chutzpah" for that kind of formulation.

INDONESIAN PEOPLE

If the Japanese are particularists, absorbed by detail, haunted by "a work psychosis," the Javanese of Indonesia in Southeast Asia is a totally different being.

Here—as in India—one wonders how much the ideal conditions for the basic necessities of life created by the climate for a small population must have established the norms for Javanese culture at some time in pre-history. Rice culture must have made the food problem the most simple possible for the early Javanese.

Even the problem of water was readily solved, with the steep slopes of the volcanic mountains providing beds for the streams that could be so easily—in the sense of technology—guided onto the terraced rice fields. Here was none of the enormous problem of China or North Vietnam, where rivers must be diked and held in check lest they wipe out huge areas of the fertile plain during the rainy season and flood tide.

Javanese culture is eclectic to a degree which no foreigner finds comprehensible. A Javanese is, nominally at least, a Moslem. But his basic fatalism, his passivity, his acceptance of class and caste, come out of the mainstream of Indian tradition which is far older.

His society is highly class oriented. Yet his village life comes close to primitive communism—or as one authority has put it, "a shared poverty." His life is controlled by a complicated pattern of European law and *adat* (indigenous but coded mores and folkways). Yet he is capable of outbursts of violence and anarchy which rival anything known anywhere in Asia ("amok" is a Malay-Javanese word from which we borrow our own "to run amuck").

No Javanese will deny that he loves intrigue; he loves intrigue even if only for the sake of plotting. At any time, even the most simple Javanese peasant moves on several levels of relationships, much as a Westerner must in his much more intense and competitive society. He is generally much more confident in his relationships with others than the Japanese. Unlike the Japanese, he assimilates to outside influence easily—if only superficially. (He is as good a linguist, usually, as the Japanese is a poor one.) After 350 years of Dutch colonial rule, the penetration of many Western concepts is probably much deeper in the Javanese village society than in most of the former colonial societies, even including India.

He is, therefore, far better at carrying on communication not only with Westerners, but also with other Asians. My own experience, for example, is that there is much more understanding between Japanese and Indonesians, largely because of this Indonesian capacity to get through, than between any other South Asians and the Japanese.

All this permits the Indonesian of today often to compromise the uncompromisable.

"Musjarawah," the traditional way of solving village issues and problems in Java, is an expression of this spirit. The villagers gather for a kind of town meeting. They discuss the issue, the decision, or the problem. But, unlike a New England town meeting, for example, where there must eventually be a vote, no outright decision is ever taken. The villagers simply continue to talk, sometimes for hour after hour, until some consensus (*mufakat*) is arrived at about how to handle the particular issue.

In 1966 and 1967 the Indonesians kept President Soekarno on in a strictly titular position as chief of state for more than two years. Only by a fluke of history was the acting president during this period, General Soeharto, not murdered in an attempted Communist coup d'état. Yet it is clear that leaders of the present regime and the majority of the political elite believe Soekarno was implicated in the attempt of the Communists to take power by force in 1965. Out of that came a bloody but brief civil war in which tens of thousands of people were killed. It brought about a virtual total reorientation of Indonesia's foreign policy (in 1965 Soekarno spoke of the Peking-Hanoi-Djakarta-Pyongyang axis).

If you look around the world at the many convulsions that have wracked the underdeveloped countries, the Indonesian ability to "slide" from one political stance to another, to preserve forms without content from one political period to another, is unparalleled. It is a product of this—sometimes maddening for Westerners—Indonesian ability to synthesize and amalgamate totally conflicting ideological positions.

THAI PEOPLE

CONTRASTED to the Javanese strong instinct of compromise and to become a part of the group is the Thai. For the Thai, in their own language "the Free People," are just that. It is hard to conceive outside Asia, and certainly not on the continent, a society so little hidebound as the Thai. Over and over again, students of Thai history and culture, comparing their society to the Vietnamese nearby, or to the Japanese and Chinese, have been struck by this vivid contrast. They are the rugged individualists of Southeast Asia.

Such ironclad Confucian doctrines in neighboring Vietnam as parental fealty are totally different in Thailand. Relations between parents and child might well fit the more permissive standards which have become popular in the U.S., post-Dewey and post-Spock. While Thai royalty and the court have all the outward manifestations of Hindu monarchy (from which they draw much of their trappings), it is significant that caste is virtually nonexistent. And, in fact, members of the royal family drop one degree of their royalty with each generation until the fourth generation again reverts to commoner.

My own experiences with villagers in remote areas of the country have reinforced the feeling one quickly gets in the cities that they are an uninhibited and outspoken people. During reporting of the insurgency in northeastern Thailand, villagers told me—in front of government officials—all sorts of damaging stories against the authorities. The most popular ballad in the 1960s, "Pu Yai Li" (Headman Li), pokes fun at a government-trained rural development worker and village official.

I would guess that this individualism is one of the principal explanations for the present rapid economic development in Thailand.

One finds village boys who have hardly worn shoes before they become truck drivers. Young girls who come into Bangkok looking for jobs within weeks dress and comport themselves like their sophisticated Sino-Thai sisters who are native to the capital. One finds young people in Bangkok, more than anywhere else in Asia with perhaps the exception of Japan, terribly current about Hollywood movies, youth styles in fashion and entertainment, and all the advantages and disadvantages of the latest transistor radio.

One of the brightest young executives on the Thailand National Planning Board says that the main Thai problem is one of waiting until present generation top officials die off. Then, he says, new standards of public office responsibility and approach to problems will come with the new, modern-trained younger bureaucrats. With them, and the technological changes going on in the private sector of the economy, Thailand could be the first tropical country to reach economic "takeoff."

These vast differences among the Asians add up to one important fact: There is no pan-Asian culture as such.

Even the classic conditions of underdevelopment, in the sense that term is used in the Western world, are not common to all

Asians. Witness the fact that Japan is a major industrial power, that India and Pakistan are among the poorest.

The colonial period in recent Asian history has reinforced these differences in myriad ways. During the last one hundred years, as communications have increased in Asia, there has been a "colonial cultural distortion." From the standpoint of what was available, of what was useful to him for his own betterment economically and socially, and what was available to him in terms of formal education, the Asian living in a colonial environment has been bound to the "metropole."

A Vietnamese middle-class student in Hanoi learned a great deal about France and French history. If he were ambitious, chances were that he thought of continuing his studies in France. If he were a Chinese in Singapore, he either followed the conservative local Chinese education—later radical, when the Communists took over in the Mainland—or British education in Singapore or in Britain itself, or went to China to study the classics. If he were a Javanese or Sumatran, Dutch became the key to opening locked doors—if it were possible at all. The Japanese, busily concerned since the middle of the nineteenth century in learning what had gone on during their centuries of isolation from the Western world, turned in on himself except for his imported technology and culture from the West.

Therefore, there was little interest, much less communication, even by next-door neighbors. Most Vietnamese, Thai, Indonesians, Filipinos, and Indians, even those who had money to travel abroad, never thought of visiting their neighbors until the past decade or so.

Even now, most of the youth who take up either seriously or faddishly ideas from abroad get them from the West, not from their Asian neighbors. Social science research, for example, which has blossomed in the Asian universities based on European and American techniques, is rarely concerned with areas outside national boundaries unless it is Europe and the U.S. Indian, and lately Japanese, films have some interest in Southeast Asia. But the American and European films are far and away preferred, even when the subject matter would seem to a Westerner totally incomprehensible to local audiences.

UNIFIERS/DIVIDERS

ALL of this is not to say, of course, that there are not unifying factors that tie parts of the Asian cultures together. Throughout South Asia, for example, the basis of all traditional art—painting, sculpture, music, dancing, storytelling, and literature—are the Indian legends of the Ramayana and the Mahabharata. And this wealth of plot and philosophical concept spreads even into Northeast Asia through the impact of Buddhism —a religion of Indian origins. The Confucian ethic is basic not only to the culture of China, but to Korea, Japan and Vietnam, as well.

Yet for all this, there are crosscurrents that block off the effects of these cultural contacts.

A few years ago I discussed with an old Indian acquaintance the striking fact that India seemed oblivious to the political influence of other nearby countries. I wondered, for example, if the young members of the Indian elite might not react, eventually, violently to the image of the growing ineffectiveness that India was giving the world. I suggested that one great factor in the political revolutions that have continually rocked the underdeveloped world was a sense of shame on the part of the new generations, in contact with their own age groups around the world, of the inefficiency, the lack of power, the "backwardness" of their countries. Would this not eventually find a reflection among young Indians?

Would they not finally seek some new radical solution to their problems simply on the basis of their *amour propre* vis-à-vis other smaller but more dynamic societies in Asia, Africa, and Europe. After all, I pointed out, had not Gandhi in part taken up the issue of Indian self-government and liberation because of his experiences as an Indian in Africa and as a believer in nonviolence with roots in the Anglo-Saxon countries, Christianity, and Russian mysticism, as well as in Indian Hinduism and Buddhism?

My friend replied he thought not, that he thought India was relatively impervious to such outside "moral" pressure. Why? Because the Indian society is so vast, so disparate, so filled with its own contradictions that it forms a "universe" unto itself. Except for relatively small immigrant groups in other parts of Asia, Africa, Western Europe, and the South Seas, Hindu society, unlike the other great world religions, has no converts beyond the confines of the subcontinent.

This Hindu "universe," with its fifteen major languages, its thousands of castes, and tens of thousands of subcastes, contains all the divisions of the great outside world. There are all religions, for Hinduism finds expression in monotheism, deism, agnosticism, atheism, animism, and hundreds of forms of mysticism, pietism, quietism, and ecclesiastical organization and ritual. Hindus are "white" and "black," Caucasian and Mongoloid, wealthy and impoverished, highly sophisticated and tribal. (There are probably fifty million tribal people in the present Indian state.)

This means that an Indian once inside his "Hindu universe" rarely compares himself to anyone outside it; he draws whatever inferences he does about his own behavior and his life from the thousands of comparisons possible inside this "universe." And, in fact, once inside India, there are no Indians—only Brahmins, Punjabis, Keralites, etc., social groups made up of the thousands of divisions along caste, linguistic, regional, and occupational lines.

Any Indian automatically finds himself in half a dozen of these divisions. And if he is English-speaking, and therefore among the elite of the population, he is also a member of a supra-caste group, the current ruling elite. I say "current" because almost any Indian caste, except the more than sixty million in the Untouchable categories, looks back to some golden past when his particular "people" were rulers somewhere in the subcontinent.

Islam, the religion of the Mohammedans, is a unifying force in Asia that sweeps across boundaries. But it is equally a disrupting influence in some national scenes. India is an excellent example. The educated Indian or Pakistani Moslem rarely questions whether some Western import in the realm of ideas or amenities is consistent with his background. It is the first question an educated Hindu puts to himself.

That means, to use Khrushchev's phrase about the Jews of the Soviet Union, that the educated Moslem in the subcontinent is a "rootless cosmopolitan." And, in fact, it was true in British Indian days that the leaders of much of the Moslem elite in Hyderabad, Calcutta, Bombay, Karachi, and even in Lucknow and Allahabad had family and close cultural ties with other areas of the Moslem world.

It explains, in part, the long honeymoon between the Pakistanis and the Anglo-Americans after independence, before Ayub Khan became disenchanted with the U.S. and switched his foreign policy to a careful game of balancing Communist China against the U.S. and the Soviet Union—and India.

I believe it is a truism that few foreigners would deny that other things being equal, a Westerner finds himself more at home with an Indian Moslem than with a Hindu. True enough that, at the level of the peasantry, the differences can be easily exaggerated. But among the educated, the Moslem is a member of an international community, varied, colorful and attractive. Whether it is as real an issue as he supposes or not, he sees himself as a member of "a people of the book," the Bible, and Mohammed's instructions were that Jews and Christians were not in the same category as "the Kaffir," the nonbeliever in the Mosaic tradition. It also goes far to explain the basic problem dividing the two new countries of India and Pakistan, so similar in so many ways.

Again, take a similarly striking example of ethnocentricity among the Chinese.

ASIANS ON ASIANS

ONE of my Asian acquaintances—actually American but born in China of missionary parents and married to a Chinese with most of her life spent either in China or among the Overseas Chinese of Southeast Asia—made a first visit to India a few years ago. Like so many of the Americans of her background, she shares all the Chinese prejudices; in fact, may reflect them more strongly than the Chinese themselves. (A Chinese friend tells me the most bitter controversies he has ever heard are between retired American missionaries who have served in China and those who served in Japan during the tragic events of the 1930s and who now live together in retirement in a church-supported institution in the U.S.)

I asked her what were her impressions of India after her trip.

23

Her reply was quick. She spat out the words: "Ha! Five thousand years of culture and they haven't yet thought to take two twigs and put them together to eat with."

The reference is, of course, to the fact that most Indians eat with their hands, and, in fact, among South Indian Brahmins, there are severe strictures against doing anything else. The Chinese, of course, traditionally eat with chopsticks.

Many, perhaps most, present-day Chinese still have little but contempt for Asian peoples outside the Chinese world. There is a grudging respect for the Westerner and his power. But the whole philosophical background of the Chinese name for their own country, "the Middle Kingdom," the center of the universe, is very real. Among Chinese with less education, it takes a form of aloofness rather than even condescension toward other Asians. It is less offensive generally to Southeast Asians—caught "in the middle"—than the haughtiness of so many Indians abroad, but it is just as strong.

Such attitudes often prevent communication among Asians. Japanese inflexibility, inadaptability outside the Japanese environment, is a constant impediment to Japan's relations with the rest of Asia. Recently, a Japanese economist took a party of high-powered industrialists on a tour of India. Most of his compatriots had never visited there before. I heard from several sources that most of the party never got over their initial shock at the poverty, the filth, and the general wretchedness of the Indian cities they visited. And, instead of providing an opportunity for greater exchange of ideas with the possibility of increased Japanese investment and technical assistance to the Indians, the expedition was a disaster.

This Japanese reaction to India is typical. I have seen on the ground repeatedly that even the Americans, for example, who notoriously find conditions in India extremely trying, do better at adjusting to the less developed parts of Asia than the more inflexible Japanese.

A few years ago a Japanese banker, an acquaintance of a close Japanese friend, quit his post as manager of the Calcutta branch of one of the major Japanese banks. It was a shock to his Japanese colleagues. For in Japan virtually no one leaves his place "on the escalator" of a career laid out in one of the major Japanese companies. Job security is one cornerstone of Japanese life. And once you begin the long ladder of slow, but seemingly inevitable, promotion toward early retirement, few professionals dare to abandon it. Fierce and unquestioning loyalty to the company is a characteristic of Japanese business life unknown in America, and virtually passing out of existence in Western Europe.

But the banker's reaction to Calcutta's poverty, filth, and degradation was so emotional that he could not support it. He came back to Tokyo and told his friend, simply: "No human being should have to live in Calcutta."

The total inability of the Japanese to understand their fellow Asians during their occupation of China and Southeast Asia in World War II equaled their brutal methods of police persecution and slave labor. My older friends in Southeast Asia all have their tens of stories about "the ugly Japanese."

One of the most humorous was told me by an Indonesian friend: Before the war, Charles Tambu had worked for a British-owned newspaper in Singapore. All his life Charles bore the scars of the petty affronts he had to suffer during his career there because of the color of his skin.

When the Japanese defeated the British, he joined—as did many other idealistic young Asians—the Japanese, believing that they really meant what they said in their slogan of "the East Asia Co-Prosperity Sphere." Charles worked in a Japanese propaganda office, translating and writing in English for broadcast to the English-speaking areas of Asia.

When a Japanese officer slapped a young Malay employee, he complained bitterly. The Japanese chief accepted the complaint, thought about it for a few days. Then one morning he called my friend into his office. He explained that slapping in the Japanese army was not a serious penalty. He then said, "Wait, I will show you." He then proceeded to call in a younger Japanese officer, revile him over some trivial mistake, and then slap him from across the desk. The younger Japanese officer was dismissed, he saluted and left the room.

The Japanese colonel turned to Charles and said, "You see." It was all my friend could do to keep from laughing. He let the whole matter drop. And the Japanese colonel, apparently, was never any the wiser. It never occurred to him that in the Hindu-Buddhist world, the head is sacred, and that one must not touch another's head, even, for example, in Thailand to pat affectionately the head of a child in passing.

I saw a striking example of the insensitivity of even Southeast Asians to other Southeast Asians during a state visit in 1965 of Indonesia's Soekarno to Cambodia. Soekarno was given a speech of welcome on the airstrip by Cambodia's Prince Sihanouk. He replied with one of his typical demagogic orations. He told the audience that he was happy to be in Phnom Penh again, for he felt "more at home in Cambodia than any place else outside my own country."

Soekarno then gave his reasons: He said that he was always glad to be there, to be with his "fellow anti-neo-colonialist fighter, His Royal Highness Prince Norodom Sihanouk." But then he gave a second reason. He said that the present kingdom of Cambodia had once been part of the Shrivijaiya empire centering on Java. Sihanouk's face fell during this reference by Soekarno, his smile froze; it was obvious that he was less than happy with any ancient claim that Soekarno might hint at against his country. Shortly afterward he was to attack Soekarno and the Indonesians bitterly.

The long destruction of traditional contacts among the Asians throughout the colonial period also leads to a reliance on almost Jungian race memory. Until recently, for example, a Thai mother in the countryside would threaten a misbehaving child with the *pu-mah*. This is a reference to the Burmese who, in a series of bitter wars in the eighteenth century, beat the Thai, sacked their highly developed capital of Ayudthia, and drove the center of the Thai state south to the present site of Bangkok.

Despite the borrowing by the Vietnamese of almost every facet of Chinese life—Confucianism, Buddhism, the mandarin system, the concept of the emperor as the son of heaven, food, and even the lovely *ao dai* costume of the women—anti-Chinese feeling is an accepted "norm." One finds even Vietnamese with great sophistication expressing the most trite racist attitudes toward the Chinese.

This diversity and vastness of the continent makes speaking of a cultural community almost impossible. The whole diffuseness of the Asian world is further spun out by two other conditions within today's Asian states: They are, in large part, geographical monstrosities created by artificial political divisions, largely the result of the colonial conquests of the Europeans. And within each of the new states such contradictions have been set up among various peoples and classes that unity at a "national" level is at best precarious. It is to these questions that we now direct our attention.

2 ✦

Countries, Not Nations

ONE of my most curious if pleasant weekends spent in Asia was a holiday on a lovely coffee plantation in one of the hill stations of South India. The tenuous connection among the guests—myself excluded—was an allegiance to the Moral Rearmament Movement.

The party consisted of my host, a retired Indian army general; his brother, a local coffee planter; a World War II Japanese general and "war criminal"; and a young Naga. The Nagas are a tribal people of northeastern India; their leaders, curiously enough, for the most part converts to American Baptism.

After a long conversation over tea, the brother of our host turned to the young Naga—both of them Indians, mind you —and said, "And what country are you from?"

It was ironic but perfectly comprehensible—and a little sad.

The planter, a tawny South Indian of tribal descent, had been discussing various subjects in a group with the young Naga. The young man, a nephew of the leader of the underground independence movement among the Nagas against the Indian central government, had punctuated the whole conversation with phrases like "we Indians. . . ." But he had not gotten through to the planter.

His appearance, Mongoloid and not unlike that of a young Japanese businessman of his age, plus his Columbia University accent, had built a psychological wall between him and his fellow

Indian. Ironically, his own political outlook was that the Nagas should remain "Indians"—remain within the Indian union with a maximum of local control over their affairs. As a believer in M.R.A., his position was that peaceful reconciliation between the Nagas and the other Indian peoples was the only way to solve the insurgency which at that time had been going on in Nagaland for more than a decade.

These kinds of racial, linguistic, and psychological barriers within the new countries of South Asia are more the rule than the exception. They are the product of an artificial creation of nations. Throughout Asia there are two dozen countries which have come into being since the end of World War II by the withdrawal of European colonial rule. Their boundaries often cut across historic, racial, linguistic, and natural divisions of traditional Asia.

The very idea of nationalism is a European concept, alien until the late nineteenth century to most of Asia. The thesis that a region inhabited by a certain people should be governed by people speaking the same language and having a similar set of ethics and values is new to most of Asia.

Even China, ruled for centuries by alien conquerors, accepted these dynasties with the weapon of nationalism only rarely raised against them. As late as the beginning of this century, Sun Yatsen's doctrine that the Manchu dynasty was "alien" rule was a radical, new idea in the Chinese world. In China's case, of course, alien rule was mitigated by the tendency repeated down through the centuries of the conquerors to assimilate and assimilate rapidly, in the Asian time-frame, into Chinese culture.

In India, one of the universals through Indian history is that the various areas of the country have been ruled by "foreign" princes. And that was true in many Indian "native" states created or preserved under the two hundred years of British rule right down to independence for all of India in 1947.

Some of the nationalist movements that triumphed in the post-World War II era had their origins in movements led by Europeans or by Europeans domiciled in Asia. They sought—as did the Hollanders of mixed blood in the Netherlands East Indies or the All-India Congress movement led originally by Britishers in

India—to gain rights in the colonial dependencies that existed in the home countries.

Even in Vietnam, with its centuries of struggle against Chinese conquest, the model for the modern nationalist movement was Sun's revolt in China.

Yet the nation-state ideal is a concept generally accepted by the elite throughout Asia today. The gap between reality and myth explains much that has happened.

Take the new nation of Indonesia. It was officially inaugurated in August 1945 with the collapse of Japanese military power and, its leaders hoped, before the former Dutch colonial rulers could return and reestablish their presence. After a long and grueling process of warfare and negotiations, largely brought on by Dutch intransigence and which undermined the role of the Indonesian moderates, international recognition was accorded the new nation-state in December 1949.

I say "accorded the new 'nation-state,'" for that was the presumption of much that was said by the Indonesians and by the international community. But this was lip service to a great fiction. From the beginnings of the Indonesian nationalist movement in the nineteenth century, it sought to overcome great differences among the peoples of the East Indies. From its earliest days, one of the slogans of the Indonesian nationalists was *satu bahasa, satu bangsa, satu tanah-air.* These Malay words literally mean: "One language, one people, one land-water (fatherland)."

But the very militancy of their assertion of these propositions by the nationalists was proof of their lack of meaning. Indonesia was a word coined first by a German ethnologist of the nineteenth century to cover the Indianized peoples of the vast island archipelago lying off the southeastern mainland of Asia. And as the lexicon of the academics gave way to nomenclature of the politicians, Indonesia became a word used to describe the Dutch empire.

The early Indonesian nationalists soon came to believe that a common language must be the basis of nationhood as it was for most of the West European nation-states. They adopted Malay, the *lingua franca* of the islands, used widely because the Malays had been the best warrior-sailors of the area. Today, the official language of the Indonesian Republic is *Bahasa Indonesia,* literally the Indonesian language, which is a conglomeration of Pasar Malay (Malay of the bazaars), Dutch, French, and English words written in Roman script rather than in the traditional Arabic script of the predominantly Moslem Malays.

Yet ironically the former British territories in the Malayan peninsula and the North Borneo coast, where Malay is the indigenous language for the great majority of the people, are not in Indonesia. And the two-thirds of the island of Java, where Malay is not spoken as the mother tongue, is the heartland of Indonesia.

As to the prayer for "one race," it was never true nor is it today. Indonesians vary from the light-skinned, hefty Dayaks of Kalimantan (Borneo) to the negroid peoples of former Dutch New Guinea. There is the devoutly Moslem but (contradictorily) matriarchal Menangkabau society of the West Sumatran coast and the Roman Catholic, highly Europeanized Minahasa in the north of Celebes Island.

The present boundaries of Indonesia are those of the former Netherlands East Indies empire. They include more than three thousand islands. And they stretch for some four thousand miles across the South China Seas dividing the Indian and Pacific Oceans. Yet nowhere are these boundaries "logical" in terms of ethnic origins of the peoples concerned, in trade routes, or in simple geographic proximity.

Take the case of the Riouw Islands, a small archipelago which lies at the very doorstep of Singapore. Even during the "good old days" of Dutch-British-French colonial stability in this part of the world, the Indies government in Batavia (now Djakarta) could not control smuggling of pepper, tin, and copra from these islands into the port of Singapore, then the hub of Southeast Asia. The Riouws were a part of the British currency system of Malaya and Singapore and the Borneo British colonies, not of the Netherlands East Indies.

Since 1945 succeeding Dutch and Indonesian governments have tried to police a rigid system of multiple exchange rates and currency controls (based on a postwar system in Belgium quickly abandoned by the more practical Belgians) with dwindling success. And they have tried to enforce it in the Riouws, too, where even in the days of the colonial police state it could not be done!

The island of Sumatra has had closer cultural and economic relations historically with Peninsula Malaya than with the island of Java. The ruling Malay sultans in former British Malaya have close family ties to the feudal families of Sumatra. The Menadonese in the Celebes are Christians, culturally related more closely to the Filipinos than to the Javanese. (And, of course, the Moslem Moros in the southern Philippines have more cultural affinity with some of the Indonesian peoples than with the rest of the Philippines.)

Almost everywhere you look in South Asia you find these geographical absurdities left by European colonialism now making claims to the status of nation-states.

SINGAPORE

SINGAPORE, sometimes called "the whore of the South China Seas," is an archtype creation of the colonial system. The city-state is ruled today by perhaps the most efficient regime in Asia. Lee Kwan Yew, the leader of the People's Action Party, considers himself a socialist in the West European social democratic tradition. His administration has pushed through a wide range of welfare state activities in the island "nation"—public housing, old age insurance, a massive free public education system—unknown even in more prosperous Asian countries.

But increasingly, the regime and the city find themselves caught in a dilemma. Singapore was spawned by European colonialism. It existed only as a fishing village at the coming of the European traders and conquerors. It was established by British capital and control as an island of stability in the frequently unstable region. It has no good natural harbor. Its resources are only the enormous talents and capacity for work and perseverance of its predominantly Overseas Chinese population.

Its livelihood has been based on the presence, first and foremost, of the British Far East military command center and the Singapore naval base. It is estimated that a fourth of the population draws its livelihood indirectly from the operations of this base. And London has decided that it will abandon this military establishment as soon as possible in its general retrenchment east of Suez.

Singapore lives off its *entrepôt* trade, serving as a way-station for raw materials departing from the Indonesian archipelago and nearby Malaysia for markets in Europe, Japan, the U.S., and the Soviet Union. It also acts as a distribution center for manufactured goods being sold in South Asia by the Japanese and the Europeans (Singapore is one of the largest single markets for Swiss watches in the world—smuggled for the most part to the rest of Asia).

To the extent the new nations around it are able to improve their direct trade patterns with customers and suppliers, cutting out Singapore's handling costs, the island faces a grim future. The very success of Lee's government in raising living standards has priced Singapore out of the market as a possible base—unlike Hong Kong, which has a continual flow of cheap refugee labor out of Communist China and which has an unreconstructed, old-fashioned colonial government—for manufacturing in the newly established clothing and other soft goods industries in East Asia, supplying cheaper products for American and European markets.

An attempt was started in 1963 to form a new federation of the old Malayan "protected" states and colonies of the British and the North Borneo British possessions plus Singapore. It would have provided at least a unified market of ten million people. But it failed and Singapore was expelled from Malaysia in 1965 by the Malaysian federal government at Kuala Lumpur.

So today Singapore is a "nation-state" of less than two million people attempting to carry on its own diplomacy, provide in some manner for its defense, soon to launch its own currency, and maintaining a quadrilingual educational system and administration! (Although Singapore is a predominantly Chinese city, it has large Malay and Indian [Tamil] minorities and uses English as its international window on the world.)

LAOS

Laos is another example of nationhood based on the vagaries of European colonial divisions in Asia. The Lao, who probably constitute only about half of the three million people in the country, live principally in the rice-growing lowlands along the Mekhong River. (There are no credible population statistics on the country.) They are an Indianized Thai people who migrated down into Southeast Asia from central Asia from the sixth to the thirteenth centuries, first cousins to the neighboring Thais (Siamese) of Thailand, the Shans of Burma, and the Thais of North Vietnam.

I remember the shock and dismay of a well-informed editor of one of the large Chicago newspapers when he turned up in the Laos administrative capital of Vientiane in 1963. It was his first visit to Asia. He had, like most Americans, been reading a good deal about the country during the long Laos crisis of 1961-62, especially after President Kennedy went on television to emphasize to the U.S. public and the Communist powers the American strategic interest in preserving the country from a takeover by forces backed by the Hanoi regime in North Vietnam and the Chinese Communists.

He could hardly contain himself during his short visit. He wanted to get back to Chicago to chide his young editorial writer who had been writing long and learned opinion pieces about the nature of the Lao "nation-state."

By no criterion is Laos a nation. Its creation was largely the product of a rivalry between France and Britain for control of vast areas of South Asia in the eighteenth and nineteenth centuries. The British were pushing out from India toward the east into Burma and threatening Thailand. The French were pushing west and north from their colony of Cochin China (now roughly South Vietnam) and their "protectorates" of Annam and Tonking in Indochina. Thailand, a very young state itself in Asian terms, had a strong monarchy. And the Anglo-French competition gave a series of intelligent and dedicated rulers an opportunity to stabilize their state in the nineteenth century.

The French agreed (in 1895) to accept the Mekhong River as the border between Thailand and Laos, in the French empire, and to accept Thailand as a buffer between French Indochina and the British. But the border is totally unreal—as U.S. policymakers are learning to their dismay today, working to help put down the current insurgency in northeastern Thailand bordering on the river.

The Lao language, another dialect of the Thai family of languages spoken in the whole area of Thailand, Laos, northern Burma (the Shan states), the western portions of North Vietnam, and large areas of southern China, is spoken by more people in Thailand itself than in Laos.

The Mekhong, far from being a barrier, is in fact an historic artery of communication in the area. The northern areas of Laos under the princes of Luang Prabang (incidentally, originally a Vietnamese warlord dynasty) and the southern areas of the country were amalgamated in 1947 by the French into the Kingdom of Laos in an effort to appease a small group of the elite agitating for independence.

The two areas have less in common than they do with the neighboring areas of Thailand. And their natural arteries of trade and communication lie through Thailand across the river.

One of the best comments on Laos nationhood is the fact that its economy's principal source of foreign exchange in 1962—discounting U.S. and other foreign aid—was earned from collect cable tolls by U.S. newsmen to their newspapers in Europe and America during the long political crisis. In more recent years, it has come from a tax on gold brought into the country legally but "smuggled" out to customers in Vietnam, Cambodia, Thailand, and Burma.

PAKISTAN

THE geographic anomaly without parallel in Asia is Pakistan. Two areas are united as one nation with a thousand miles as the crow flies across Indian territories separating them. Not only are the "two wings," as they are called in English language parlance, divided by a two and a half-hour flight by jet aircraft, but they are totally different on almost every score.

West Pakistan is the Middle East—semi-desert or desert, tribal to a considerable extent, feudal in the pattern associated with other Moslem lands, and relatively sparsely populated.

35

East Pakistan (where more than 55 per cent of Pakistan's more than 115 million people live) is a part of Southeast Asia. It is one of the most densely populated regions of the world. The climate is monsoon, the land engulfed for four months of the year when two-thirds of the area lie under the flood waters of the Ganges-Brahmaputra River system.

West Pakistanis are often tall by Asian standards, robust physically, light-skinned. The Bengalis of East Pakistan are small, dark, more closely resembling the other peoples of Southeast Asia, with a slight Mongoloid cast about their eyes.

The West Pakistanis tend to be direct, even brusque, pragmatic. There is a cult of masculinity. The most famous professional soldiers in the Indo-Pakistan region come from the northern area of West Pakistan.

The Bengalis are quiet spoken, if garrulous, taking great pride in their sophistication, their love of ritual, and are incorrigible romantics.

The West Pakistanis speak several languages (usually taciturnly)—all of them looking strongly toward Arabic and Persian for their roots. The Bengali of East Pakistan is a derivative of Sanskrit with a magnificent literature, one of the richest in the subcontinent. The most celebrated modern Indian-Pakistani poet, Rabindranath Tagore, was a Bengali, originating from the area now in East Pakistan.

It goes without saying that among the chief common problems the two regions share is underdevelopment. But the reasons for it and any proposed economic and social solution must be, in the nature of things, vastly different.

The *modus vivendi* that now holds the two areas together is fragile. West Pakistan is the source of the military power that provides internal stability under a military dictatorship. Virtually the entire Pakistan armed forces are recruited in West Pakistan. The Bengalis provide a large portion of the bureaucrats and political *savoir-faire* for the state.

But probably the only real tie between the two wings is the Moslem religion, which holds them together in the face of their fear of the threat of India as a majority non-Moslem state. (It needs to be said quickly, of course, that India's Moslem minority of nearly fifty million is half the population of the two Pakistans.)

CAMBODIA

CAMBODIA, again, represents another irrationality of the nation-state concept as it has been artificially introduced in Asia. During the eighty years of French rule of Indochina (the present states of Vietnam, Cambodia, and Laos), Cambodia had virtually ceased to exist except as an administrative unit of the French empire.

For centuries the once mighty Cambodian (Khmer) empire, under the onslaught of the more aggressive and dynamic Vietnamese descending down the coast from the valley of the Red River and from the Thai expanding out of their cultural center on the Chao Phya River, had been contracting.

As any Vietnamese intellectual will tell you at the drop of a hat, the very existence of a Cambodian entity was probably only saved by the coming of the French. Otherwise, it might have gone as did the Indianized Buddhist state of Champa in what is today central Vietnam, which gradually disappeared in the seventeenth century after fourteen centuries of existence. Only a few scattered Moslem tribesmen, using the name Cham, architectural ruins, and exquisite pottery remain to attest to that great and thriving culture.

It is significant that the present Cambodia flag carries a silhouette of the famous ruins of the once great city-state of Angkor. For Cambodia's main claim to national identity today rests on that memory of the splendor of those edifices built from the ninth to the fifteenth centuries.

Not much else is left. During the colonial occupation, Cambodian commerce flowed through the colonial creation, the South Vietnam port city of Saigon—founded by the French for the express purpose of getting out the rice and rubber. Its internal and external commerce today lies almost completely in the hands of the Overseas Chinese community—at least six hundred thousand people out of a nation of five million. Artisans are almost all from among the Vietnamese minority, at least another million people.

Its rice bowl in Battambang province on the Thai border is farmed by people who are as much Thai as Khmer. There is a Moslem Cham-Malay minority of another two hundred fifty thousand.

The ethnic Cambodian peasant, himself, lives in villages, as he has for centuries, as a largely subsistence farmer. Physiologically he is a distinct type from his Vietnamese and Thai neighbors—generally much darker, a larger frame, often with curly hair.

Interestingly enough, the present power elite in Phnom Penh, which is so voraciously nationalistic, is very far removed physiologically and culturally from this Cambodian type. In 1965, at a state dinner given by Sihanouk, I noted that in the huge open banquet pavilion, with several hundred people in attendance, only my table companion, the chief of protocol of the royal household, could be identified as belonging to the classic Cambodian type.

The rest of the assemblage—and not the least notably Sihanouk, himself—represented descendants either of the Chinese or Vietnamese minorities, or of the ethnic group called Khmer Khrone. The latter are Cambodians or Vietnamese of mixed Cambodian-Vietnamese descent—for remember that before 1954 the border between the old French colony of Cochin China (today South Vietnam) and Cambodia was only a line on a map.

At this writing Sihanouk's government is dominated by Khmer Khrone, as it has been from 1945, many of them actually born in the provinces of South Vietnam. The leader of the principal underground opposition movement to Sihanouk—incidentally, an independence fighter and nationalist when Sihanouk still played the role of puppet to the French colonial rulers—is a member of this clan. And his brother is a leading South Vietnamese Buddhist politician.

Not only do most of the new states of South Asia, like Cambodia, not represent nation-states in the tradition of the Western concept, but they are often "multinational." The most striking example, of course, is India.

INDIA

A PAKISTANI Communist friend, commenting once on this problem of nationalism and the nature of the new states of Asia, said, "If we are in dire distress in Pakistan, trying to make believe we are a 'nation' because we are all Muslim (Moslem), the Indians are in even worse shape: They are trying to create a nation-state on the basis of a myth of unity that never existed."

The myth to which my Pakistani friend referred is the dream that a united India restores the state ruled by Ashoka, the great Buddhist emperor of the third century B.C. Ashoka has much the same role in the subcontinent's history as Alexander of Macedon does for those of us bred on the Judeo-Graeco-Roman tradition. In a golden age, he did conquer much of what is modern India today. And like so many successful soldiers, he turned peace-merchant after his conquest, establishing pacifist Buddhism as the religion of the state with toleration of other creeds.

But Ashoka's victories—like Alexander's—were short lived, and the breakup of the empire came shortly after his death. His Buddhism, too, became just another creed in the huge pantheon of the subcontinent's religions and in India was reabsorbed by Hinduism.

Nehru saw his regime as a continuation of the traditions of Ashoka. The present Indian flag uses Ashoka's symbol, the Buddhist wheel of life. But if that was its significance to Nehru, it meant more as Gandhi's *charka*—the spinning wheel of his movement to defeat the British by reactivating India's folkcraft industries.

Using any of the European standards of nationhood—identity of race, language, physiological characteristics, or historical unity —India does not exist as a nation-state. When Mohandas Gandhi turned to traditionalist values of the Indian subcontinent to wage a "war" of liberation against British conquerors, he also had to turn to much narrower nationalisms. The Congress movement achieved little success when it functioned as a movement of English-speaking intellectuals in the nineteenth century. Its success came when Gandhi organized it on the basis of local "*pradesh*

39

committees," largely along linguistic and sometimes caste lines, appealing to individual "national" identities in the vast array of India's plural society.

This appeal reached its "logical" conclusion in 1956 after independence when, under the Congress Party government of Jawaharlal Nehru, the States' Reorganization Commission recommended a political reorganization of the country on basically linguistic lines. This decision, often blamed by critics of current policies as the root of much of the present political disorder, had a certain inevitability about it.

Thomas Babington Macaulay, one of the most influential men in the history of modern Asia, proclaimed in his reform of education for British-dominated India in 1835: ". . . it is possible to make the natives of this country thoroughly good English scholars and to this end our efforts ought to be directed." When independence came in 1947, less than 5 per cent of the Indian population could handle the language.

But the English language, along with the *raj* of the British itself over the whole of the subcontinent, had been the great unifier. Indian leaders were able to talk among themselves—as they had not been since Sanskrit as India's universal language fell into disuse before the Christian era. But English brought with it more than just a vehicle of communication. Shakespeare and the Bible became as much a part of the Indian intellectual's baggage as the Upanishads and the *Bhagavad Gita*. European science joined yoga and the Buddhist *sutras*.

Yet it was inevitable that a government of universal suffrage and pseudo-Western party politics had to bow before the will of the great mass which needed to conduct its affairs in languages it understood. The "return" to the fifteen official languages of today has unleashed a welter of local, regional, and linguistic "patriotisms."

On almost every recent trip to Bombay, I have found a new statue of Shivaj Maharaj, the seventeenth century hero of the Marathas guerrilla campaign against the Moghul emperors and the British. It can be and has been argued that Shivaj is an "Indian" national hero. But the present Shivaji cult in the new

Maharastrian-speaking state created by the states' reorganization is an agitation of the majority Maratha population in India's huge second city of Bombay against the present status quo.

The Marathas are by and large the hewers of wood and the drawers of water in their own state while Bombay—India's most Westernized city and perhaps its most cosmopolitan and the state capital—is dominated by a non-Maratha, non-Maharastrian-speaking elite.

The Shivaji-Maratha-Maharastrian cult has thrown up a semi-clandestine Maratha vigilante group which threatens to dispossess the present Bombay Establishment. If its power continues to snowball, it could threaten the whole business-educational-social complex at a time when the talents of this elite must be used to the maximum to meet the growing economic and political crisis, not only in the state of Maharashtra, but in India as a whole.

The excesses of this "nationalism" are not unknown in the West, of course. One might make a comparison, for example, between the Black Power advocates and the Shiva Sena, the Maratha political movement. But whatever its claims for social justice, the threat of chaos it poses to any progress is apparent in the present Indian context.

On a "national" level, take the problem of the Indian army. Perhaps its most talented younger general may not make it to chief of the army staff, in no small part because a few years ago he criticized the nature of the propaganda about Shivaj as a soldier. He pointed out, for example, that recent equestrian statues of the guerrilla leader had him astride a horse that was unlike any of the small polo ponies traditional to Indian horsemanship and certainly not available to Shivaj when he was holed up fighting in the Western Ghats.

That lecture at an army staff college was enough to bring on a court of inquiry and a reprimand. The conflict arose from the fact that important units in the Indian army are Marathas, one of India's so-called martial castes, and the current Minister of Home Defense, Y. B. Chavan, one of the most powerful in the cabinet, is a Maratha who has built his political following in Maharashtra state on appeal to his "caste brothers." And they chose to take umbrage at what they considered a slur on their "national" hero.

The power of these nationalisms, below the countrywide level, is almost universal throughout South Asia and the new countries.

MALAYSIA

In Malaysia, for example, the careful balance between the 40 per cent of the population which is Overseas Chinese—mostly immigrants during the colonial period—the 40 per cent Malay, and the 20 per cent Indian and other minorities is the greatest problem of stability for the state.

The Overseas Chinese is more aggressive, harder working, and takes advantage of formal schooling. The Malay is far more content to follow his traditional pattern of subsistence farming, fishing, and soldiering. The Chinese is also susceptible to the call of a strong China, the Chinese Communist exploitation of this theme, a long cultural tradition of his forebears on the mainland of China, and his strong family ties. The Malay is equally sensitive to the Moslem tradition of militant religious intolerance, his refusal to accept "Kaffirs." And when he becomes a "victim" of superior Chinese drive and domination of his economic life, he turns to violence.

When the feud between Singapore—led by a predominantly Chinese government under Lee—and the Malay leader of Malaysia, Tengku (Prince) Abdul Rahman, reached a fever pitch in 1965, the Tengku told me he had no choice but to break it off.

"When an old man in the *kampong* (the village) takes a young wife and they cannot get along, it is better that he divorce her," the Tengku said. His reference was to the "marriage" between his regime in Kuala Lumpur, dominated by his own Malay, with old guard Chinese leaders in former British Malaya, and the younger Lee and his socialist government in Singapore. Rahman said repeatedly at the time of the crisis that had he not chosen "divorce," the Malay nationalists would have resorted to violence. Most observers on the scene thought he was correct.

A few months earlier Lee, himself, described in an interview the basic problem that Chinese and Malay leadership faced in any bi-racial state in the area. I asked him why he, as a Chinese politician with a predominantly Chinese constituency, had chosen to enter the then Malaysian federation taking, in effect, second-class citizenship for the Chinese. He said, "I would hope that any Chinese politician would understand that if we push the Malays too far, they will commit suicide and take us with them."

The barometer of Chinese-Malay antagonism goes up and down. As I write, riots have broken out in the predominantly Chinese port city of Penang in Malaysia, ostensibly over the question of the British devaluation of the pound in December 1967 and Malaysia's decision to go along with it and devalue, too. There is little doubt that this time, as earlier, the agitation is part of the political in-fighting among the Chinese parties and factions in Malaysia. Chinese Communists also exploit it. (The remnant of the Overseas Chinese guerrillas who kept a twelve-year insurgency going against the British in Malaya until 1960 still exists and is active in the Malaysia-Thailand border area.)

But at the root of the problem is the basic bi-polar character of the state which will not disappear for generations—if ever—given the nature of the differences between the two peoples. Experience of assimilation between races in other parts of Asia, and in the world generally, indicates that the "balance" may continue to be precarious for years.

INDONESIA

In Indonesia the same problem, but in different dimensions, exists with the Overseas Chinese community, probably numbering more than three million in a total population of 110 million. Here, too, the Chinese dominate the commerical machine.

But a long-term problem also exists between the Javanese and the non-Javanese peoples in the archipelago. The Javanese was originally native to the central and eastern portions of the island of Java. He belongs to one of the oldest cultures in Asia. His language, his music, his plastic arts, are among the most sophisticated found anywhere in the region. But he is generally less aggressive, less pragmatic, less innovating than the Malay and other peoples of the so-called Outer Islands of Sumatra, Borneo, and the Celebes.

43

His numbers and his statecraft—exemplified in the role of Soekarno himself, born of a Balinese mother and a Javanese father —have given the Javanese the paramount role in the country since it was founded in 1945. Repeated revolts and maneuvers by the peoples of the Outer Islands, who have the big advantage of holding most of the country's easily exploited natural resources, have failed. Power is still largely centralized in Djakarta, dominated by the largely Javanese army. And probably more than at any time in the history of the nationalist movement, resentment, bitterness, and friction are greater and appear to be growing faster between the Javanese and the non-Javanese portions of the population.

It finds expression in various forms. But its derivation is basic. The peoples of the Outer Islands tend to be largely more religious Moslems (or Christians in Celebes and the Moluccas) than the Javanese, who have a stronger pre-Moslem Hindu heritage. The political movements of the Outer Islands emphasize decentralization, individual liberty, plurality. The Javanese emphasize personalities (what the Sumatrans call "the Javanese maharaja complex"), centralization, a steam-rollering nationalism.

The Outer Islanders want free enterprise, a decentralized economy in which they can run their own more prosperous affairs, welcoming foreign capital into oil, mining, and plantation agriculture. The Javanese want, generally, a regimented economy which will assure a deficit Java of a major portion of the state's earnings. When it is viewed in this light, then, the reason the Indonesian Communist Party (the PKI) is almost exclusively a party of the Javanese is easily understood. The PKI's toeholds in other parts of the country are almost exclusively where Javanese plantation workers migrated during the colonial period; for example, North Sumatra around the city of Medan. For this reason communism versus anti-communism becomes increasingly an ethnic as well as a politically divisive force.

VILLAGES

ALL of these differences must be put in the context, of course, of pre-industrial societies. Asia—with the exception of

Japan—is villages. If, as the old Chinese proverb has it, "The emperor's writ stops at the village gate," the converse is also true: The villager's loyalties—and even his interests—largely halt at the village gate.

India is a nation of 600,000 villages, despite her huge cities of Calcutta (6 million people), Bombay (4.6 million), Delhi (2.6 million). These villages are unbelievably (for the Westerner) remote from the main course of world affairs, or even national concerns.

In 1956 on a visit to India, I had been shown a model village near New Delhi, where the so-called community development program was being undertaken. I suspected—if for no other reason than that the village was so near New Delhi and had as a board of benefactors the half-dozen most important political names in the country—that it was atypical.

On the spur of the moment, I hired a taxi and we drove out onto the highway into the nearby province of Uttar Pradesh. (The name itself is an interesting anagram, a comment on what has happened in India in recent years. In British times the province was called United Provinces, an amalgam of old princely states and directly administered areas of British India. When the states' reorganization turned it into one of the new linguistic states, the initials UP, which had become a byword even among non-English-speaking Indians, became Uttar Pradesh, literally Northern State, an example of that strange continuity so often seen in Indian history.)

At a spot I designated, I asked the driver, who came from a nearby village, to take me into a local environment. He hesitated; it was a puzzle why the *burrah sahib* wanted to see the poverty-stricken villagers. Finally we went to a cousin, a local veterinarian. After he had satisfied himself that I was not a government official, but just a mad American tourist, he suggested that I walk five miles into a nearby village that he knew. The village had only an ox track connecting it with the outside world.

I shanghaied the taxi driver as interpreter and off we went. We spent the morning and the afternoon in the village. For the first few hours I attracted a good deal of attention. A former British Indian army soldier, an old man now, hung about to talk to me.

45

The village children tagged along until they became tired. It was all a great carnival for the villagers. But in the course of the day their excitement over my presence began to wear off and I managed to ask a great number of questions, perhaps got a few honest answers.

My most dramatic memory of that day—aside from the wretched poverty which I had seen innumerable times in hundreds of other Indian villages—was that I could find no one in the village, less than fifty miles from New Delhi, the country's capital, who knew who Jawaharlal Nehru, the Prime Minister, was. A few of the villagers volunteered that they knew the name of "Gandhiji"—but they were not quite sure who he was.

The villages of the Indo-Pakistan subcontinent are perhaps an extreme case—in the dimensions of their isolation. But I have had the same sort of experience in villages in Burma, Laos, Java, Thailand, and Vietnam. There were—at least until very recently— villages in northeastern Lao-speaking Thailand where the photograph of the king of Laos was displayed rather than the king of Thailand. I don't think that this was so much a political act as simply that contact with the Laos side of the Mekhong River was stronger than with Bangkok, the Thai capital.

Political events over the past two decades in Vietnam and Java have led to intensive propaganda seeping into every village. But certainly the villagers' understanding of the issues propagandized is quite a thing apart from the small urbanized population.

Burma today, where Rangoon's writ carries no further than the physical presence of the Burmese army—and sometimes not even that far—is a prime example. The majority of Burmans, living in the central plain of the Irrawaddy River and who dominate the central government, have tried to force Burmese nationalism on the Karens, the Shans, the Kachins, the Chins, and the Nagas, and the Moslem community. (Non-Burman peoples made up 40 per cent of Burma's population in 1956; there are at least sixty languages and dialects spoken in the country.)

They have expelled Indians and Pakistanis—many of them native-born to Burma. And riots against Overseas Chinese in the summer of 1967 seem to preface a move against the Chinese too. It has ended with a half-dozen different revolts stewing throughout the country, twenty years of chaos and stagnation in vast areas, and alienation of a large part of the population.

Local nationalisms, village isolation, and the demands of an urban elite, however small, for political progress—generally understood to mean strongly centralized government—is one of the most important features of almost all these new Asian states. It leads to a kind of schizophrenia, a self-perpetuating and constantly accelerating conflict of loyalties: The central government seeks to increase its allegiance by increasing its role in local affairs. The resistance of local concentrations of power to the center produces crisis after crisis. This brings greater strain on an already overtaxed central government bureaucracy. And while the proponents of centralization seek concentrated power in a national government as the only way toward the idealized nation-state, their attempt to speed up the process of assimilation inevitably brings resistance which not only defeats the whole program, but sometimes jeopardizes the state.

3 *

The Brown Sahibs

A BRITISH banker who has spent a long career in various parts of Asia tells a not atypical story of the pre-World War II colonial societies:

He "came out to India" as a very young man to serve the usual apprenticeship as a clerk. Although his background is carefully camouflaged these days—as I write, he is in his sixties—by a proper broad-A accent, he "came of no family." And in the Madras of those days, a young Englishman without a public school education and university had his "place."

In the normal run of things he struck up a tennis-court acquaintanceship with a young, attractive British Indian army officer. The young Indian was one of the new breed being groomed for officership in the Indian army forces. Until just prior to World War II, most officers in the British Indian army were Britons. Indians were relegated only to so-called "viceroy commissions," a kind of supernoncommissioned officer between the ranks and the "King's commissions," the British officers.

The young Indian officer was a good tennis player. And the young banker continued to play with him, the game on the courts leading to a broader friendship. Within a few months it had become a "problem" at the bank. The young Englishman was called in, told in no uncertain terms that friendship with a "native" was prejudicial to his career and that he should discontinue seeing the Indian.

Perhaps because it was on the eve of the great events that would sweep Asia after 1940, perhaps only because my banker friend is a rather stubborn fellow, he disregarded the advice given by his elders. Years later—after Indian independence in 1947—the Englishman had become a veteran banker in New Delhi. And the Indian army officer had become the very popular chief of Indian army staff, Kodendera S. Thimayya, one of the most important officials of the capital's new independent regime. In fact, he was a "most important contact," my British friend wryly concludes.

That atmosphere of discrimination and intolerance was certainly the rule rather than the exception in the colonial societies. I have never met anyone who actually saw the legendary sign in the Shanghai club (or park) which purportedly said: NO DOGS OR CHINESE ADMITTED. But there are thousands of Asians, and non-Asians who lived in the East in the decades between the two World Wars, who believe it existed. And whether it did or not, the vicious racism that the story symbolizes was part and parcel of the European colonial system in Asia.

Hundreds of millions of people were ruled through a system that was based on a simple principle: A white skin was proof of superior intelligence and morality. In theory, of course, there were options open to the Asians to crack this barrier. In Indochina the French built a university in Hanoi which turned out doctors and lawyers. A good French accent—like a knowledge of Dutch in Indonesia—could get a certain kind of acceptance by the European establishment.

Yet even the French who gloried in their disregard for race at home in Paris had much the same kind of restrictions on memberships in clubs in Saigon that were enforced in the British colonies. In India the restrictions—no more rigid nor complicated, of course, than the traditional Hindu concepts of caste and "contamination" by lower caste groups or outcastes—had far-reaching ramifications. Calcutta, for example, the great business center, had two chambers of commerce, two principal clubs. (The duality hangs on without meaning to this day.) One included British and other foreign firms and one was for Indian merchants and industrialists.

The Japanese victories of the early months of World War II in the Pacific area against the Americans and the European colonial regimes, and their demonstration of knowledge of twentieth-century power and technology by an Asian people, cataclysmically swept away the old system. But as late as 1950, there was a great hoo-hah in Singapore when the new American Club announced that admission was open to Chinese, Malays, and Indians, as well as Europeans.

European racism in Asia produced a strange kind of schizophrenic reaction among the local urbanized, educated elite. On the one hand it brought on a violent nationalist reaction. On the other, it produced a set of ideas and values which simply were an attempt by Asians to copy the Europeans. In everything from language to styles of dress, there was a whole code of intellectual snobbism based on an often-distorted version of European values. And the two extremes—total rejection and imitation—were equally caricatures.

In Indonesia, for example, the Japanese—incidentally through the easy defeat of British and Dutch forces in Southeast Asia and then deliberately with political indoctrination—set off a wave of reverse racism down through the society. When the Dutch began their efforts to reconquer their colony in 1945, the nationalists announced their freedom in words paraphrasing the U.S. Declaration of Independence. But at the same time there was the widespread "Bamboo Spears" movement—an almost atavistic attempt to answer Western technology and military force with bare hands and fanaticism. And in East Java, there was a massacre of former European and Chinese prisoners of the Japanese (in part the result of racist tirades broadcast by a European woman from Soerabaja, who still travels about the world on her credentials as an Indonesian expert).

Everywhere, of course, in the colonies were those who made their peace with the colonialists. In India they were called "toadies"—those who worked so closely with the British that they received rewards in terms of jobs and contracts (they were also sometimes called *wogs*, Western Oriental Gentlemen, a term of derision). Some were given a kind of social acceptance and were "knighted," at least as members of the British Indian Empire peerage. In Cochin China a French-trained bureaucracy combined landlordism and intermarriage with Overseas Chinese merchants to form a new class.

The combination of the old ideas of the traditional Chinese society and the new ideas of national revolution, largely from the West, produced an atmosphere of violent emotional reactions.

NEW AND OLD IDEAS

"THE thoughts of the Chinese youth underwent the most drastic change about the time of the May Fourth Movement," writes Chang I-p'ing, a writer quoted in Chow Tse-tsung's study of the May Fourth Movement. "At the time, most of them protested in an uproar against the family system, the old religions, the old morality, and the old customs, in an effort to break up all traditional institutions. I was then studying in a summer school in Nanking. I knew a young man who abandoned his own name and substituted the title 'He-you-I.' Later when I went to Peking, I met at the gate of the School of Letters of Peking University a friend of mine accompanied by a young girl with her hair cut short. 'May I ask your family name?' I asked her. She stared at me and screamed, 'I don't have any family name!' There were also people who wrote letters to their fathers saying, 'From a certain date on, I will not recognize you as my father. We are all friends, and equal.' T'ieh-min was among those who had denied their fathers; but when his father died in 1921, he wrote a very touching poem to explain his grievous mourning for him."

In the long run of history, the period of direct European domination of these past 450 years may pale.

Traveling about the Indo-Pakistan subcontinent, I begin to get the feeling that as older cultural strains come rising to the surface the brief—two hundred years in some five thousand years of recorded history—British sojourn may be only a ghost to future generations.

If you travel up the steep, winding slopes of the foothills of the Hindu Kush toward the famous Khyber Pass in West Pakistan,

51

you pass hundreds of mementoes of the British occupation. Here is a monument to a famous British soldier and governor. There, painted or cut into a cliff, is a graffito by a British regiment.

But more important than these scratches on the stone faces of the roadside are customs and modes of behavior which date from prehistory. I am sure that the ceremony of the *maliks*, the village leaders, bringing sacrificial fat-tailed lambs as an offering to Jacqueline Kennedy when I traveled this route as a member of her press party in 1962 was not too different from that which greeted Baber, the Moghul conqueror, when he passed this way in the sixteenth century en route to the conquest of northern India.

Once, watching a group of Baluch Rifles officers and men of the Pakistan army (a regiment in the old British Indian army) playing a kind of rough and ready polo in Gilgit, a tiny state in the Himalayas of northern Pakistan, I was reminded of the earliest Western accounts of a similar game played on horseback by Scythians in accounts by Alexander's generals more than two thousand years ago. The wolf carcass then used has been replaced by a wooden ball. But the rough and tumble in which a rider can be wrestled off his horse has more to do with the Scythian game than the very proper polo played by His Royal Highness Prince Philip and his friends.

LANGUAGE PROBLEM

Yet, for the generations reared in colonialism—which still direct the affairs of Asia today—the European domination is real and still a controlling factor. Colonialism has produced an elite in much of Asia alienated from the mass it directs. Often these leaders do not speak their peoples' languages—literally as well as figuratively.

An Indian friend of mine tells an amusing anecdote about his own problem. As a reporter, he had occasion in the early 1950s to call on officials of the Soviet Embassy in New Delhi. The Russians he met were products of the early wave of carefully trained young bureaucrats who opened Soviet missions in the newly independent countries of Asia after World War II. And as a shining product of Moscow's very prestigious Institute of Oriental Languages and other Russian Communist training schools for subversion in Asia, they insisted on speaking Hindi to my Indian friend.

The Hindi they spoke was very stylized, heavily dependent on Sanskrit for adjectives, using nouns which had been concocted by the orthodox Hindu academics in Benares and elsewhere to meet such twentieth-century needs for nomenclature as "automobile." My friend, whose Hindi is rudimentary and has been used in his travels about India only for dealing with servants and occasionally to capsulize an Indian concept, just couldn't understand what was being said. For, like tens of thousands of other Indians, he speaks English at home, or on occasion his own mother-tongue, Gujerati. And, as a product of Oxford, he is far more at home in English in any kind of political discussion.

At one of his last press conferences, Prime Minister Nehru was asked if he understood the Hindi then being used by All-India Radio for news broadcasts. He said no. And he, too, admitted that the artificiality of the so-called national language made it incomprehensible to him. (When asked why the government radio continued to use it in spite of other protests, he said because "Indians are a long-suffering people.")

Indians have, of course, a very special and difficult problem for there is no real national language spoken throughout the country. Even Hindi-Urdu, which is the *lingua franca* of the north, is not universal since it is spoken, even in a primitive way, by only a small minority in the south. The regional languages are spoken by millions. Some have centuries of tradition, vast literatures, and huge vocabularies for philosophical and literary work—if not for technology. Then, too, English was the language for the educated elite for more than two hundred years.

The problem is universal throughout the former colonial countries. Two Vietnamese friends of mine startled a mutual American friend at a dinner party in Saigon with their own personal language problem. We had just finished a two- or three-hour discussion of the vast complexities of the South Vietnamese election scene preceding the balloting in the fall of 1967.

The Vietnamese had described in a head-reeling fashion all the contingencies involved in the elections—the candidates' person-

53

alities, the political movements, the regional conflicts, the possibility of cheating, etc. We veered off onto the subject of the appeal of any citified candidates to the peasantry. And the problem of language came up. Both of my friends, fervent nationalists throughout their lives with one now in his mid-fifties, the other in his mid-forties, explained that they had "lost" their command of Vietnamese during a long residence abroad as students and exiled politicians. In fact, neither had ever studied written Vietnamese until he came back from abroad when he had to "learn" his own language.

I was told by Vietnamese friends with Communist connections during the French Indochina War (when I spent a year in Hanoi as a correspondent in 1950-51) that meetings of the Communist party politburo of the Viet Minh were held in French. Certainly, at least in the early days of the Communist-led nationalist movement against the French in the immediate postwar period, the language problem was a critical intellectual concern for the Communists.

Truong Chinh, one of the leading figures of the Hanoi Communist politburo, wrote an essay in the early postwar period in which he advocated the Vietnamese returning to the use of Chinese ideographs in which Vietnamese had once been written. The Romanization of the language by Alexandre de Rhodes, a Jesuit missionary priest in the seventeenth century, using a combination of French, Spanish, Portuguese, and German diacritical marks, is the only successful attempt to alphabetize any of the Far East tonal languages. It accounts, at least in part, for the relatively large-scale literacy in Vietnam.

And it is the type of formula which the Chinese Communists had originally hoped to follow in order to make Chinese more amenable to modern technological developments in the West. But Truong Chinh saw it as a barrier to close collaboration with his friends the Chinese Communists. Needless to say, nothing has been heard of his proposal since. Not only has the Hanoi regime had other more difficult problems to think about, but the Romanized language has become part and parcel of modern Vietnamese life in both Communist and non-Communist zones of the country.

In Indonesia during the height of the resistance against the return of Dutch rule, from 1945 to 1950, the cabinet meetings of the Indonesian Republicans in their stronghold of Djogjakarta were often held in Dutch. The new national language, Bahasa Indonesia, was too primitive for political discussions. The more sophisticated Javanese, spoken by most of the officials, was politically unacceptable because of the non-Javanese representatives' fear of "Javanese imperialism." And most of the cabinet had been educated in Dutch schools in Indonesia or in Holland itself. More recently I have heard government officials in Djakarta often give their more critical instructions to their office staff in Dutch. (Ironically, the word "Bung" used in the Indonesian nationalist movement as "comrade" was taken from the dialect of Dutch spoken by Indonesian-born Hollanders and Eurasians, groups which after World War II became among the most bitter opponents of Indonesian independence.)

Language is more than a medium of expression. I find my Vietnamese friends have a different personality in English than in French. I can only guess that they express still different nuances when they speak Vietnamese.

GROWING DIFFERENCES

THE problem of the use of an alien language by the elite is only an evidence of a far greater influence of foreign cultural values. It is only one aspect of the lives of the elite which is far different from the mass of the population. Everywhere the former European colonial masters' criteria of the good life are accepted as the norm.

I was horrified to find, on my last visit to Bali, that the beautiful Balinese landscape is being littered with little Dutch bungalows—the type once built by Hollanders in Java and now favored by Javanese officials living in Bali or by the few Balinese who have moved into a higher income bracket and "want to keep up with the Joneses."

Older Thai houses—built on stilts to get out of the monsoon wet which floods lowlands for much of the year and to provide a breeze on the hottest summer nights—are being replaced by rather bad imitations of Californian bungalows. They are totally unsuited, with their large glass surfaces and low ceilings, for the Thai tropics.

At the home of an upper middle-class Vietnamese family in Hanoi, I was surprised to find chopsticks propped on the little glass or plastic blocks which the French *bourgeois* set beside the plates so that the silver may not mess the tablecloth.

One of the South Asian chiefs of state is famous for his ability to communicate with Americans. A U.S. ambassador with long experience in Asia suggests more policy decisions than he likes to reckon with are the result of that political figure's ability to "mix a good martini." But the same Asian's wife is still in *purdah* —the traditional seclusion for Moslem women.

Air-conditioning has become a common item in the households of Indian businessmen, government officials and other members of the middle class. Yet often within a stone's throw in New Delhi, servants are living in what are called "hutments," lean-tos built out of refuse.

In a political discussion with an old Vietnamese friend, I once asked him to define what he meant when he said that the new kind of leadership that South Vietnam needed must be found among people with Vietnamese values. He immediately gave me one criterion: A leader who did not have the habit of drinking French wine. It is a rare Saigonese politician who does not take pride in his knowledge of French wines. Yet the mass of villagers knows only locally-made rice grog, or beer at most.

I heard a discussion a few years ago among my friends in Lahore at a dinner party about the "fast set" of young Pakistani teen-agers, sons and daughters of government officials and army officers in the city. They were posing some of the same kind of problems for their parents that suburban Connecticut mothers and fathers worry about. The fashion of the young girls at that moment was the "teddy chemise," a very tight version of the traditional long blouse and pantaloons that Punjabis wear. Only a few minutes from the new suburbs of the city where these children live, women live in polygamous households as they have for centuries.

My friend Tarzie Vittachi, one of Asia's best journalists, has described the problem brilliantly—if perhaps bitterly—in his book,

The Brown Sahib. I have borrowed his title for this chapter describing the new elite, in South Asia particularly, because it connotes so much for those of us who have lived there. Vittachi says:

> Who are they? They appear in many guises and operate at various levels of social and political life. In any officers' mess in South Asia you can meet a Brown Sahib playing the blimp, imitating and caricaturing his predecessors in the colonial armies. He is recognisable, too, in social and sporting clubs: the made-over Englishman bemoaning the passing of the Empire with the arrogance and nostalgia of the *Daily Express.* In the political life of South Asia he becomes more complex: his domestic life and private manners will be indistinguishable from those of the brown-skinned Englishmen . . . but his political philosophy and public attitudes may well be violently nationalistic, anti-British and anti-West. A strange feature of such a man's "progressiveness" is that while he will clamour for a return to a simpler, less materialistic and more "Eastern" way of life for his compatriots, he takes great pains to secure for his own children the best Western education that money and influence can buy.
>
> The tragedy is that these Brown Sahibs, hobbled by doctrinaire political philosophies or burdened by their cultural heritage as they are, often have the talent and training to bring decent human living conditions to the people of Asia; but while they are straining and stretching to ease themselves out of their self-contradictions, another kind of Brown Sahib—the Asian Jingo —is winning the power struggle.
>
> The Asian Jingo is a semi-westernized, half-baked, pseudo-politician, abiding by no rules, uninterested in any principle, unattached to any political philosophy, system or party except insofar as it serves as a vehicle to carry him at once to the centre of power. He does not hesitate to arouse communal, caste, linguistic or religious passions to achieve his goal. He claims that he represents "the people," which is true to the extent that the Westminster-type parliamentary systems imported to South Asia can provide for such representation.
>
> But this representation is only formal, and therefore largely illusory.

It would be a moot point whether the divergence between these members of the elite and the masses of Asia is narrowing or growing. In some areas it may be diminishing, but only because a new elite is taking over and an old one is being modified.

The Indian army, again, is a good example. At independence it was commanded at the top echelon by British officers. But rather quickly (in part because of Nehru's determination to spin off commanders in order to vitiate the threat of an entrenched military machine taking over from civilian nationalist leadership) a type of Indian army officer came to the fore.

Leaders at independence belonged to an Anglo-Indian elite which had been formed in the British Indian army and which had received rapid promotion during World War II. Although they came from the so-called martial castes of the country, they in fact formed a kind of supra-caste. They spoke English in their homes, affected British officer's accents, mannerisms, and dress. Their code of conduct was that of the gentleman and officer of the British army. And they shared the community of interests and a code of ethics with their comrades-in-arms around the world.

Today this Indian army supra-caste is rapidly disappearing. Time is taking its toll of the generation reared in the British tradition. A Sikh (a bearded member of the Hindo-Islamic religious community of the Punjab) is far more Sikh today, even if he is an army officer, than he was twenty-five years ago.

Not long ago in Calcutta I chatted with a group of senior Indian army officers of the old school. We got onto the subject of a Jesuit mission in a neighboring state. It turned out that the Jesuits, dedicated not only to their church but to acquiring a vast and very pragmatic knowledge of the Indian communities and problems, were good friends of the officers.

One of the officers indicated that the two groups—the Jesuits with their long tradition of militant, realistic efforts in India and the former British Indian army officers with their military discipline—had spoken often of their common problem: The changing world around them. Both apparently felt the same emotional reaction to a central authority—one in Delhi, the other in Rome—which no longer could or would take a strong, single line.

The Brown Sahibs

THE dual allegiance of the members of the Asian elite to their own Asian traditions and to the new, imported technology, standards, and ideas of the international community (I prefer "international" to "Western" because of the universality of many of the ideas current in the industrialized West) is greatest for the Asian intellectual. And here we need to define our terms. Much more than in the industrialized countries of the West, "intellectual" in Asia is a word setting one apart.

No one has put the whole problem more poignantly than my friend Soetan Sjahrir, the Indonesian socialist leader, writing to his wife from the death-hole in New Guinea where the Dutch colonialists had imprisoned him in the 1930s. In an entry in his diary dated June 20, 1935, he writes:

> Am I perhaps estranged from my people? Why am I vexed by the things that fill their lives, and to which they are so attached? Why are the things that contain beauty for them and arouse their gentler emotions only senseless and displeasing for me? In reality, the spiritual gap between my people and me is certainly no greater than that between an intellectual in Holland and, for example, a Drents farmer, or even between the intellectual and the undeveloped people of Holland in general. The difference is rather, I think, that the intellectual in Holland does not feel this gap because there is a portion—even a fairly large portion—of his own people on approximately the same intellectual level as himself. And that portion is, moreover, precisely what constitutes the cultural life of Holland; namely, the intellectuals, the scientists, the artists, the writers. . . .
>
> In substance, we can never accept the essential difference between the East and the West, because for our spiritual needs we are in general dependent on the West, not only scientifically but culturally.
>
> We intellectuals here are much closer to Europe or America than we are to the Boroboedoer or Mahabharata or to the primitive Islamic culture of Java and Sumatra. Which is our basis: the West, or the rudiments of feudal culture that are still to be found in our Eastern society?

59

So, it seems, the problem stands in principle. It is seldom put forth by us in this light, and instead most of us search unconsciously for a synthesis that will leave us internally tranquil. We want to have both Western science and Eastern philosophy, the Eastern "spirit," in the culture. But what is this Eastern spirit? It is, they say, the sense of the higher, of spirituality, of the eternal and religious, as opposed to the materialism of the West. I have heard this countless times, but it has never convinced me.

Sjahrir died in Switzerland in 1966, a victim of Soekarno's regime which had imprisoned him for years. He lived to see that despot overthrown. But I believe he also learned that the struggle for the kind of internationalism he sought was much further away than he had thought in the colonialists' jails of the 1930s, or even when political independence came, finally, in 1950. The "feudal culture" he mentioned has so far proved stronger than the dynamics of Western political institutions grafted on to the Indonesian body politic.

One of my first introductions to Vietnamese intellectuals was during a long, grim winter in Hanoi. I became acquainted with perhaps the most important scholar in the country—a mathematician, linguist, and litterateur. We met because of his interest in politics and because he had, briefly, at the end of World War II, played an active role in Vietnamese politics.

At the end of the period of which I speak he was what was then called in Hanoi an *attentiste*—a "waiter." His sympathies were with the Communist-led and dominated Viet Minh fighting the French. But he is a scholar, admirer of the old Vietnamese Confucian forms, and simultaneously a disciple of European humanism (which he has absorbed as have other Vietnamese intellectuals to a lesser or a greater degree through their exposure to the French).

I felt then, and it appeared to be confirmed when last we met in Paris where he is in exile at this writing, that his conflicting loyalties were very much a product of his being pulled by Vietnamese nationalism on the one hand and his revulsion against the brutality, the anti-intellectualism of the Communist movement on the other.

His solution, known throughout Asia, was to sit the whole conflict out, attacking all partisans from the sidelines. In practical terms, too, it was typical of what I have seen so many Asian intellectuals do. His livelihood was assured by his wife, a typical, aggressive, hard-working Vietnamese businesswoman, who ran a retail business.

The pattern is a well-known one, not only in Vietnam, but in Korea, Japan, China, and throughout South Asia. Mother earns a living, often by means that are less than those idealized by the sages of the old cultures. Father, meanwhile, studies the old philosophies and tries, usually not too successfully, to adapt them to the precarious modern situation.

JAPANESE INTELLECTUALS

In Japan, where the clash between old and new is superficially less pronounced, the dichotomy nevertheless exists. The *interi* of Japan, the intellectuals, play a much smaller role in their nation's everyday affairs than in Western societies. And, in fact, less than they did at the great changeover of Japanese society in the second half of the nineteenth century when it came out of partial isolation and its pre-industrial past to emerge quickly as one of the leading industrial nations of the world.

E. Herbert Norman, in his classic if overly Marxian work, *Japan's Emergence as a Modern State*, explains how the "revolution" which set the country on a new path was a work carried out by an alliance of soldiers, merchants, and scholars.

Norman writes:

> Political theories of countries other than China had as yet made little impression on Japan, or if one recalls "the cult of antiquity" in the French Revolution, when the most ardent republicans and Jacobins could think of no better model for their ideas than those inspired by the heroes of the Roman Republic. In this sense the fundamental document of the Meiji Revolution, the Imperial Oath of March 14, 1868, was an expression, in terms familiar and acceptable to the anti-feudal aspirations of the masses of the people throughout the land, envisaging as it did the need for consulting public opinion in the administration

61

of affairs for the benefit of the nation and the encouragement
of foreign knowledge.

. . . The Meiji settlement which laid the foundation of a modern
state in Japan . . . was carried out under the brilliant leadership
of *Samurai*—bureaucrats who, in the teeth of opposition directed
against them even by members of their own class, wisely pursued the path of internal reconstruction. . . . The machinery
for the epochal changes accompanying the restoration was a
government formed from the ablest, most self-sacrificing of clan
military bureaucrats who utilized to the full and with remarkable dexterity those autocratic powers which they steadily
strengthened. In looking back to the strong years of that period, whatever one may think of the words "military" and
"bureaucrat," it seems an incontrovertible fact that these military
bureaucrats were the spearpoint of advance, the vanguard of
modernization, in the establishment of a modern state in Japan.

K. M. Panikkar, the Indian historian, points out that while Ram
Mohan Roy, the brilliant Indian intellectual and reformer, was
corresponding with Condorcet on philosophical subjects, Japanese scholars were translating textbooks on mathematics. The
Japanese scholars were interested only in what was called
"Dutch learning"—their only exposure to European technology.
And as Panikkar and others have noted, the defeat of China, the
land of Confucius, during the Opium War of 1839-42 convinced
them that they must turn to the West for power.

Today the Japanese intellectual is like a man with one foot on a
ship, the other on shore, and the whistle has tooted. The boat is
bound for that promised land of the industrialized society, an
equalitarian world where technology is king. But on the shore are
the traditions of the past. Not the least of these is the honor and
special status accorded the scholar in his ivory tower. Over and
over again sacrifices have to be made for the new kind of life. The
forms of the past must give way.

I think of a trivial but typical exhibition of the problem seen
often at the entrances of the Tokyo subway system. On crowded
downtown corners of Tokyo groups of people gather to say
goodby to each other. They often do so in the traditional Japanese
fashion with an incessant ceremony of bowing from the waist. I

don't know a more difficult protocol than maintaining oneself upright in the midst of a Japanese subway crowd, much less continuing the graceful act of bowing to one's elders or friends.

I remember a long, continuing, fraternal argument between two of my Japanese friends. Both had been revolutionaries in their youth—members of the Communist Party in the 1920s, dissenters from the militarist war policies of the 1930s and the 1940s. In post-World War II both had finally achieved some measure of intellectual contentment by finding that Japan had begun to rebuild the society on more democratic lines, as they had always hoped. But what about the traditions? One friend loved the old dancing and music of the *geishas*. But, his friend said, the *geishas* are a relic of our feudal past. You cannot have *geishas* without feudalism, and we do not want feudalism to continue. But, the friend answered, the *geishas* are a part of our culture, of our heritage, of the kind of life of fulfillment, including art and music, we want for all our people. And we must preserve it.

The argument was, of course, never settled. One of my friends is dead—a victim of an illness brought on by his long years during the war in solitary confinement when he refused to be released, freedom that could have come had he only been willing to sign the militarists' pledge of absolute loyalty to the Emperor.

Today much of the Japanese intellectual class—the artists, the university professors, the scholars—find themselves considerably isolated from the mainstream of Japanese life. There is much less interchange than in the U.S. or Western Europe between the academic community, for example, and the government in such subjects as economics; the big Japanese companies only rarely use the academics. The university economist rarely contributes to the whole—and extremely able—complex of Japanese government trade control bureaucracy and long-range target planning.

"Why is the tradition of the intellectual's participation in national life of the nineteenth century lost today?" Takeo Naoi, one of Japan's most respected journalists and independent minds, writes me. "This is a most crucial question for honest intellectuals. One can point out that Japanese education from its beginnings (after the Restoration) was dominated by German culture with its abstract way of thinking. Even German professors invited by our government, like Dr. Bertz and Dr. Koeber in the Meiji Era, referred to the adverse influence of the German system in Japan."

> Intellectuals became proud of their role as members of the "ivory tower," aloof from the dirty business of politics. Even today, academicians, administrators and clerks are looked up to while businessmen, technicians and politicians are regarded as a species of a lower grade.
>
> I should also like to point to another reason. In Meiji Japan there was a common goal of all Japanese whether they were businessmen, politicians or scholars: To build a "standard nation." All their efforts and earnings were concentrated on this single goal. It was achieved with the victory over Russia [the Russo-Japanese War] in 1905.
>
> With the national goal achieved, self-satisfaction led to a process of differentiation and disintegration of the society spread. Each group—politicians, military and businessmen—began seeking their own ends instead of, and apart from, the national interest. The single-minded, austere way of life gave way to frivolous and indulgent ways in every corner of society. (It was recognized and an imperial edict was issued to request the people to maintain self-discipline and self-restraint.)
>
> In these circumstances, Japanese intellectuals, disgusted and disillusioned, turned more and more to the "ivory tower." Their interest shifted from the outer world to their own inner life, from national interests to individual pursuits. [Dr. Tomonaga, professor of philosophy at Kyoto and father of the recent Nobel-winner, has published a famous book entitled *History of the Awakening Ego in the Modern Era* on this theme.]
>
> The process of differentiation continued. At the same time, the struggle for supremacy in national affairs was contested by several groups. In the end, the military clique won the race which led to the national catastrophe of 1940.
>
> I have little hope in the old intellectuals who had "disengaged" for a long period and have suddenly sprung back on the platform after the War with a crippled sense of reality. I have hope in the younger generation, assistant or associate professors of the universities who have little experience with "disengagement."

Periodically a political crisis like the planned Eisenhower visit of 1960 erupts. And it generally finds the overwhelming weight of the political community and Japanese business on one side, the intellectuals on the other, flamboyantly in defiance of the government.

"You will ask then (considering his important role in the nineteenth century)," writes another old friend and one of the most astute foreign observers of the Japanese scene, "why does the Japanese intellectual feel and act so alienated most of the time. I think a lot of it is attributable to the image which the Japanese has of himself as a person—corresponding less to fact than do most national images—that is, of himself as *samurai*, swashbuckling warrior, who strikes the most absolute poses, *zenttai mitomenai*, *zenttai* this, *zenttai* that. Absolute opposition to this, that or the other, while actually compromising all the time.

"You may remember the strike a few years ago in Kyushu, where the number one union, wearing their headbands, was assembled like an army of warriors to do battle, while the number two union looked like another army, and the air rang with absolute denunciations of each other and the company. It finally developed into a small scale naval war. In the same way, mild-mannered college professors who would never dream of doing anything forward as individuals get caught up in a demonstration wearing *hachimaki* headbands and snake dance through the streets. They're absolutely loyal, determined, and resolute *samurai*—for a few hours."

Many of today's leftist Japanese intellectuals are the same people who were most compromised by their subservience to the militarist regime that precipitated Japan into her war with China in the 1930s and with the U.S. in 1941.

Obviously, the disaffection of Japanese intellectuals arises out of myriad causes in Japanese history. But in no small part it is a result of the absorption by the Japanese intellectual of methods of thinking and working on problems derived (and I think in a thwarted pattern) from the West. The government-business complex, on the other hand, uses the techniques of other industrialized societies but maintains a definite Japanese pattern in its basic approach.

I defy any economist—Marxian, Liberal, Keynesian, or one of the New Economics breed—to explain in their conceptual terms the startling comeback of the Japanese economy in this past two and a half decades since World War II.

Basic to Japanese progress has been the application of peculiarly Japanese techniques. For example, Japan has today in outward respects an economy of private initiative. But it would be a foolhardy observer who would describe it—even in relation to our systems in the Western capitalist states so radically modified after the great depression and in World War II—as free enterprise. A complicated set of checks and controls, compromises and orders, between the Japanese business complex and the Japanese government, gives Japan "a planned unplanned economy."

Where the elite have scored successes in Asia in the past fifty years, it has usually meant this kind of strange amalgam of the traditional and the modern. Often the twentieth-century exterior belies the traditional methods by which problems have been met and dealt with.

GANDHI AND NEHRU

An INDIAN friend is fond of saying that the great difference between Gandhi and Nehru was that Gandhi was an internationalist using Indian traditional methods to accomplish his aims. Nehru, on the other hand, he says, was a traditionalist camouflaging his actions by a Western or internationalist façade.

Thus Gandhi sought to establish a system of representative government in India based on principle and sought after Indian independence to disassemble the Congress freedom movement, to turn it into a vast social service organization. He foresaw that one-party government would end up in a kind of despotism that had been traditional in India's history.

Nehru, on the other hand, faced with the practical problem of governing a nation-state that did not in fact exist, carried on to make the Congress Party a great adjunct of the state. And as often as not, behind the scenes he maneuvered in the star-chamber manner of the traditional Indian autocrat.

Nor is it an accident, I think, that Gandhi was a Gujerati, a member of an Indian family of sea-coast and caravan peoples

66

that for centuries has felt the fresh currents of international thought. The Gujeratis are among the best traders in India. Their people have gone to far-flung parts of the British Empire—especially to Africa where Gandhi himself worked as a young man. Nehru was a Kashmiri Brahmin, a Hindu priestly caste that by guile and intrigue has managed for centuries to keep the upper hand even when they existed in communities which were predominantly Moslem, like the Vale of Kashmir itself.

Yet this fundamental difference between Gandhi the revolutionary and Nehru the maintainer of the *status quo* has been obscured by their methods. Nehru spoke in a Cambridge accent, a convert to Fabian socialism. Gandhi spoke in the role of the *mahatma*, the traditional Indian holy man. Gandhi was thus able to move millions of Indians, only vaguely aware of his political objectives, behind his demands for Indian freedom without a resort to violence which he felt would destroy any hope of basic changes in the Indian people's daily existence. Nehru obfuscated his inability to deal a revolutionary new hand in the structure of Indian life after independence with slogans of socialism and secularism.

Paradoxically, of course, Gandhi's use of Indian traditions to mobilize the masses for a gigantic effort at national revival could, in the long run, threaten the aim of introducing an international humanism. The poet Tagore warned of this trend. The Gandhians reawakened not only old Indian loyalties, but also much of the narrow prejudice that had kept India backward for centuries.

And it was, in fact, Gandhi's appeal to ancient Hindu tradition that played a big role in the alienation of the Moslem political leadership—especially secularists like Mohammed Ali Jinnah, founder of Pakistan, who decided that the only security for the Indian Moslems was in a separate state. Irony of ironies was that Jinnah, a near agnostic, had to use Islam as his rallying cry for founding Pakistan as a separate state.

The partition of the subcontinent into two countries in 1948 led to bitter and bloody strife, and a permanent arms race in the subcontinent with the constant threat of flare-ups like the 1965 Indo-Pakistan War.

The duality of the Asian intellectual's personality has often immobilized him when confronted with growing problems of his society. I asked my old friend, Soetan Sjahrir, the last time I saw him, before his imprisonment and death, why his own brilliant group of young Indonesians had failed so dramatically in achieving their post-independence goals.

In the late 1940s they were the most promising and attractive of the young revolutionaries. Sjahrir, in his diary written from isolated Dutch colonial jails, had brilliantly dissected the world scene of the 1930s—far more astutely than Nehru in his emotional biographical works. A nucleus of bright young intellectuals who followed Sjahrir had formed an intellectual elite in Indonesia and had created a small, but presumably potent, Indonesian socialist party pledged to the concepts of both personal liberty and economic development.

Yet by the late 1950s they were in total disarray. Some had been bought off by Soekarno's demagoguery. (Soebandrio, the gray eminence of Soekarno's foreign policy in the '60s, which envisaged at least a tacit alliance with Communist China, was the best example.) Some were in Soekarno's prisons. Others had simply opted out of politics and leadership.

Sjahrir said, "I guess the only explanation is what you would call in Americanese 'no guts.' "

Yet why? These were the same young men who had been willing to sacrifice their lives for freedom in the fight against the Dutch. They—along with their close friends in the liberal Moslem community—had forced Soekarno to go on with the fight in 1948 when he was ready to knuckle under to the Dutch during the so-called "second police action."

The mellowing of age, the awareness that the great paradisical society they had envisaged during the fight for independence would not be brought about in their lifetime, was certainly a factor. The growing recognition after independence that political freedom from the Europeans was only the beginning of a reconstruction of their societies was another.

But I believe far more important was that inability to mix their two heritages. Too often they explained Indonesian happenings to themselves, as to others from the outside, in a framework of political analysis that was already useless in the West and which never had much application to Asian conditions.

THE GREAT MYSTERY

IT is worth noting here that few Asian intellectuals or other members of the elite have turned their attention to the most important mystery of Oriental history: Why did the technological revolution come in the West and not in Asia?

At a time when the feudal states of Europe were still struggling with the most elemental needs of their people, when their elites were semi-barbarian, great societies of enormous wealth had already risen and fallen in Asia. Not only were the Asian courts and great cities wonders of development to such stray Europeans as arrived—such as Marco Polo, who visited China in the thirteenth century—but many of the breakthroughs that were to usher in the new industrialization of the West were first found here.

The Indians had developed the concept of the zero in mathematics, not passed on to Europeans for several centuries, even after the Arabs picked it up from the Indians. The Chinese had invented gunpowder, probably before the Christian era. They developed paper in the time of Christ, and movable type at least four hundred years before Gutenberg printed his Bible. The Grand Canal of China—eight hundred miles of navigable waterways and irrigation channels, built in the seventh century and rebuilt in the thirteenth century—is still a monumental construction.

The great monuments of Angkor are architecture which dwarf the Gothic cathedrals of Europe built in the same period. The Chinese examination system for government officials existed before Julius Caesar and the consolidation of the Roman Empire. Dr. Hu Shih, the great Chinese philosopher of our times, once told me he thought that the whole concept of *laissez-faire* ("A government governs best which governs least"), one of the axioms along with the "Protestant Ethic" which led to Western industrial development, had been introduced by the Jesuits through the French *philosophes* from China to Europe.

69

Only a few Western scholars have given this question their full attention. Marx formulated, although he did not elaborate it in any great detail, his theory of "the Asiatic mode of production" in which he sought to set the Asians apart. Later Max Weber, the founder of modern sociology, was to pick up the subject and examine Indian and Chinese societies for their differences with Europe. And in our time Professor Karl Wittfogel and his theory of the hydraulic society (and resulting Oriental despotism) has tried to give an answer.

But it is a question to which Asians, despite their centuries-old heritage of speculative thinking, have given little thought. It is, indeed, a question which they studiously ignore today.

K. M. Panikkar, the brilliant Indian historian whose work, *Asia and Western Dominance*, is one of the few attempts by an Asian social scientist to examine this problem, still avoids the fundamental question of why small numbers of Europeans were able to subjugate the continent. Panikkar's view was also distorted by his bitter anti-Americanism, his pro-Russian sentiments. When I saw him in 1961, he insisted that Asia's only problem was the extension of American power into the continent. He brushed aside any suggestion that there were basic psychological and social problems which had made it impossible for Asian societies (always excluding Japan) to cope with the technological revolution.

Yet it is these same elite-intellectuals who are trying to lead their countries to the modern industrialized world. I believe there are two reasons why they avoid the fundamental question of why industrialization did not come first in Asia: On the one hand, an explanation would lead to the formulation of a concept that there is a chasm between the cultures of the West and the East. And that superficially smacks of the same kind of racism which existed in the colonial period. That is, such an acceptance of basic differences, given the present tendency to equate industrialization and human progress, would imply to a facile mind a basic inferiority of the Asian cultures and peoples.

Secondly, I believe they avoid it because those nontraditionalist thinkers in Asia who might attempt to wrestle with the problem are the victims of what I call the "feedback" from Western political, economic, and philosophical thinking. This theory and analysis are based on conditions and elements in the industrialized world that have little to do with the Asia of yesterday—or of today. And among these, of course, are the Asian activists who have been seduced by Western Communism's promise of a road map into the future.

4 ✦

Autocrats in Search of Machines

IT was one of those hot, sticky nights in Bangkok. We were all sitting out in a garden of an old Thai-style house—the living floors raised on stilts above the ground with an open area below. There was a loud chorus of bullfrogs and tree crickets, singing out of the *klong* and the trees along it just across the high hedge of bamboo that separated the little garden from the road.

My host was a small, soft-spoken Vietnamese. With him was Souphanouvong, a Lao prince, and his wife, a lovely, diminutive Vietnamese woman.

Ostensibly our host was "a private person," a refugee from the war which had broken out in Indochina earlier that year (1948) between the French and the Viet Minh—the Communist-led nationalist movement. In fact, he was the chief of the local mission of the Viet Minh, whom the Thais tolerated to function in Bangkok as a propaganda and communications center for the Vietnamese insurrectionists.

I had come with Jim Thompson, an old friend who had been with the catchall intelligence services, the Office of Strategic Services (OSS), during World War II. He had been scheduled to be parachuted into French Indochina to work clandestinely against the Japanese when the war ended abruptly after the bombings of Hiroshima and Nagasaki, and knew something of the Vietnamese nationalist aspirations. Jim had fallen in love with Southeast Asia, settled down in Bangkok, and almost single-handedly revived its dying silk industry.

Like myself and some of our friends, Jim had hoped that the predominantly nationalist Viet Minh movement might somehow be weaned away from its Communist leadership. (Jim, whom the newspapers were to call the "silk king" of Thailand, was to disappear mysteriously years later—in 1967—while on a vacation in Malaysia.)

We had been invited to dinner and after the meal we were shown a 16 mm movie in the garden. It was a propaganda film smuggled out of Vietnam, showing an attack by a Viet Minh guerrilla group against a French convoy moving along the roads outside Hanoi.

The film was of extremely poor quality. The cameraman himself was obviously a participant in the attack. And as he ran and jumped during the action, the film swayed and dimmed. Processing also had been poor and at times it almost blacked out. Nor was our projection equipment the best then—in a Bangkok that had little to do physically with the modern, bustling city of two decades later.

But the film was intriguing and spectacular. The climax was a sally by a group of young Vietnamese against a French tank. A young student attempting to knock out the tank was shown grabbing a grenade, clutching it to his chest, and literally throwing himself against the tank. He was successful—blowing himself and the tank to smithereens.

The film ended on that note. We were all a bit shaken. My host said almost to himself, "It is *affreux*—that children must die in war."

Almost before he got out the words, Madame Souphanouvong, jumping to her feet, screamed at us, "No. It is necessary. No sacrifice is too great for the fatherland—for the cause of national independence and liberty."

We were then treated to a staccato ranting mélange of Vietnamese, English, and French. It was a May Day diatribe on the glories of the national liberation movement in Vietnam and throughout Asia.

73

It was my first exposure to the realities of Communism in Asia. I had known Asian Communists in New York and Paris. But they were of a different variety, men who for the most part had lived long years in the West and whose vocabulary was the standard cant of the long period of apology for Soviet tyranny through the 1930s.

Souphanouvong was then, and still is at this writing, the titular leader of the Pathet Lao—the minority Communist guerrilla organization directed by Hanoi which has produced a *de facto* partition of Laos since 1954. Madame Souphanouvong was the same kind of Vietnamese fanatic I was to encounter over and over again in the next decades—not unlike the much more famous Madame Ngo Dinh Nhu.

Looking back on this incident over the years, I think it was fitting that my introduction to my first acknowledged Asian Communist acquaintances should have been a Lao prince and his Vietnamese wife.

For I believe one of the dominant themes of Asian Communism is its appeal, not to a starving proletariat, but to the highest echelons of the old feudal elite which has governed Asian societies in one form or another for centuries.

APPEAL TO ARISTOCRATS

THE appeal of Communism to an old aristocracy is not a phenomenon limited to Asia. Max Nomad, a no-nonsense chronicler of the whole history of rebellion and humanism in the Western world, has written, in an essay entitled "Capitalism without Capitalists," of the attempt by the Prussian authoritarian Bismarck to seduce the first prophets of "scientific socialism," Marx and Engels themselves, into his camp. Bismarck toyed with the possibility of creating a kind of Junker-Communism—a combination of feudal paternalism with Marx's call for concentrating resources in the hands of the government.

Throughout South Asia in the former colonial countries, Communism has recruited much of its leadership from the old elite. Unlike Europe, there was little scope for an appeal to dispossessed middle-class intellectuals. Only among the Overseas Chinese do you find a milieu which approximates the middle class of Western Europe. The intelligentsia, as in Imperial Russia, is largely the sons and daughters of the landlords, the mandarins of the bureaucracies of the old kingdoms, re-formed but largely intact after the conquest of these areas by the European colonialists.

Many of the rebels, the real radicals, were sloughed off by Communism in Asia in the early decades of the movement.

Almost from the Revolution, Russian foreign policy has seen the colonial problem and its heritage in Asia as a target from which it could mount an attack on its enemies in Western Europe. There is no evidence that the slogan, much quoted by both Communist and anti-Communist writers since 1945, "The Road to Paris lies through Peking," was ever enunciated by either Marx or Engels, or even Lenin. As I have pointed out, Marx and other early socialists did not see the possibility of socialism arising in Asia because of its different conditions. And, in fact, Marx considered British imperialist rule in India as "progressive" in introducing into the static and despotic society the beginnings of capitalism.

But as early as 1921, the Third Congress of the Comintern did go on record as favoring a massive Communist effort in Asia. "Without a revolution in Asia, there will be no victory for the world proletariat revolution," a circular of the Comintern said. "This must be firmly grasped by every proletarian Communist."

Yet "the Eastern question," as it came to be called in Communist circles, was not even discussed at the Third Congress, a fact which M. N. Roy, the most prestigious Asian present, protested strongly. The refusal of Communist leadership to do more in Asia, the alliance between Communist parties and "bourgeois" nationalist parties in the popular front governments in Europe of the 1930s tended to disillusion many sincere Asian revolutionaries. And it was one of the reasons why such people as Roy, the Indonesian Tan Malaka, and others were eventually to break with Moscow. Sometimes they argued that the Russians were selling out the Asians to European nationalism, at other times that Moscow was trying to use Asian "bourgeois" nationalism at the expense of Asian Communists and more "revolutionary" elements. But essentially they all found that European Communism was an import which could not or should not be sold in Asia.

The Asian political woods are thick with ex-Communists—their experiences not too different from the "god that failed" generation in the West. Today, for example, the young Westernized Parsis of Bombay, who joined the Communist movement in India under its guise of fulfilling the promises of Western European humanism, have become the most virulent anti-Communists. Their pattern of allegiance and defection is not unlike that of the sons and daughters of Jewish immigrants to the United States who joined the Communist movement in our own country at about the same time.

Others like Mohammed Hatta, one of the most important leaders of the Indonesian revolution against the Dutch, earlier rejected Marxism as a political platform for the building of the new state in Asia. As a student in Holland, he had initially cooperated with the Communists in forming the League Against Imperialism. But he broke with the Communists and the organization quickly.

Through Hatta's writings run several themes concerning Marx and the Communists which are common in the thinking of most non-Communist Asian leaders—from the more conservative to the more radical. Hatta, with a very thorough grounding in German philosophy and economics, accepts Marx as a social scientist, one among many, who points the way toward methods of inquiry that may be helpful in Asia. But Hatta says that Marxian socialist theory is not helpful as a political program in Asia because of basic differences from Europe. He points out that Islam, itself, and the village life of Java, have themes of mutual self-help that exist in European socialism. But he rejects the determinism of Marxism, which he says has little to say about the development of socialism in the lands of the East because their evolving societies will be dictated by their own history and culture.

A large base of Communist leadership in South Asia in the last forty years has come from another type of revolutionary. They are members of the old elites who see Communism as a short cut to the twentieth century—a way of modernizing their own weak and incompetent states in the struggle for power on the world scene.

They often carry their whole autocratic ritual with them. In Indonesia, for example, in the years when Soekarno was playing a game close to the Communists, his minister of education was a member of the Javanese *priyayi* (nobility)—the old Javanese aristocracy which traces its beginnings to the Shrivijaiya empire of the seventh to the fourteenth centuries.

The minister was awarded a Lenin (formerly Stalin) prize for his services to Indonesian and world Communism. Yet Indonesian non-Communist political observers were always amused that he used Javanese court language in addressing Soekarno, the special forms reserved for the sultans of the old feudal courts of Central and East Java. And this great Marxist-Leninist revolutionary backed out of Soekarno's presence, bowing and stooping in the fashion which Asian courtiers have used from time immemorial.

As I write, the central Indian government has just engineered the suspension of a nine-month government in the state of Bengal dominated by pro-Peking Indian Communists. Yet many of the important leaders of this movement—including the central figure behind the scenes—are sons of Hindu princelings of East Bengal (now East Pakistan). These men have had every advantage afforded Indians during the colonial and post-independence period, wealth and the trappings of the feudal order.

I was privy to an interesting session between one of these leaders and some of his followers a few months before their government was ousted by an increasingly anxious national government in New Delhi. Police had broken up a demonstration by strikers on the Calcutta waterfront. The strike was under the direction of radical Communist student and trade union leaders.

I was interviewing one of the aristocratic Communist leaders in his office when several of the young men involved in the altercation on the docks burst into his office, bruised after a bad mauling by the police. The conversation was partly in Bengali, partly in the Calcutta Urdu dialect. I understand only a few words of the latter.

But the manner of the Communist leader toward these men was

77

easily discernible—that of a typical high-caste Hindu, an aristocrat of the old order, talking to inferiors. And when he said *jao* (go) to clear his office and get on with our session, it came closer to an order to a servant than a command of a Communist leader to his comrades in revolution.

MANDARIN COMMUNISTS

REVOLUTIONARY slogans, often borrowed from European Communists, cannot camouflage the basic "elitism" of the new regimes set up by the Communists in Asia where they have taken power. It is significant, I think, that no member of the North Vietnamese Lao Dong (Communist) Party politburo is a "proletarian."

All are of the mandarin class which has ruled Vietnam, even indirectly under the French colonialists, for centuries. Vo Nguyen Giap, the military genius who commands the Vietnamese Communist forces, is notorious in Vietnamese circles for his haughty manner and disdain typical of the old-fashioned Vietnamese *lettrés* (schooled in the vast knowledge needed to write Chinese characters) for his social "inferiors."

Even in Communist China, which might prove the exception to the rule since its party came to power on a wave of peasant following, the appeal of Communist propaganda emanating from the Russian Revolution was to elitism rather than to humanist traditions which carried so many European intellectuals from romantic socialism into the hard line of left-wing social democracy and finally Stalinism.

Chang Kuo-tao, one of the founding members of the Chinese Communist party who later broke with its leadership, writes:

> At the time of the May Fourth Movement [1919], a number of the radical scholars and youths began to display an admiration for the Russian Revolution and to lean toward socialism. After the Chinese Communist party was established (1921), quite a few of the youth joined its ranks. In reality these young people were not genuine Communists; they had not even studied Marxism-Leninism, much less begun to have faith in it.
>
> They also had an imperfect knowledge of the theory and

practice of the Soviet Union and the Comintern. Almost all of these young people had a sense of desperation concerning China's weaknesses and degeneration. What they dreamed of was an independent and free China which would be rich and powerful.

That was the situation then, and it has not changed during the last thirty years. Why? This is what those who study modern history should explain.

An old friend and Chinese scholar, Hsieh Chen-ping, suggests that this same situation is at the root of the conflict current, as I write, between the followers of Mao Tse-tung and Liu Shao-chi which has split the leadership and following of the Chinese Communist party.

Liu began his political career as a leader of the Chinese Liberation Movement, a group of college and high school students working for "national recovery," not for Communism. I believe that we can assume that many of the Maoists' charges against their enemies as bureaucrats fighting, from their privileged position as technocrats, the more radical line of the Mao group are true. In effect, the conflict is—at least in part—a fight between those who would continue the "permanent revolution line" of Mao leadership and those members of the control organization who want to pursue a more cautious program which will not endanger the bureaucracy.

BUREAUCRAT COMMUNISTS

If the idea of the Communist state appeals to the old aristocracy of the pre-industrial past, as I have argued, it also appeals to the new aristocracy of the new states' growing bureaucracies.

Everywhere in Asia the new states have thrown up enormous bureaucratic structures that dwarf anything existing during the colonial period. The argument can be made, of course, that colonial regimes were simply control and tax-collecting organizations. As the new states attempted to begin the expansion of social welfare activities, health, education, and other kinds of social engineering, it was inevitable that they should have to expand the bureaucracy.

79

But the expansion has been beyond any justification of it on this score. India, for example, which was governed by some 300,000 central government employees before World War II, has a federal government bureaucracy of nearly three million today. And this does not include the massive growth of the states' governments, on a ratio far exceeding anything seen in New Delhi itself.

You get a picture of this incredible load of the new regime by looking at the ministerial levels of the states. The recently-created Harianna state—carved from the Indian Punjab after the creation of the Punjabi Subhi demanded by the Sikhs—had a total of twenty-three ministers and deputy ministers compared with a total of only thirty seats for the ruling coalition in the legislative assembly. And this is in a state which, by and large, includes only the deficit areas, which in terms of relative Indian poverty means food deficit, of the old Punjab!

The growth of the Indonesian bureaucracy is equally fantastic. The Netherlands East Indies was governed by a bureaucratic force of 35,000 higher civil servants, most of them Netherlands-born Hollanders, and some 170,000 other employees—part time— in the villages. The latest estimate of government employees for the current situation in Indonesia is over two million. It is almost superfluous to add that most of these are paid less than a living wage, that they must earn their livelihood from other jobs, not excluding pure and simple bribery.

To this new class of bureaucrats Communism has great attraction. It preaches total central control of authority. That means decisions cannot be questioned either by a representative assembly or by mass public opinion. It preaches highly detailed, central economic planning. That means that the bureaucrats will make the economic decisions made in Western and Japanese economies through compromise between private entrepreneurs and government. It preaches government control of cultural activities. That means a noncritical press, the use of the arts and artists by a privileged few in the government.

DEMAGOGUE COMMUNISTS

NOWHERE has this coming together of the old-style auto-crat and the new Communist doctrine of "dictatorship of the pro-letariat" exercised by a small group converged so dramatically as in Indonesia. Soekarno was not a Communist. But as his "reign" continued, he moved closer and closer to the Communists until, in 1965, he was at least informed of if not a participant in a Com-munist attempt to take power by coup d'état.

I got some foretaste of where his despotic tendencies would take him back in 1950. At that time I was a young, very naive newspaperman. I had come to Indonesia to try to found an Eng-lish-language paper. I and my backers anticipated that English would soon have to replace Dutch as the Indonesians' main tool for access to modern technology. And as had already happened in other Asian countries, we speculated on the possibility of a small but extremely influential and profitable English-language daily in Djakarta.

Over the course of almost a year I negotiated with Indonesian government officials to start the paper. They threw obstacle after obstacle in the way. And it became apparent that, whatever their other objections, the principal one was that the paper would play too significant a role to be left in the hands of foreigners. I aban-doned the project. But I stayed on to report as a free-lance for several American, European, and Asian newspapers.

Soekarno "picked me up," as he has so many other young and not-so-young American journalists since. I was treated with great deference. And I accompanied him on trips throughout the coun-try. One weekend I was invited, along with another American newsman and a Dutch journalist, to accompany Soekarno's entou-rage to East Java. The occasion was the birthday of Soekarno's mother, a handsome old Balinese lady who lived simply in retire-ment in Blitar, the small town where the President had grown up.

We all sat one evening relaxing on the porch of the little Java-nese house in which Soekarno's mother lived. We listened to the orchestra of the Sultan of Solo, a *gamelang* playing softly under the frangipani trees in the garden. It was a great concession to

81

Soekarno that the players had come. For the orchestras of the Javanese sultans and their dancers traditionally had not left the *kraton* (palace) of their lords even in Dutch colonial times. And it had its political implications, too. The Sultan of Solo had been a partisan of the Dutch in the fight of the Indonesians for independence while Soekarno headed the republic.

The conversation turned, of course, to politics. I was baiting my Dutch colleague, a socialist, about the compliance of the Dutch Labor Party in the colonial war which the Netherlands had waged periodically between 1945 and 1949 to regain control of the Indies. And I pontificated that while I was convinced that if the American socialists had failed because they had taken too dogmatic a position and alienated the great mass of the U.S. voters, the Dutch socialists had gone too far in the other extreme by participating in a government that had waged an out-and-out colonial war in order to preserve their place in the coalition postwar governments of Holland.

It was at this point that Soekarno entered the conversation. He said that the essential problem of political life was one of maintaining authority through "agitation." He predicted—and I remember that he used the English slang phrase "out-agitate"—that he would be able to out-maneuver the Communists by such appeals to the masses.

Soekarno said it was for this reason that he had, within months of the signature of the new agreement setting up a condominium between the United States of Indonesia and the Netherlands over the former Dutch New Guinea, begun to demand its transfer to Indonesia. It was, he said, an example of how he snatched an issue from under the Communists' noses.

As time went on, it became clear that the differences between Soekarno and the Communists were narrowing on the domestic political scene. Soekarno's Nationalist Party was left without a *raison d'être*, its one slogan and aim gone when political independence came. It turned increasingly to Communist formulations of policy through Soekarno and its left wing, recruited among the same masses in Central and East Java where the Communists have had a following since the early 1920s. By the early 1960s, front groups in Java labeled "nationalist" were in fact largely in the hands of the Communists.

THE STATE CAPITALISTS

PERHAPS even more attractive to the new bureaucratic classes of the underdeveloped states in Asia is the Communist espousal of total government control of the economy. Capitalism for the newly independent states' elites is synonymous with the exploitive colonial systems they knew.

From the days of the British East India Company and the (Dutch) United East India Company, one of the main images of the European domination of Asia has been the vast European trading companies and their industrial offshoots.

Even as late as 1950 in Indonesia, the Big Five Dutch and British trading combines were the principal arbiters of commerce in Indonesia, along with the monopolistic Dutch inter-island shipping company, an Anglo-Dutch oil company, and the Dutch international and domestic airlines.

But if the rationale for state capitalism in the new countries has been that private entrepreneurial enterprise was synonymous with the old monopolies of the colonial system, the reality has been that the bureaucrats wanted in their own hands the power afforded by control of the economy. No better example exists than the State Trading Corporation of India.

It has grown into such a Frankenstein's monster that it threatens to eclipse Indian private international traders. Its notorious inefficiency and corruption is one of the scandals of the current Indian scene. Its origins go back to the early 1950s when the Indian government decided to begin extensive trading with the Communist bloc in Europe. Prime Minister Nehru's advisers in the foreign office warned that the Communists could use profits from the trade to fund the Indian Communist movement. And, indeed, it was common gossip that Russian newsprint was being sold at bargain prices, with profits used to fund local Communist journalistic endeavors.

The S.T.C. was created to give the Indians a government body with which to deal with the government agencies trading for the European Communist economies. But almost immediately its fief began to expand. In part, it was unavoidable. The S.T.C. argued, for example, that it could not import cement for a fluctuating market if it did not control all cement imports. And this meant that imports of cement from non-Communist sources, too, were rerouted through the S.T.C. Gradually the S.T.C. has moved into fields for which it was never intended.

A good example was told me by a Calcutta business executive. An exporter was selling coal to a Hong Kong utility company. The coal was priced marginally because of the bitter competition from petroleum. Suddenly a coal export corporation was created under S.T.C. auspices. The exporter was forced to go to the coal export authority for a license to ship. The license simply meant adding another 2 or 3 per cent to the cost of the coal as the coal export authority's "handling costs." And the exporter lost his Hong Kong customer to more efficient sources of supply. The incident is not untypical. The Indians have, for example, lost a large portion of Japan's mushrooming iron ore market for the same reason.

But the S.T.C. has provided another huge reservoir of jobs for bureaucrats. There is the usual nepotism involved in such bureaucratic expansions in Asia (and, I might add, in the West). But I think that it is as significant that after the fall of the Russian fellow-traveler V. K. Krishna Menon from power in the disaster brought on by the Chinese Communist invasion of India's Himalayan marches in 1962, several of his former lieutenants found jobs there.

Soekarno again provides the example of the appeal of Communist ideals for art in the new states. His collection of modern Indonesian painting is, according to most connoisseurs, one of the greatest heaps of rubbish in the underdeveloped world. But he played *grand seigneur* to a few hundred Indonesian artists who painted on command.

The collection was housed in the old Dutch colonial governor-general's palace in Djakarta and was seen only by those who were admitted to "the royal presence." (The Chinese Communists, in a move to win favor with Soekarno, published an enormously expensive volume with full color plates of the collection. Perhaps rarely has so much attention and expense been lavished on such worthless artistic material.)

His authority over the press was hardly less than that of the Communist states themselves. My good friend, Mochtar Lubis, one of Asia's most brilliant young journalists, was jailed for nine years—with no charge, no trial—for *lèse majesté* against the person of Soekarno.

Ironically, this reinforcing of traditional forms of Asian despotism by "socialism" had been foreseen by its earliest proponents. Marx, Engels, and even Lenin feared a combination of the bureaucratic strength of the traditional Oriental tyranny and the new socialist ideas. Lenin, in fact, warned of an "Asiatic restoration" in Russia which might come if the socialist revolution did not come concurrently in the West.

ASIAN COMMUNISM

If Communism's appeal in Asia is to the old and the new aristocracies—in part sharing that same appeal to these classes in Europe and particularly Eastern Europe—it also has important features in Asia which are unknown elsewhere. It has become a cliché to say that the great appeal of Communism in Asia is to nationalist sentiment.

Again, Sjahrir, himself a social democrat who knew what Marxism and Communism were and had rejected Communism, wrote from the New Guinea prison:

> With respect to the first prisoners who were sent here after the famous [Communist] uprising of 1927, the largest part of these men, who followed the command of the P.K.I. [Indonesian Communist Party] at that time, did so with the same sort of disposition that they would have followed any *prince* [my italics] or venal quack or lunatic. . . .
>
> They are, simply and fundamentally, Indonesians: that is to say, Javanese, Menangkabauers, Bantammers, or Soendanese. If one wishes to understand them, one must regard them in this light first of all, and only then can one really evaluate the so-called communism that many of them profess. And if one then

85

makes such an evaluation, one finds that it is a strange sort of communism, indeed, a mythical Hindu-istic-Javanese, Islamic-Menangkabau, or Islamic-Bantam sort of communism, with definite animistic tendencies. There are not many European communists who could recognize anything of their communism in this Indonesian variety!

Certainly under the oldest doctrine in the world of politics—"My enemy's enemy is my friend"—the elites of the new states, weaned on the milk of anti-colonialism, were bound to look with some favor on those who the former colonial masters in the West (the British, the French, the Dutch, the U.S.) felt after World War II were their principal enemies (the Soviet Union and its allies in Central Europe).

But I believe that this equating of the Communists' appeal to nationalism with what we think of as nationalism in the West is too facile.

The "nationalism" of the old Asian societies is a distinct phenomenon. It is true, of course, that Western nationalisms also are very specific entities. The basis of Czech nationalism, for example, is the Czechs' bitter love-hate for the Germans and their long memories of Austrian tutelage, and now twenty years of Russian domination. Or the prime ingredient of Mexican nationalism can be said to be "anti-*gringo*-ism" developed in the almost two centuries of living in the shadow of the "colossus of the north."

It is this aspect of nationalism as a single, unique appeal to one facet of loyalty—rather than an appeal to loyalties to a multitude of concepts embodied in the nation-state idea which has rarely existed in Asia—that is most significant.

CHINESE NATIONALISM

I OFFER the case of the Chinese. Their ethnocentricity is notorious and could be called Chinese nationalism. But I believe no one who has only read about it can appreciate its intensity or its quality until he comes into contact with it on a personal basis.

A few years ago I was being feted by a party of Chinese friends in Tokyo. They were a highly sophisticated group. All were refugees from Communist China. Some departed the Mainland before the Communists consolidated their power in 1949 because of their long-standing hatred and struggle against the Communists. Yet they are also opponents of the nationalist regime in Taiwan, bitter enemies of the policies of Chiang Kai-shek on the Mainland which, they believe, brought on the Communist victory. Younger members of the group are former Communists who joined the movement in the 1940s, lived to regret their mistake, and escaped from the Mainland through Hong Kong.

In the course of our conversation that evening we discussed the problem of China and her relations with the rest of Asia. All admitted, and some even went so far as to annotate, China's history of "great nation chauvinism" toward her smaller neighbors. But only a few minutes further along in the conversation, they turned to the subject of the Japanese. And for more than half an hour, I and a member of my family with me, were treated to the spectacle of emotional, inflamed rhetoric on how the Japanese had simply copied everything they had—culturally, socially, economically— from the Chinese!

The argument, of course, holds some water. But no member of that highly sophisticated group, all speaking Japanese and with a great knowledge of Japan's history, would have denied, if the question had been posed, that the Japanese transformation of the past century into an industrial giant during a period when China went further into decline was not, in fact, a tribute to the basic differences between the two countries and their cultures.

The Chinese, through the ages, from their position at "the center of the universe," could equate the behavior of the Western "barbarians" with the North Asian tribes who have invaded China over the centuries. The foisting of opium on China even when it was illegal in the West, the "pig trade" in Chinese coolie "shanghaied" labor in the mid-nineteenth century, the burning of the Summer Palace during the Boxer Rebellion were acts of barbarism committed by Westerners on the Chinese seldom equaled by representatives of any civilized society. But even in the midst of their humiliating experience with the power of Western colonialism in the past century and a half, China's elite had their fabulous history to look back on.

I wonder if today one of the most powerful influences in the

Russo-Chinese conflict over Communism is not the intellectual arrogance of the Chinese: The assumption that, of course, it would "naturally" be Chinese leadership which would perfect the Marxist-Leninist dogma to find a synthesis of ancient patterns of conduct and modern technology instead of the Russian "barbarians."

Nowhere do you see more this use by Communist propagandists of "Chinese nationalism" as the main prop for their proselytizing than among the more than twenty million Overseas Chinese in Southeast Asia. (My estimate is of all ethnic Chinese, whatever their citizenship or their current status vis-à-vis their acknowledgment of their Chinese ancestry.) These Chinese are the descendants of immigrants from the Mainland who had gone abroad, drawn by the opportunities to lead a better economic life. They are, on the whole, from the lowest echelons of Chinese society on the Mainland. Most came as illiterate workmen, often as coolies indentured to the big European companies.

Today, much of their subculture is typical of a middle-class society anywhere. There is a drive for physical comfort, for economic security. They have been, generally, apolitical—content to live outside the main political stream of the former colonial societies where they made their living. (The notable exception is, of course, their support—largely monetary—in the early 1900s of Sun Yat-sen and the leaders of the Chinese revolution against the Manchu dynasty.)

They had a preferred, or at least a special, position in the colonial system: They were middlemen through whom the economic system worked. Ambitious, pragmatic, hard working, urbanized for the most part, they provided the yeast necessary for the large European enterprises to market their products, to collect their raw materials for export to the industrialized countries, to overcome the inertia of the peasant societies of Southeast Asia.

Material success has brought some integration into the power elites of the countries in which they live—in Thailand, Burma, the Philippines, and to some extent Vietnam. Even in Indonesia they penetrated slightly into the world of the Dutch-speaking Eurasian community with its special status.

In one Southeast Asian country today two of the most important members of the cabinet are by race pure Chinese. And, incidentally, they are the two most outspoken anti-Communist, anti-Peking members of the government. Ne Win, the present dictator of Burma, was born of a Chinese father.

In fact, they repeated what Chinese have been doing for centuries. Emigrants descending into Southeast Asia have been crucial in the history of the region. For example, the present kingdom of Thailand was in fact founded by a Chinese warlord adventurer. The Thais themselves earlier came down off the central Asian plateau in what is now China.

The advent of European colonial rule and steam sea transportation turned the traditional slow "Chinese" movement south into a mass migration. Whole Chinese families came—and often maintained at least a tenuous contact with their relatives at home. They organized in clans, mutual aid societies, and set up Chinese schools.

When the Overseas Chinese were barred from integration, as has often been the case, they turned back to their Chinese heritage. Second and third generation offspring who went into law and medicine became aware of the great Chinese past. They sent their children to Chinese schools. Sometimes they sent them back to Mainland China for education, aspiring to have a scholar in the family, the culmination of traditional values in the Chinese society.

The advent of the Chinese Communist regime in China was cataclysmic for these populations. In the early 1950s, it was a commonplace to say that China would eventually gobble up the whole of South Asia. The new Chinese Communist diplomatic missions, where they were allowed to operate, began preaching the word. They denigrated the new non-Communist leadership of the new Southeast Asian states. In Indonesia, the Chinese Communist ambassador was declared *persona non grata* in 1950 because he had written a book in which he attacked the then vice-president, Mohammed Hatta. In Laos, a Lao-Thai-speaking former school teacher and editor of a Communist Chinese newspaper in Bangkok, expelled from Thailand, turned up as the leader of the Chinese Communist Embassy.

The Communist officials infiltrated and sometimes took over

the old mutual aid societies of the local Chinese communities based on their community ties from old China. They "taxed" local Chinese Communists to pay for Communist subversion. But most of all, they promised the Overseas Chinese—caught in between as the enemy of the impoverished peasantry as middlemen and as the victims of discrimination by the new nationalistic governments seeking to curb their economic power—that they would be the new *Herrenvolk* of an Asia dominated by China.

OVERSEAS CHINESE VIS-À-VIS PEKING

ONLY slowly did the events in China boomerang. Slowly the "underdog" Chinese resident of Java or Cambodia heard that the new regime in China was antagonistic to the very classes of small entrepreneurs that he represented. He learned that the Chinese Communists were out to destroy much of the old cultural heritage that the Overseas Chinese, just beginning to have economic and intellectual resources to appreciate it, had begun to take pride in.

The events of the late 1950s turned the tide against Peking. The hard line and success of the Americans during the 1958 Taiwan Straits crisis, when the Chinese Communists made a feint toward the remnants of the Nationalist regime in Formosa, destroyed the myth of the "inevitability" of Peking's control of Southeast Asia. (A significant part of the Chinese community in Singapore and Malaysia comes from the Fukien coast and the Offshore Islands, intimately involved in the dispute.)

Meanwhile, the Chinese themselves, with the greatly increased communications, began to make a new appraisal of what the Communists were accomplishing in China and at what cost.

There were changes in Southeast Asia, too. In Singapore, a bright, ambitious and pragmatic group of Chinese took control of local government as the British relinquished their colonial hold. Under the leadership of Lee Kwan Yew, a program of social welfare and an attempt to build local loyalties were begun. The Overseas Chinese in Singapore began to calculate that the new "wave of the future" might not be the Chinese

Communists. The best indicator was the fact that the two-to-one ratio of Chinese choosing whether to study in Singapore's Chinese or English language schools reversed between 1950 and 1960. Young Chinese saw their hope of advancement rested largely on the basis of knowing the English language and not traditional Chinese learning.

The story is not over, of course. Since 1965 there has again been a sharp turn in the fortunes of the Overseas Chinese and their problems. American commitment in Vietnam, the failure of the Chinese Communist-backed coup d'état in Indonesia in 1965, the movements—however feeble—for regional grouping in Southeast Asia behind the American shield for mutual security against the Chinese threat have had peculiar side effects.

In Indonesia the Chinese have been the victims of a series of "pogroms" in the wake of the anti-Communist reaction to the failure of the Peking-backed Communist coup d'état. In Burma, where anti-Communists and neutralists cooperated from the early 1950s in a policy of buying peace with their huge Chinese neighbor to the north at any cost, the government of General Ne Win has given tacit approval to local campaigns against Peking—with the prospect that they will turn repeatedly into attacks on local Chinese, such as occurred in Rangoon in 1967.

It remains to be seen how much Peking can continue to exploit the situation of the Overseas Chinese—caught as he is between his own and very personal anti-Communist sympathies, his visceral allegiance to China as the fatherland of his culture, and local persecution and opportunities afforded in Southeast Asia.

GROWING-UP CHINESE

THE human tragedies involved are the essence of the struggle. Not long ago I visited an old Overseas Chinese friend and his family in the Indonesian mountain capital of Bandung. Bandung has been the center of the anti-Soekarno, anti-Communist agitation on the island of Java since 1965.

My friend is a Westernized Chinese; during the past decade he and his family and Chinese friends have been among the chief victims of the Soekarno regime's oppression of the small entrepreneur, the anti-Communist professionals.

He speaks no Chinese, although he does speak Dutch and English and was educated in Europe. The family chose Indonesian citizenship on independence in 1950. And his only Chinese identity is his physiognomy. Yet when a wave of anti-Communist agitation broke out in 1963, in part organized for political purposes by Soekarno's enemies, it turned anti-Chinese. My friend's house was one of the first to be attacked and partially destroyed. I saw him not long afterward. Both he and his wife were in a state of shock—victims of a persecution for which they had no real psychological defenses.

Again, the dilemma of the Overseas Chinese was poignantly presented to me during the same trip to Indonesia. I looked up a former trade union leader in Djakarta. He was an ethnic Chinese, and in the immediate post-independence period in 1950 he was an organizer of a socialist office workers' trade union—virtually the only honest bread-and-potatoes organization in Djakarta, where Communist propaganda organizations posed as trade unions. He was a confirmed European-style social democrat, an anti-Communist. And he was trying to bring non-Chinese Indonesian leadership into the union, understanding that his role as a Chinese handicapped its ability to recruit non-Chinese workers.

But by 1965, he was terrified of the growing anti-Chinese feeling in the largely Moslem anti-Communist movement. He told me that he had arranged to emigrate to join relatives in Australia. And he argued that only Soekarno, who had made an unpublicized speech before the Chinese Chamber of Commerce in Djakarta a short time earlier proudly relating that he had "Chinese blood," stood between the Chinese and massacre. The problem of Soekarno's alliance with the Communists and Peking was no longer his concern, caught as he was in the growing atmosphere of racism.

The other side of the coin is the insensitivity of much of Indonesia's non-Chinese leadership to the nature of the predicament. After the Bandung rioting, I spoke to one of Indonesia's most honored and sincere anti-Communist leaders. He is a man known throughout the country for his humanitarianism and liberality. Yet, he told me that "the Chinese have brought this on themselves." He pointed to the fact that Chinese students at the Bandung schools had tape recorders, radios, bicycles, and other material advantages that the non-Chinese and poorer Indonesian students could not afford. He pointed out that the Chinese merchants rode about in big American cars which the profits from their retail businesses made possible. And he was very close to saying that the Chinese had brought on their persecution not only by their affiliation, either real or imagined, with the Communists, but also by their very energy and ambition.

The moral dilemma—like so much of the race problem in the U.S., in East Africa between the Negroes and the Indians, or in a hundred other places around the world—is extremely complex and difficult of solution. And there is no reason to believe that it will not be a source of political problems for a long time.

COMMUNIST NATIONALISTS

THE exploitation of Chinese chauvinism and persecution is only one of the traditionalist themes that is used by Asian Communist leadership. Today in India the Communists—along with their supposed arch-enemies, the traditionalists—are among the chief exponents of Indian separatism and local "nationalism."

In Bengal, for example, the pro-Peking leadership of the party is trying to use the conflict between the Bengali-speaking population of Calcutta and the rural areas and the predominantly non-Bengali Calcutta industry and business leaders. And through its domination of the many splinter political groups working against the Congress Party, ruling in New Delhi, it is appealing to "Bengali nationalism" against the all-India government.

Bengal has a long history of separatist currents dividing it from the rest of northern India. The Bengali intellectual is extremely proud of his nineteenth-century heritage of Hindu reform, a literary renaissance, and the role of Calcutta as the chief gateway

93

for the entry of Western ideas to India for the long period (until 1912) when it was the political and economic capital of the British Indian Empire. They are still fond of quoting a proverb of the nineteenth century: "What Bengal thinks today, India thinks tomorrow." It is typical of Communist tactics in Asia that they should try to harness this feeling against the central non-Communist Indian state.

The Communist insurgency in Northeast Thailand, among the Malay population and the Chinese of peninsula Thailand, and in the isolated Chinese community of Sarawak in Malaysian Borneo are all examples of this attempt to use local "nationalism" against the central government. The first Communist attempts at organization in Thailand in the 1920s were, in fact, among the Overseas Chinese at a time when integration had gone much less far than today.

Yet for all the effectiveness of Communist propaganda in Asia, for all the power demonstrated by the new centralized state they have built in China, the efficiency of the politico-military machine built by the North Vietnamese Communists in Indochina, the discipline demonstrated by the North Korean regime, Communism is faced with a basic problem in Asia:

Can it prove itself as a relevant ideology, an intruder, too, along with other European concepts from its very different origins in Western and Eastern Europe, transplanted into the Asian environment?

For beyond its determinist aspects—that is, its doctrine of the inevitability of class warfare and socialism—its preaches progress and must bring hope of solution to Asia's vast problems.

Once, a few years ago in a frank conversation with a Bengali Communist, a pro-Peking partisan, we talked about the enormous technological problems faced by any Indian regime. I asked him if he did not, as a highly sophisticated, Western-educated professional man of great competence, believe as I did that Communist dogma offered no solutions for what Nehru once called "the nightmare city of Calcutta."

His answer was succinct: "Certainly not." I asked, then, what he believed his Communist friends were trying to do. His answer again was brief: "They are trying to create chaos." And he told me that he had warned an intimate friend, one of the leaders of the Bengal movement, that "he must be careful, for this is the real *Lumpenproletariat* and, once unleashed, there is no telling where they would lead us."

But only two years later my acquaintance was part and parcel of a Bengal state regime dominated by the Communists, following just the course of which he had expressed fear.

I am convinced that he reflects the thought and feeling of many South Asian Communist leaders. They are caught, many of them, in a net of a lifetime's pursuit of a program which they no longer believe is relevant. But they know no other place to turn.

It is this problem of Asian adaptation (along with the strength that the Chinese Communists have shown in coping, at least until the chaos of the Cultural Revolution from 1965, with the problem of control in China) that has made Mao Tse-tung the leader of much of the Communist movement in Asia despite the Russians' superior resources. In India, for example, the Russians have been left with the bulk of what Stalin once called "the seat warmers"—old party hacks who have followed the Moscow line for thirty years through all its torturous turns and who have a vested interest in not turning their backs on it now.

Pro-Moscow leadership has also paid a high price in Asia for the twists and turns of the Comintern line, the slavish following of Soviet foreign policy objectives rather than the revolutionary goals of the Asian leaders. In India, the Communist leader Dange fought the nationalist leadership of Gandhi when it opposed Indian participation in World War II—even turning informer for the British police. But only a few months earlier, he had been willing to take an anti-war position in the brief period between the Hitler-Stalin Pact and the Nazis' invasion of the Soviet Union which suddenly turned an "imperialists' war" into a "people's war."

In Indonesia, the 1948 attempt at a coup d'état against the Republic while it was fighting the Dutch was ordered as part of Moscow's whole "Calcutta line"—the beginning of the wave of Communist insurgencies against the new so-called bourgeois nationalist and independent regimes forming in India, Burma, Malaya, the Philippines, and Vietnam. Earlier, during much of

95

the 1930s, Asian Communists found their "comrades" in the European colonial countries soft-pedaling or even opposing independence because it conflicted with their attempts to form popular front governments to resist the growing menace of fascism in Europe. I believe it is easily explained, psychologically, how an older generation which managed to survive the mental torture of the Communist discipline "rides" with it now, whatever the events.

MAO'S APPEAL TO ASIANS

EVERYWHERE in Southeast Asia the young, intelligent, dedicated party workers are swinging over to the Peking line, if for no other reason than that it presents a relatively simple and clear-cut analysis of the contemporary scene. In India, for example, Moscow and its Indian followers by and large have supported the New Delhi government in the international arena. This forces the pro-Russian Indian Communists to modify their criticism of the present regime. The pro-Russian Communist line often comes down to a simple promise that they would work the Congress Party's program better were they in office. The pro-Peking leadership, on the other hand, starts out with the fundamental revolutionary statement that the *status quo* is untenable, that it must be blown up. It is a frank statement that they are have-nots and that the haves are in power. It is also a flagrant appeal to racism. In the early 1960s, one of the most widely distributed Chinese Communist posters was a picture of Mao in a group of colored Asians and Africans in national costume with the simple title, "Mao Tse-tung and the Family of Nations."

To many sincere young Indian radicals, the choice of which is most pertinent to his own situation is clear. He sees around him starvation, stagnation, demoralization. Action, even if the end is not in sight, seems a clear path. The pro-Peking Communist leadership has even been able to overcome nationalist sentiment brought on by the 1962 attack of the Chinese Communists on India, explaining it as provocation by an Indian government backed by "the imperialists."

In fact, their basic antagonism to the Moscovite leadership of the party was heightened by collaboration between the pro-Moscow leadership and the Indian government during the period of the Chinese invasion. It was no secret in New Delhi that a list of "Chinese" Communists to be arrested under emergency decrees at that time was prepared for Nehru by the Russian-backed wing of the party.

For most Asian Communist intellectuals, the choice during the past twenty years has been clear: Either they must adapt their essentially European dogma of Communism—or abandon it. Some of the most illustrious revolutionaries have done just that and quit the Communist movement—M. N. Roy of India, one of the few Asians ever to reach the top rung of the Comintern, Tan Malaka of Indonesia, perhaps the most dramatic and charismatic figure in the whole Indonesian revolution, Ch'en Tu-hsui, one of the founding members of the Chinese Communist party.

All three of these men—so different in personality, yet so similar in their roles as activists who dominated the radical movements in their own countries during much of their lifetime—changed their opinions violently in the great events between the Russian Revolution in 1917 and the approach of World War II. But all three finally broke with the Moscow-led Communist International movement. The individual episodes which brought on the break were quite different. But, I believe, the essential similarity was their intolerable position, caught between the demands of Russian foreign policy and Communist dogma and their own vast knowledge of the local, particular problems of their own countries.

Much of what they said at the time they broke with the Communists has either been destroyed or couched in such polemic terms as to obscure the basic disagreements and difficulties. But a letter of Ch'en Tu-hsui publicly answering charges of the Chinese Communist party against him and his former leadership on December 10, 1929, succinctly sums up the issue of the revolutionary opposition to the Moscow leadership:

> I, who was not clear in perception nor in decision in upholding my opinions, sincerely carried out the opportunist policy in the Communist International, and became the instrument of the narrow Stalinist faction. I could not save the Chinese

Communist party nor the revolution. For this, the other comrades and I are responsible. . . .

For many present-day Communists, the dilemma has led them to Maoism—either in its entirety or as an example of how the tenets of Marxism-Leninism may have value in the Asian environment.

As early as 1947 Anna Louise Strong, the American Communist journalist, pointed out what Mao was trying to do. Her article, which first appeared in the American magazine *Amerasia*—and for which she was arrested and deported from the Soviet Union—anticipated the long feud between Moscow and Peking leadership that would finally erupt in the earth-shaking Soviet-Chinese breach.

Ironically, the article was based on long conversations Miss Strong had with Liu Shao-chi, today's arch-enemy of Mao and the Maoists. He said, she wrote then:

Mao Tse-tung's great accomplishment has been to change Marxism from a European to an Asiatic form. Marx and Lenin were Europeans; they wrote in European languages about European histories and problems, seldom discussing Asia or China. The basic principles of Marxism are undoubtedly adaptable to all countries, but to apply their general truth to the concrete revolutionary practices in China is a difficult task. Mao Tse-tung is Chinese; he analyzes Chinese problems and guides the Chinese people in their struggle to victory. He uses Marxist-Leninist principles to explain Chinese history and the practical problems of China. He is the first that has succeeded in doing so. Not only has he applied Marxist methods to solve the problems of 450 million people, but he has popularized Marxism among the Chinese people as a weapon for them to use. On every kind of problem—the nation, the peasants, the strategy, the construction of the Party, literature and culture, military affairs, finance and economy, methods of work, philosophy—Mao has not only applied Marxism to new conditions but has given it a new development. He has created a Chinese or Asiatic form of Marxism. China is a semi-feudal, semi-colonial country in which vast numbers of people live on the edge of starvation, tilling small bits of soil. Its economy is agricultural, backward, and dispersed. In attempting the transition to a more industrialized economy, China faces competition and the pressures—economic, political, and military—of advanced industrial lands. This is the basic situation that affects both the relations of social classes and the methods of struggle towards any such goal as national independence and a better, freer life for the Chinese. There are similar conditions in other lands of Southeast Asia. The course chosen by China will influence them all.

Miss Strong has, of course, overstated her argument. But Maoism is still a clear, clarion call to other Asian radicals. And it was seen as such when it first appeared. The article was published and received with much attention in India by the Communist Party before the Russians forced a change in party leadership, the publication's recall, and expurgation.

The future impact of Communist appeal on other Asians will depend, as Liu told Miss Strong, to a considerable extent on the Chinese Communist successes. And the outcome of the current struggle between the followers of Mao and the "bureaucrats" could be crucial.

Yet, in the long run, the problem for the advocates of Communism in Asia is the same as for the advocates of non-Communist systems: What will work? And it is clear, as I shall try to point out, that the magnitude of the problems dwarfs any of the present approaches to their resolution. But first, let us turn our attention to the phenomenon of Americans in Asia.

PART TWO ❀

THE
AMERICANS

5 ✴

The Establishment for Export

THE middle-aged couple reminded me of our neighbors when I was growing up in a mountain village of North Carolina: Warm, good, solid American Protestant farmers—the kind that serve heaping dishes of nutritious but lightly seasoned food, often two or three starches on the same plate. They were indeed described by that phrase, "the salt of the earth."

Yet the whole scene was misplaced. For they were living in a medium-sized city of South India, the only foreigners except for two American Peace Corps girl volunteers in the local hospital. Potable water for washing and cooking had to be brought from a great distance. The house was as neat as any Midwestern American farmhouse inside. But my host, an agricultural technician working for the AID mission, told me when his wife was out of hearing that constant human defecation in the garden had "upset" his wife.

They had been there for almost two years when I visited them. And in that time, the American foundation executives supervising the project in New Delhi, who had suggested I visit them, had come only once to see how the work was coming. "Work," itself, was advising Indian agricultural extension officials in a rich, delta farming area. But in order to get what was decent housing by American standards, the couple lived some fifty miles away from the central office of the project, to which the husband commuted every day over rough Indian roads, past bullock carts and miniaturized donkey pack trains.

103

The couple had come with the kind of missionary spirit that infuses most American officials abroad in Asia. But they had been worn down by the difficulties of the problem itself—of trying to revolutionize even a small part of Indian agriculture in a pilot project—by the lack of realism in the U.S. Embassy in New Delhi about the project and official instructions passed down. And there was constant friction with the Indian bureaucracy, more concerned with higher echelons in Delhi than with the farmers it was supposed to be helping.

The tone of their whole stay had been set early on. The housewife, in the "neighborly" way of rural Americans, had invited local wives to her house for tea. But here, as in many places in South India, the local leadership was Brahmin. They came. But they could not eat or drink in the house of a foreigner, an "outcaste."

The housewife recounted the anecdote. She said she understood, but it was obvious that neither of them could quite accept the situation. When this rebuff—or what they felt was a rebuff —was multiplied by others over the weeks and months, they withdrew to a solitary existence.

And when they awakened me at four o'clock in the morning to catch a train in a tour of American aid projects (they had packed me some sandwiches and tea so that I might not risk a bad case of diarrhea from eating on the train before my next stop some nine hours away), I left feeling almost as heartsick about them as they seemed to feel themselves about their efforts.

The incident is not typical, perhaps. But it is common enough. And I think it gives some insight into the enormous problems of the bureaucracy trying to carry out our foreign policy in Asia.

GOVERNMENTAL MISSIONS

THAT bureaucracy is immense. All told, there are some fourteen thousand employees (excluding off-embassy Central Intelligence Agency employees) of the American government in Asian embassies of the U.S. from Suez to Hokkaido. Only about 18 per cent of these are officially "diplomats"; that is, employees of the Department of State. The vast majority are specialists, their operations being extensions of the activities of the various American government agencies directly concerned with foreign affairs, AID or the Defense Department, or indirectly related to its problems, like the Commerce and Agriculture Departments.

Few Americans, even those informed on the larger issues of American foreign policy, are cognizant of the ramifications of this bureaucracy. Everywhere it is attempting to fill the vacuum created by the withdrawal of West European colonial power and the growing ambitions and needs of the new Asian governments:

An American representative of the U.S. Civil Aeronautics Administration in Bangkok, the hub of East Asia's airlines' systems, plots traffic-growth patterns and plans with Thai officials for a new airport.

U.S. Foreign Agricultural Service officials work with the Indians on new methods of crop census.

An official of the U.S. Atomic Energy Commission in Tokyo helps arrange financing and training of technicians for half a dozen experimental reactors in as many East Asian countries.

A United States Information Service representative in Trivandrum, Kerala, on the southwest coast of India—the only U.S. official within six or seven hours' plane ride—helps a local newspaper with technical problems of getting and printing news.

You get some idea of the growth in the past two decades from a few figures: Today the U.S. maintains seventy-seven diplomatic missions and posts in Asian countries. In 1939 there were only fifty.

Problems for this bureaucracy begin and end with the most mundane—what we may call, for lack of a better over-all term, the problem of creature comforts.

Americans are a race apart when it comes to living standards. And they take their whole elaborate material life with them wherever they go.

During the 1963-64 political crisis period in Vietnam, before the entry of American troops in mass, I was startled to find the deodorized material for cats' refuse boxes on sale in the military retail store in Saigon! And later, when the U.S. troops arrived in large numbers, the incredible array in the military retail stores compared favorably with any American supermarket. Once, standing in line, I heard an American soldier complain bitterly that while he had been able to purchase an ironing board, there were no ironing-board covers!

At Da Nang, some five hundred miles north of the central discharge point for American goods at Saigon, I found in 1964 elaborate high-fidelity radio and phonograph equipment. Again, the display would have matched anything available in a shop in the U.S. That equipment had to be purchased in Japan, transported to Vietnam for sale, and then carted back to the United States as "hold baggage" of American soldiers and civilians. Once, visiting an American army unit in an isolated area of central Vietnam, I found it difficult to walk through the bunker-quarters where the men lived for the mass of electronic gear—I counted three tape recorders, two phonographs, and five radios. There were only five men—one officer, one civilian, two sergeants, and a G.I.—in the unit.

Problems associated with these creature comforts are often aggravated for the American bureaucracy by local government. For example, some Asian local governments forbid Americans in government service to resell their automobiles because they bring such high prices on the local market restricted by import controls. That can mean that a local embassy employee must bring a car in with him—there is rarely adequate local transport—and then the U.S. government must ship it out again when he leaves. The amount of time and expense involved in getting such shipments of household effects through local customs, ports which often are subject to wholesale theft and mishandling, and from one isolated area to another is astronomical.

American tourists who ride the magic carpet of the international airlines, served caviar and champagne over six continents with little variation, and moving from one "international style" hotel to another in all parts of the world, see little of the problem. But few Americans today can maintain a hectic office schedule, or bounce around an Asian country on field trips, without having as a "base" living quarters along U.S. lines. At best that is difficult and expensive, if not impossible to provide.

Posts in the Asian tropics are enervating. Few Americans live in India for six months without coming down with some kind of disease—often a not serious but nagging abdominal complaint or a fungus infection. And tens of my friends, veterans of diplomatic posts in Asia, have more serious semi-permanent maladies like amoebic dysentery, malaria, or simply chronic bad digestion. The atmosphere of poverty, the general misery, the tensions brought on by living in an alien environment but working on a more or less Stateside schedule take a heavy psychological toll.

Wives have an even tougher time than their husbands. In much of Asia, American women find housework impossible. Shopping and many of the ordinary functions of U.S. housekeeping are not possible because of the language barrier, because of local custom, and sometimes just physically impossible.

Servants are generally available, of course. But their supervision—a lost art to most Americans reared in the new age of domestic appliances—is difficult. And the American is not used to the whole complicated "feudal" obligations toward the servant's family and problems he is expected to assume.

There is endless entertaining—ironically, because of American wealth now expected of U.S. officialdom abroad by most local capital city societies in Asia. Official life is so entangled with this entertaining that most jobs for the U.S. government official in an Asian embassy become twenty-four-hour affairs.

Take, for example, the case of a Southeast Asian mission that I have known over many years. Twenty years ago, the ambassador's wife was a highly motivated, aggressive and competent woman who initiated with wives of embassy personnel a modest, American style social-work program. Local officials and businessmen's wives were brought into the projects. Now it has mushroomed in size—and cost—with a growing city. The mission wives today are hard pressed to keep up with the vast commitment of time involved. Charity bazaars and other expenditures are also a real financial sacrifice and embarrassment—particularly for the wives of the younger and less well paid embassy officials.

U.S. FAMILY PROBLEMS

Unless the husband and wife are resourceful, they may find themselves isolated. The constant moving—most tours are for two or three years, and rarely does a State Department official serve more than a maximum of five years in a "post"—increases the burden. There is a constant process of making new friends, stabilizing a home, getting into a routine. Most Oriental languages are difficult and rarely have any international currency. About the time a couple (and their children) may feel they have begun to settle in, have a group of local friends, begun to have some knowledge of the enormous (but extremely important) nonofficial aspects of the society of the host country, it is time to move on.

Rearing American children presents equally difficult decisions. In many posts there is no American- or English-language school. That means that children must be sent off to school at an early age—something most American families feel is a personal sacrifice (just as they would at home) even if most of the cost is borne by the government. There is the continual worry that they are not leading "normal" young American lives, that they may become strangers to their own country and never quite belong to any of the societies in which their parents are posted.

An American in Asia, official or nonofficial, must periodically draw up a balance sheet: Is his job, however interesting and rewarding materially, compensating for what he is missing "back home"? Most American embassy personnel in Asia are alert, reasonably intelligent, educated, middle-class city dwellers. They are paying a heavy price in the "extras" of life back home—everything from seeing TV to going to concerts or on weekend excursions by automobile (not possible in much of Asia).

With the revolutionary changes in U.S. life, greater than any society in the world, there is a great possibility of estrangement. The feeling of "foreignness" in American society often consists of a composite of minor things. A diplomat friend told me, after his last visit home, quite serious and shaking his head over the experience, that he hadn't been able to dial a long-distance telephone number. "Isn't that a comment! Not to be able to dial a telephone when you get back home, because you have been away so long," he said.

Attempts to compensate the employee overseas for what he is missing can never really succeed. And most Americans representing their country abroad in whatever function don't really expect it; they hope to find compensatory satisfaction in the dignity, the novelty, the importance, the prestige that comes with the job.

But the attempt to compensate him materially only to the degree that living abroad is made as comfortable as possible produces new problems. It can lead to "the Golden Ghetto"—the creation of a "little America" in a foreign country that isolates the U.S. mission members from the realities of life in the country in which they serve.

Other reporters have made a great deal of it during the past twenty years. (Incidentally, they usually are reporters who, themselves, have made quick, flying visits, have worked out of luxury hotels while they lambasted the American bureaucrat for his "luxurious" life.)

The problem is constantly debated in the inner circles of the Foreign Service. Does an American serve his country better by trying, insofar as he can, to live the life of the people with whom he works in the host country? Or is he a better representative of his country if he tries, insofar as he can, to maintain the standards of life he would know at home?

One of my Indian friends, a man with a deep sense of pride in his own traditions but a sophisticated journalist with a wide acquaintance and long residence abroad, commented once on an American diplomat who sent his children to a local Indian school, "It's all very well, I suppose. But I would want my children to get the best education they could." The same incident also provoked bitter criticism from career Foreign Service officials who saw it as a gesture by a politically appointed chief of mission who would stay abroad at most two or three years. They pointed out that their children faced a whole school career, most of which would be spent out of the U.S. in different countries.

There is, however, great risk from "the striped-pants mentality" to effective implementation of policy in any mission. I have known not a few prize prigs in the U.S. Foreign Service. There was the deputy chief of mission in a South Asian country who once returned a clipping from a local newspaper to an officer his junior, pointing out to him on a formal inter-office memorandum dictated through a secretary that it should have been forwarded through the internal embassy mail with a formal "buckslip"!

The most crucial element in the equation is, of course, the ambassador, himself, the chief of mission. Although it may sound trite, he does have a position analogous to a captain of a ship. In periods of emergency, particularly, his powers over the members of the mission are total. In routine times, he sets the mood, the pace, the dedication of the mission.

His duties are enormous. His chief responsibility is directing the reporting of events in his host country for Washington's enlightenment. But he is also the chief administrating officer for a large establishment—one of the smallest Asian missions had a budget in 1966 of $325,000 excluding salaries of twenty-five embassy personnel. (A complicated accounting sytem rebills back to other agencies in Washington costs which are not covered by State Department appropriations.) He must direct his own State Department staff, supervise the local aid program, if there is one, mesh gears with the local Central Intelligence Agency's representative, supervise the activities of the U.S. defense attaché's office and any military stationed in the country, lay down the political line for the local propaganda functions of the United States Information Service.

THE AMBASSADOR'S VOICE

THE mission chief's name is signed to all reporting messages that leave the embassy for Washington. Reading, editing, and sometimes writing his own messages instead of turning them over to his staff, is an enormous job. The amount of this paper work has reached incredible proportions. Dean Rusk reckoned that four hundred thousand words a day flow into the State Department from U.S. embassies abroad. Much of it can only be skimmed by officials at home and goes into files that—hopefully— are used by the Intelligence and research organizations of the Washington headquarters. But the ambassador often feels that he must make his voice heard, must be on record as to the important events happening in the country of his assignment. He must protect himself: Often minor developments may indicate a trend or be critical when viewed with hindsight at some future date.

One American ambassador to Laos, for example, filed such

lengthy cables that the whole U.S. government signals operation from the Far East to Hawaii and Washington was awash in his dispatches. During John Kenneth Galbraith's sojourn in New Delhi, he kept such a constant avalanche of wordage flowing to Washington—much of it gratuitous advice on matters not affecting U.S.-Indian relations—that it was common gossip around the White House that President Kennedy was extremely annoyed.

Visitors take up a great deal of the ambassador's time. Recently there were some hundred official visitors scheduled through Bangkok in less than a month, many of them congressmen during a recess. The ambassador has to take special pains with the local representatives of the American press or visiting journalists if they come through, for a word from them may jeopardize his whole political approach in the country—or his job. (Although not an official part of their functions, hundreds of man-hours of many U.S. Information Service officials are taken up helping visiting or resident American journalists.)

Some of these visitors can be unbelievably demanding. A few years ago when then Vice-President Lyndon Johnson toured Asia, instructions preceded him on exactly what brand of Scotch whisky was wanted, where the bed should be in relation to the air conditioner, a description of the kind of toilet paper that should be available, and menus for all meals.

The relatively trivial visit of Jacqueline Kennedy to India involved a great portion of the New Delhi Embassy staff and their wives for weeks. Her arrival date was changed no fewer than five times. There was a "practice run" to make toasted cheese sandwiches by the women of the New Delhi Embassy. When the trip finally got under way, the itinerary was constantly changed. For example, with less than two hours' notice, the itinerary of the President of India's train was suddenly shifted to take her from Agra to Benares on the Indian railway's Grand Trunk lines. It was the U.S. equivalent of mucking up the Baltimore to Philadelphia section of the Penn-Central—at a time when Indian railroads were already almost breaking under the strain of increasing freight traffic and other problems.

One visiting congressman almost caused an international incident in the early post-World War II period during my residence in Bangkok, when he visited the holiest temple of one of the Buddhist countries of Southeast Asia and started tapping walls with his cane, barking out questions on the quality of the teak. The ambassador's wife made the apologies and hushed up the whole incident, apparently with the senator never knowing that it had occurred.

In theory, the ambassador is trained for all such emergencies, a product of years of experience as a junior officer. If theoretical personnel planning has worked out, he should have served in various areas of the world, should have had various assignments— as an economic reporter, a cultural officer, an administrative officer—as well as the traditional duties of diplomatic representation and political reporting for Washington. He may have had language training.

And with luck, he had served earlier as a junior officer in the same country as his present mission-chief assignment. That means that he has wide acquaintance in the bureaucracy of the host country, may have personal contacts with former younger officers and politicians who have moved up in echelons of their government just as he has.

But that's only the theory. As I write, of the total of thirty-two missions in Asia, six are headed by political appointments— men chosen by presidential appointments outside the career Foreign Service. (Three posts are temporarily without chiefs and four are temporarily closed.)

In some cases, these men are veterans in government service and with long records of dealing with foreign policy matters. Chester Bowles, twice ambassador to India, is a typical example. Some are mere political appointments, made to pay off "campaign debts."

There has been a strong tendency in recent years to make another kind of political appointment. It is the choice of an ambassador, often from academic circles, who has demonstrated through his writings or scholarship a deep interest in the host country or economic and political problems of which it is a good example. In some cases these men have been effective diplomats.

But, on the whole, they come to their job without the techniques of diplomacy, which is a trade like any other, and without the long history in vast detail which inevitably precedes any particular problem reaching a crisis stage.

These appointments bring up the basic question about the American diplomatic service which is in constant dispute: Many acquainted with the problem of American foreign policy argue that diplomats are made, not born—nor created out of the air by Presidential appointment. They argue that only with an elite, career service, carefully selected and trained, can any of Washington's policy decisions be made effective in the field.

This point of view is opposed by those who argue that such a service tends to become inbred, removed from the realities of American political life at home, incapable of effecting a policy made by a democratic, representative government. The advocates of a broader-based overseas bureaucracy argue that American resources, including systems and educational techniques, can substitute for old-fashioned diplomatic career experience.

EUROCENTRISM IN THE STATE DEPARTMENT

THERE is a further projection of this argument—and an extremely critical one in Asia—"universality" versus "specialization." Unfortunately, universality during the past twenty years has meant for the most part wide career experience in Europe. Our Asian policy has suffered greatly from the fact that the Department of State has been dominated by men whose experience and whose view of the world has totally centered on Europe. Ironically, despite World War II in the Pacific, the Korean War, and the Vietnam War, we are just getting over this disability.

I was almost bodily thrown out of the office of one of today's most senior American diplomats, then serving in Paris, when, returning from Hanoi in 1951 to the United States, I brashly and heatedly warned that the French were lying to us about their armed strength in Vietnam, that their policy was headed toward certain defeat. One bright, young career diplomat, in the Saigon Embassy in the early 1950s, was packed off into oblivion—not to reappear until the Kennedy administration—because he dared to oppose the "Eurocentric" line of the then ambassador.

This "Eurocentrism" expresses itself in subtle ways. On my recent sabbatical in the U.S., I heard a brilliant exposition by a former high State Department official of the problem of Vietnam. He talked at great length, justifying his opposition during his years in State to our growing commitment there. (He did not explain his earlier and disastrous role in advocating unqualified American aid to the French from 1945 to 1954, to enable them to fight the war in Indochina.) But when he spoke of the Saigon regime, the government of South Vietnam, he used the word "primitive" to describe its leadership. I could accept—if only for the sake of argument—almost any other adjective he might care to use, "parochial," "opportunist," "venal," "weak," etcetera. But anyone who has dealt with the crafty old politicians of the Saigon scene, or even the politically inexperienced young military officers, has tremendous respect for their shrewdness. "Primitive" they are not. And I am afraid that this *lapsus linguae* of a very articulate and experienced diplomat is simply a projection of a subtle racism picked up in the effete foreign ministries of West Europe.

If one is to look for the "original sin" of our failures in Vietnam, you can trace a good part of the problem to this refusal to see the problems of Asia in their own light. It was perfectly obvious to me—as it was to hundreds of other nonofficial and official U.S. observers—as early as 1951 in Hanoi that the French could not win against a Communist-led nationalist insurgency without the support of a disciplined minority, at least, of the Vietnamese. That could have been brought about only by sweeping and generous concessions in French policy toward Vietnamese nationalism.

Yet American policy, dominated in Washington by career service officials and the France desk, looking toward France and European problems exclusively, brought little pressure to bear on the French to make these concessions. And that was in spite of the fact that it was the enormous American military and nonmilitary aid problem (a total of more than $4 billion between 1945 and 1954 that kept the French effort afloat in Indochina).

In 1950, for example, the then American ambassador to Saigon, Donald Heath, made a speech on a visit to the U.S., saying that France had given Vietnam a status equivalent to that of one of the members of the British Commonwealth. It was patently ridiculous. And the French used it in Vietnam against the nationalists to enforce their argument against further concessions. When the late Robert Blum, then the U.S. aid administrator in Indochina, insisted in 1951 that nonmilitary American aid should go directly to a Vietnamese administration, the French demanded his recall, and Washington acquiesced.

In the long run, this policy did not serve us in Europe. The economic and psychological drain on France which the war effort in Indochina entailed, and the ultimate failure of her policy there, helped produce the crisis of the regime which developed into a return to Bonapartism under de Gaulle. And it helped to alienate the French, especially the left, from any possibility of a long-term alliance with America.

In Vietnam, itself, of course, the effects of this American-supported French policy are self-evident. Not only did the French lose, but they helped to bring down the whole structure of non-Communist nationalism among the Vietnamese—a structure that we were still trying to rebuild during the 1960s. They added credibility to the Communist argument that only they and the Communist bloc could speak for real independence from colonial rule. And they associated the whole West—from which the U.S. ultimately cannot detach itself in Asian minds—with their policy.

Yet if we must be wary of Eurocentrism in the U.S. diplomatic corps posing as universality, there is also the problem of local Asian specialization turning into a disease well known among diplomats—"localitis."

Once talking with an American consul general in Pakistan, I had an archtypical experience in this attitude: The diplomat said to me during a long, discursive conversation on Pakistan and her problems, "If *we* had not lost the Eastern Punjab . . ."

(my italics). I feigned deafness and asked the diplomat to repeat himself. Again he said, "If *we* had not lost the Eastern Punjab. . . ."

The reference was to the partition of the old Punjab Province of British India in 1947, with its former Moslem majority, between the two new countries of Pakistan and India. He had so come to identify himself with Pakistan's interests that he slipped into expressing a point of view totally out of keeping with the necessity for objectivity. That objectivity was essential in the highly emotional political confrontation which has been continual since independence came to the two successor states.

We went right ahead with the interview, my companion totally oblivious to what he had indicated.

The phenomenon is not limited to Asia, of course. Lack of objectivity is perhaps the inevitable concomitant of specialized knowledge in any diplomatic venue—and, for that matter, in other human pursuits.

But working among the small elites of Asian countries in which diplomats and other members of the American establishment move, the risk that communication with the local society never gets out of a small cocktail-party circuit is extremely grave. Several times U.S. missions in Asia have taken surveys of the acquaintanceship of officers among citizens of the host countries. And the results have been shocking, for, sifted down, the total acquaintance is small and tends to overlap from one diplomat to another—usually the relatively small circle of English-speakers.

(Nor is it limited to the official American missions. In Japan, for example, the Rockefeller Foundation, one of America's largest nonprofit organizations with a long history of local operations, is notoriously inbred. Its educational program, locally, and grants for study in the U.S., its research projects, and its propagandists are all limited to a very narrow section of the English-speaking Japanese society.)

The problems, the failings, and the failures of the official American missions abroad are only part of the picture, however, for the U.S. establishment goes far beyond that.

The Establishment for Export

THE U.S. business community is an important entity. The numbers of Americans working for U.S. firms in Asia is relatively small. There is almost always the local representative of the major oil companies, the airlines, the banks. But in much of South Asia, they are relatively new arrivals. Even today, many American firms find it more convenient to be represented by citizens of the former colonial powers in the various countries. (In India, for example, no residence visa is required for a British Commonwealth national, but U.S. firms must elaborately prove their need for American personnel.) He often works for a lower salary and has more long-time knowledge of the country.

The professional diplomat likes to believe that the businessman's view of what is happening is narrower than his. And certainly there are times when he creates problems for the local mission. But some of the most astute observers of the local scene in Asia are veteran U.S. businessmen, whose very economic existence depends on being well informed on local political, as well as economic, currents.

One big problem is that home offices don't always listen to them. I can think of one case where a big international company refused to pick up its options for new stock in one of the big five Japanese electronics companies in the mid-1950s. Its ownership in the Japanese company was thereby diluted. And it was at a time when it was already obvious that Japanese electronics would be a world leader in the coming decades. Or another friend, who represents a vast American international oil company in South Asia and has had to pick up the pieces over and over again when his head office refused to follow his advice.

Yet total American investment in all of Asia is small—probably not more than $3.9 billion (almost half of this in Middle East oil) compared with $28.3 billion in Canada and Latin America, and $16.2 billion in Europe. A case might be made that if the U.S. did have imperialist interests, of which the Communist world accuses us, and a huge American business establishment in Asia, our foreign policy might be more solidly based and carried out more effectively.

Yet American business presence in Asia is a potent force for changing the old societies. Take the small but widespread example of the gasoline filling station. Because the international oil companies know no other way to operate, they have spread throughout Asia the typical U.S. installation. It brings—out of its context, to be sure—a simple example of efficiency of operation and management unknown in the majority of Asian business communities.

Raul Haya de la Torre, the revolutionary hero of Peru and an old acquaintance, discussing this whole phenomenon with me in Tokyo a few years ago, put it this way: Lenin was right, he said, in saying that imperialism was the last stage of capitalism. But that is the view as seen from the developed countries. Seen from the vantage point of the underdeveloped countries, it is the first stage of capitalism and a modern technological society. Compare the fate of a Peruvian worker, he said, who works for a foreign mining company in Peru, with that of the landless Indian on the hacienda of one of the *latifundistas*. However much he may be exploited in terms of modern industrial wages, his fate is far better. He has modern medical treatment, a standard wage, and sometimes housing. On the *finca*, he is worked without regulation and may be fed *coca*.

You can make the same general argument for Asia, I believe. And proof is that with the exception of Japan, after positions in the government bureaucracy, jobs with foreign-owned companies are the prized situations sought by young people throughout the continent. The very fact that there are trade unions in many of these companies, far exceeding their development in locally-owned companies, is partial proof of their generally progressive character.

MISSIONARIES

A THIRD pillar of the American establishment in Asia is the missionaries.

In part, perhaps, because I am a Jew, I have always been appalled at the basic implication of Christian missionary activity in Asia. The very idea of approaching the old cultures, if decadent societies, of Asia with the concept of "the Word" presupposes a kind of moral superiority which the West would be hard put to defend in her 450 years of dominance in her relations to the continent.

Many of the missionaries realized their ambivalent position. And many changed their view fundamentally over the years they served in Asia.

Contrast the views of Henry Winters Luce, father of the founder of the publishing empire Time, Inc., on his arrival in Asia in 1897, with his attitudes after a long career as a missionary: On his arrival in Japan, he writes:

> In Tokyo, we got our first close look at heathenism. We made our way to the Shiba temples and shrines. . . . As we looked into their [worshippers'] faces, the younger ones filled with unrest and hopelessness, the older ones taking on the placid, vacant expression of the Buddha they worship, we felt as never before the greatness of the message we were bringing, so full of hope and cheer and *life*. Japan has an awful need, and as we saw this need, so much greater than we had dreamed of, our hearts were weighed down with the burden of heathenism.

But returning to Asia in 1935 on his last visit, after a period spent studying in America, Luce visited the famous Buddhist cave-temples of Yun Kang near Peking in northern China. This time he wrote:

> These great sculptures are a monument to their [Buddhist monks'] aspirations—an outward symbol of a great inward and spiritual grace. To stand in these caves amid all this beauty is close to being lifted into heaven.

No educated Asian can contest the fact that the Christian missionaries—largely financed from Britain in the nineteenth century and increasingly from America in the past fifty years—have done enormous beneficial work in education, medicine, and social welfare. The church-supported universities throughout the area have turned out tens of thousands of leaders—including, ironically, many of the middle-echelon figures of the Chinese Communist movement. In 1950, more than half the figures with university education listed in the Chinese *Who's Who* were graduates of mission schools.

Lower schools have provided many countries—and still do—with the best pre-university training. There is hardly a major city in Asia without its mission hospital. These hospitals and medical schools have not only succored the ill, but have carried out research in and treatment of many of the tropical diseases virtually unknown in the temperate West.

Such figures as the almost legendary Sister Theresa working in the Calcutta slums have given Asians an ideal of practical social responsibility which is largely absent in all the old societies—even in their organized relgious practices.

There are today some 35,500 non-Asian Christian missionaries in non-Communist Asia; half the more than ten thousand Protestants are American citizens. Increasingly, their missions have become oriented to medicine and education, rather than proselytizing. More than once, I have talked with missionaries who see "good works" as an end in itself, rather than conversion.

The dedication of these people is remarkable. A few years ago, I happened on a young American couple in a hotel in South India. They were studying the local language for six months in preparation for establishing a medical and educational mission in a predominantly rural Moslem area. The wife was the daughter of missionary parents. Her husband was studying medicine in the United States when they met. He told me frankly that he had no interest in proselytizing. But they were committed not for a tour, or two tours, but for a lifetime career in a totally isolated village in the interior—even the small town where we met had no air transportation.

The mission plan conceived of a seventy-five-year program. Violence often overtakes individual converts to Christianity in a South Indian Moslem environment, they explained, so that their effort was part of a decades-long program of good works intended eventually to convert a village *en masse*. I frankly was fascinated that the young couple, their three tow-headed youngsters—all under ten—were seemingly no different in their other attitudes from hundreds of thousands of young Americans of their own age group back home in the U.S.

This couple's pessimism about conversion prospects appears realistic. Except in the overwhelmingly Roman Catholic Philippines, the growing secularization of the Asian elites coupled with their nationalism, which views Christianity as a Western phenomenon, dims increasingly any prospect of large Christian communities.

(Actually, of course, Christianity in South India is probably as old as any place in the world and certainly predates the conversion of northern Europe. The so-called Syrian Christians of Kerala State on the west coast of India can document their communities from the fourth century A.D. and claim to trace their beginnings to St. Thomas, the Doubter, who came there after the Crucifixion to convert a still more ancient colony of Jewish traders. It is within the realm of possibilities, according to local historians, because of the relatively gentle trade winds that, since time immemorial, have made possible navigation of small Arab craft on ancient trade routes across the Indian Ocean from the Persian Gulf.)

The older, established American churches have, to a considerable extent, accepted the pessimistic outlook for proselytization. And just as many attitudes are changing radically in both the Catholic and the Protestant churches on other old issues, the aims of the missions in Asia, too, are being radically revised and with tremendous speed.

The Rev. Jitsuo Morikawa, speaking at the annual assembly of the home missions division, National Council of Churches, in Atlantic City in 1961, enunciated the new creed:

"Jesus Christ is no parochial God, or partisan respecter of persons. He doesn't belong to the Christians and isn't confined only to religious activities."

Many of the oldest missionary groups in Asia now accept this kind of approach to their activities. In several countries, in part pushed by the growing nationalism of Asian governments, in part by their own Christian fellow-believers in Asia, church organization and government are being turned over to local organizations as fast as possible.

Since the end of World War II, there has been a rapid growth of missionary activities by the American pentecostal groups. They probably represent more than half of all American missionaries overseas. To a considerable extent, many of them still hold to the old idea of "faith" missions. But, increasingly, they, too, have augmented their efforts at conversion with medical, educational (particularly linguistics research and training), and social welfare activities.

THE MILITARY IN ASIA

EQUALLY radical changes have overtaken the U.S. military presence in Asia—an integral part of the Establishment. Although the U.S. has fought two wars in Asia since the end of World War II in 1945, the nature of warfare and the global commitments of the U.S. have changed the whole approach of what might be called "the permanent American military establishment" in Asia.

Thirty years after the sinking of the *Panay*, a small vessel of the Yangtze River Patrol in 1937, an American "spy" ship, an electronics intelligence craft, was captured by the North Korean Communist regime. The *Panay* intensified the U.S. debate over "intervention" versus "isolation." But public opinion was in part assuaged by the Japanese ambassador to the U.S. making a public apology by radio, deploring the incident as a "shocking blunder."

But in 1968, when the *Pueblo* was fired on and taken into a North Korean port, the U.S. sought by every means possible to negotiate a settlement with a totally recalcitrant—if small— Pyongyang regime.

The comparison, of course, like all historical analogies, is not wholly valid. When the *Pueblo* was captured, the U.S. was already engaged in a major war in Southeast Asia. Paramount was the fact of whether or not the ship was in North Korean territorial waters; it was a point hardly mooted by most Americans in the days of gunboat diplomacy. The *Panay* was on the Yangtze to protect American lives and property in a period of Chinese internal turbulence during the Japanese attempt to conquer the country. Few in the U.S. contested her right to be there. The *Pueblo* was testing electronics communications systems of the whole Communist world, part of a worldwide system. It was engaged in electronic espionage to prevent any surprise attack on the U.S. that might come in minutes with new intercontinental ballistic weapons systems delivering atomic warheads that could destroy a whole civilization.

It is possible that the future will see such a refinement of weapons that "forward" U.S. military bases common in Asia in the two decades between the end of World War II and the Vietnam War will no longer be practical or necessary. Already as I write, there is speculation about the huge American base on the island of Okinawa. The development of an atomic weapons delivery system by Communist China could make such a base virtually useless.

It appears likely, however, that for the next decade or so the U.S. will maintain at least some military communications (and warning) bases in some areas of the East. The presence of military personnel in these countries is, under the best of circumstances, a political irritant.

Take the example of Thailand. The U.S. has a force—as I write —of some forty thousand men in that country. Most of them are in relatively isolated base camps away from the larger cities. But there are large numbers of American servicemen on vacation in Bangkok, Thailand's capital and one of the great tourist attractions of Southeast Asia.

The Thai are wholly committed to the U.S. alliance—not only the present government, but the King, extremely important in Thailand's political system, and the majority of the educated. They see the alliance as the only defense against Communist China, its ally the North Vietnamese, and the Communist-backed insurgents operating in several areas of the country.

Yet friction between the Thais and the Americans is growing. It is largely the result of Thailand's first exposure in her history to the obligations and risks of a long-term alliance with a major foreign power. In part, it arises out of what the Thai leadership feels is unfair criticism leveled by American newsmen against Thai inefficiency in combatting its own social and political problems. It has been exacerbated by the public debate over the U.S. policy in Vietnam which the Thais see as critical to their own strategy.

But repeatedly, Thai friends have voiced their most strenuous objection to one thing: The conduct of American servicemen with Thai women. What passes for innocent holding hands, "necking" in the old American parlance, and other public expressions of affection infuriate the Thais. (The clash of cultures is curious, and sometimes inexplicable. Americans might be equally upset by the common public holding of hands by Thai males.) And American commanders appear unable to do anything about it.

This irritant is only a small example of what seems to be the inevitable repercussions of a "permanent" American military presence in an Asian country. In Japan, and even Korea, after some explosive episodes in the early 1950s, this friction appears relatively minor because of the prosperity and flexibility of societies which have seen such vast changes over the past twenty years. But in the more static societies of South Asia, it will be a continuing problem.

Although the military bring—like other parts of the American officialdom—prosperity into the small local economies where they live in Asia, this does not offset the increased political problems they create. An automobile accident, a barroom fight, an altercation with a landlord can quickly blow up into a major incident.

NEED FOR TRAINED PERSONNEL

THESE are only some of the problems that any American mission has to live with in Asia. And, as our commitment grows in complexity, it will take more and more highly skilled diplomatic talent to cope.

Are they being prepared?

Before answering that, we have to go back and look at what has been the mainstay of our diplomatic missions during the period since the end of World War II in Asia. It is a difficult task, of course, because we are lumping together two dozen countries and a series of very different crisis situations. And there are no more bitter arguments than those concerned with separating policies, techniques, and personalities in the U.S. diplomatic establishment.

Ultimately, in discussing the American bureaucracy in Asia, you get into the same problems that affect any large organization in modern American life. Personality clashes explain as many situations as differences over "substantive" issues. I can think of one South Asian country, for example, where three U.S. ambassadors were unable to complete their tours without considerable fireworks. In no small part, it was because they have had to deal with a brilliant, but extremely difficult, foreign minister in the host country.

Washington demands "conformism" that plays havoc with any attempt to find original answers to very specific problems. In the State Department, for example, the road toward becoming head of a mission lies more through pleasing superiors back home than through a real understanding of problems in the countries where an aspiring officer works. Or an even better example is the AID administration. Congress has imposed so many instructions and restrictions on the agency's operation—where and what it may purchase, what kind of policies it shall take, limiting short-term commitments—that administrators must spend more time meshing their programs with Washington than with the needs of the country where they are stationed.

However, I would question to what extent this criticism of the U.S. overseas bureaucracy is valid beyond its application to all large organizations in the U.S. I have had enough acquaintance with American business, for example, to question the great myth of its efficiency. I doubt that more American ambassadors abroad are oriented toward pleasing their bosses than overseas managers of U.S. firms. "Careerism" is a pretty common phenomenon in all walks of American life.

I would argue that the backbone of our personnel in Asia in the past two decades has come from three sources: The offspring of missionaries; the group of dedicated bureaucrats who cut their teeth on the Marshall Plan in Europe; and a generation tempered by the U.S. Great Depression of 1929-36.

If I am asked who I believe is the most knowledgeable and balanced expert on China at the State Department, several names come to mind—and at least three of them are offspring of missionary families. (Incidentally, a large number of Japanese and Chinese studies scholars in the academic community share these origins.)

Or the CIA official I consider most well informed about the South Asian country where he is posted is the son of a famous missionary educator.

The list is long wherever you look in Asia. I believe their influence and competence has been far greater relatively than their numbers. The reasons are apparent: They know the area, speak the languages in the countries where they grew up, and feel no great deprivation in their service for long periods abroad. They also have a sense of the American entity, the U.S. as a whole, in world affairs. And, in my experience, perhaps as a reaction to the idealism of their parents, they are profound realists about the countries and peoples where they serve. They temper an academic knowledge of Asian cultures, which can so easily tend toward idealization, with practical personal experience.

In a different way, the young economists and officials who came out of the West Europe recovery experience had something to offer. If they were not aware of Asian problems—and usually they were not—they did know "the ropes" in dealing with the Washington bureaucracy on terribly complicated financial and procurement matters. And, in fact, they "grew up" with the whole methodology and burgeoning bureaucracy of the aid concept. The success of the European recovery program—granted, of course, mainly due to the Europeans rather than to the Americans —gave them a "psychological momentum" for tackling the much more difficult problems of economic development in Asia.

I spent a week a few years ago traveling through rural India with one of the most devoted American civil servants I have ever met in Asia, George Knierim. A hallmark of his peculiar qualities was that Knierim was the only man in the AID mission in India ever to ask for a pickup truck as his personal vehicle. It was the only car he could have driven through the countryside where he tried to get a look at agricultural problems as they really were— instead of viewing them through the eyes of Indian bureaucrats far from the immediate problem.

He was away from his wife for as long as a week at a time several times a month, constantly traveling and visiting agricultural experiment stations, colleges of agriculture, and individual farmers themselves. I realized that he was a real "dirt farmer" with scientific training early during our tour together.

But it was only later, when we talked at great length about personal experiences, that I began to understand his motivation, why Knierim had had a certain amount of success with Indian farmers—if not always with Indian agricultural executives in New Delhi or with U.S. officials there. As a young man, he had grown up in the arid stretches of the American Southwest. He had had to quit school during the Depression, then work his way through agricultural college. He was deeply religious. And his "feel" for the problems of an Indian farmer—not unintelligent, but conservative, unable to take "chances" with new ideas—was through this personal experience.

Contrast Knierim's experience with that of the next generation of farm specialists now going to Asia. Many of them do not know how to milk a cow by hand; their experience is with tractors and combines, not mules and hand plows. The best, over long periods, learn to accommodate themselves to Asia's bullock agriculture. Many do not and simply spend their time shuffling papers. Or they join their colleagues, the Asian agricultural bureaucrats—usually drawn from urban environments—in heaping scorn and blame for the lack of development on the "backwardness" and the "stubbornness" of Asia's farmers.

All three of these groups of Americans with experience that fits them for the job in Asia are rapidly disappearing. The normal attrition of age will not carry many into the next decade. For the moment, there appears to be no replacement available.

Much of the fervor has gone out of the whole program to develop the backward countries. The programs of the past twenty years have not, on the whole, been successful. There is little of the *élan* among specialists that characterized the Marshall Plan generation.

Missionary families and their offspring may be dwindling; and, in an age of more rapid communications, even those Americans who are reared abroad tend to identify completely with their own age group at home in the U.S., rather than with the young people around them. Few live in foreign posts almost completely isolated from the mainstream of events at home in the U.S., as mission children did forty to fifty years ago.

It takes a peculiarly sensitive young American, reared in the atmosphere of unbelievable prosperity (as judged by the rest of the world) since the end of World War II, to understand the whole concept of poverty as the ancient societies of Asia have known it. How can Americans, even when a portion of our people live at substandard levels on welfare schemes which give them in a week more than the equivalent of the annual per capita incomes of such countries as India and Pakistan, understand what it means to be poor in South Asia? How much understanding does it take the intelligent, middle-class American recruited into the Foreign Service to empathize with a leadership in most of Asia, much less a populace, which virtually has no economic security?

One new source of talented, dedicated and, to some extent experienced, young personnel is the Peace Corps. It is the general consensus among Americans in Asia that the Peace Corps will never have more than the most marginal effect on the local situations in the countries where they work. But the experience of living and working in the underdeveloped societies will give at least a few young Americans an appreciation of the totally different life of two-thirds of the world's population. Some of these young people are going on into the overseas bureaucracy—so far, 210 into the State Department, another 62 into AID, and 26 into the U.S. Information Agency.

THE GROWING BUREAUCRATIC CRISIS

YET as American problems in Asia grow increasingly complicated and complex, there is a growing crisis in the bureaucracy. The State Department, itself, is badly in need of a gigantic overhauling. Overlapping jurisdiction, overstaffing, vague definitions of duties and services, all frustrate the individual bureaucrat.

The Department of State has mushroomed to such size that its branches are often stumbling over each other. Arnold Beichman, in an article on "The 'Other State Department,'" points out and documents with examples that the U.S. mission at the United Nations has a life of its own and often takes policy decisions at variance with the Department of State in Washington. "Because of this [vast popular] support for the U.N., the U.S. Mission has enjoyed particular privileges and powers and the unique distinction of being an embassy which can, when the U.S.U.N. Chief feels it necessary to, defy the State Department with impunity."

But even more basic is the problem of recruitment of the kind of material that is needed for future diplomats. Let me cite an example of the kind of long-term problem that is presented:

Bengal, East Pakistan and West Bengal in India, is a region of a hundred million people. Its population is growing at more than 3.5 per cent annually.

Indian Bengal, with its capital and port city of Calcutta, is one of the most vital parts of that country. More than half India's exports flow through its port. Calcutta is the largest city in the country.

East Bengal (East Pakistan) is an equally crucial area. Its problems of overpopulation, rural poverty, and political instability are almost classic for underdeveloped countries. Both areas have militant, radical political factions including dynamic Communist movements in the hands of leadership which is presently pro-Chinese Communist.

The area will be a principal concern of U.S. policy-makers in Asia for the foreseeable future. The U.S. overseas agencies need to recruit now young officers who will know the area, who ten years from now will have seasoned judgments in making policies affecting it. They should get language training in Bengali. (Perhaps the whole question of language has been exaggerated. It is one element, an important one, in the diplomat's equipment. Knowledge of Asian languages can, of course, lead to insights into problems and human relations. But one of the most incompetent diplomats I have known speaks half a dozen languages brilliantly.)

Yet neither Dacca, the capital of East Pakistan, nor Calcutta is the most comfortable place to live. Physical amenities can be provided for Americans living in either area. But a young man or woman who spends long periods in either place will have to sacrifice many of the commonplaces of living in the U.S. today. If expertise is to be the criterion, a career as a Bengal expert is likely to mean long tours in both areas with only occasional assignments back home in Washington or elsewhere.

For an ambitious young man, the prospects of becoming an eventual chief of mission in either India or Pakistan are slim. (Both embassies are headed by political appointees as I write.) Perhaps even more important to a career-conscious young man is the fact that the top echelons at home in the State Department are increasingly filled by political officers instead of career personnel. As I write, of the top sixty-three jobs at State in Washington, only twenty-nine are filled by career men. In 1959, there were forty-three jobs of equivalent rank, with twenty-nine of them filled by career service people—meaning that the whole increment in the department's growth at the top in the past decade has been filled by political appointment.

Attrition—marriage for women officers, more attractive foreign job offers, a decision to leave Foreign Service for life at home—will cut heavily into the officers recruited now. Salaries are attractive, but for the young man or woman capable of passing the Foreign Service examination to qualify for foreign posting, many other opportunities are open in business and academic life at home and abroad.

In the past, the lure of the diplomatic service, its prestige and power, attracted large numbers of qualified applicants. But almost instantaneous communications between Washington and posts abroad have increasingly turned even the most astute ambassador into a messenger boy in crisis periods. The growth of foreign travel, available to a great part of the American public, make Kyoto, Den Pasar, Siem Riep, and Agra only stops on a world tour, no longer distant and romantic places. Foreign Service for the U.S. government is no longer the exotic role it once was.

The U.S. presence is Asia cannot but be profoundly affected by the revolutionary changes that are going on in American life.

Those changes, to a considerable degree, are lengthening the gap between life in the U.S. and life in most of Asia. And that is why, more and more, the problems of American life at home are being exported to our bureaucratic establishment in Asia that must, in the final analysis, carry out any policy.

6 ✦

"Beautiful India, Beautiful America"

FOR years I stomped about the East infuriated by the European's concept of the naive American abroad in the world, armed with tremendous power, blissfully making a mess of everyone's life by a total misunderstanding of what goes on about him. The whole theory was spread by the former colonial administrators who had seen the pre-World War II *status quo* vanish. They blamed anti-colonialism, naively held, of Americans for the great changes. It was sometimes summed up in the whole argument "we know our natives."

But it reached a slick apogee in Graham Greene's novel, *The Quiet American,* written in the early 1950s. In that almost feline way that Greene has for sensing the mood of what is happening in a foreign environment, he captured much of the atmosphere of Hanoi and Saigon under the conditions of the French Indochina War. It was an admission I wouldn't make for years. For in addition he had tagged on to what was an essentially French-Vietnamese confrontation, a view of the Americans as the real devil in the situation.

I was in Hanoi during his first visit. And I suspected at the time that his analysis simply came from his own frustration at finding the attitudes of Vietnamese Catholics repugnant, that he was looking for a scapegoat.

Greene has plunged into such depths of anti-Americanism in more recent years as to indicate just how emotional and illogical a

132

route he was on. "If I had to choose between life in the Soviet Union and life in the United States of America," he wrote in 1967, "I would certainly choose the Soviet Union, just as I would choose life in Cuba to life in those southern American republics, like Bolivia, dominated by their northern neighbour, or life in North Vietnam to life in South Vietnam." This takes that anti-Americanism which passes for sophistication in some British circles from the smart to the ridiculous. (One would think that the whole squalid Philby-Burgess-Maclean scandal would have shown the absurdity of this hackneyed attitude of a jaundiced British circle.)

But reluctantly I have had to admit that there is a good deal more to the argument about American naiveté than I would concede formerly. And that admission has largely arisen out of the events in Vietnam in 1963 and the martyrdom of Ngo Dinh Diem on the cross of American credulity.

Indelible in my memory is a scene at Saigon early in that fateful summer. It was a stag dinner arranged for a visiting Washington dignitary. For over an hour I had listened to a bitter denunciation of the Diem regime, delivered by my young and earnest colleagues of the American press.

In exasperation, I finally said, "Assuming for the sake of argument that all the things you say about this regime are true, what do you propose to substitute for it?"

NEWSMAN A: Anyone could do a better job than Diem.

SANDERS: Name one person you think could do a better job.

NEWSMAN B: General X.

SANDERS: That's nonsense. I have known General X for fifteen years; he is a member of a racial minority, a military type who knows little of civilian government. He would be the first one to tell you that he couldn't run this country.

NEWSMAN A: But anyone would be better than what we've got now.

SANDERS: That's all very well for you to say at a cocktail party. But it isn't that way that Washington can make policy. Policies are made from real alternatives.

133

Little did I know that that was exactly the way policy was being made back in Washington. And that at that very minute, some U.S. officials were plotting to pull the rug from under Diem and deliver South Vietnam into virtual chaos for months.

American naiveté in dealing with Asia and Asians is a constant source of consternation to friend and foe alike. It is much too late in the day for "Beautiful India, beautiful America," incantations to wish away the enormous difficulties that lie in the way of understanding and an effective policy in Asia. Uncritical, *pro forma* invocations of the clichés about mutual appreciation and understanding between Asians and Americans are just not adequate in the present critical lack of understanding on both sides. Yet this is still the level at which many intelligent Americans view the problems.

How many times have I heard, for example, the thesis that "getting to understand one another" is the solution to all our problems? No one in Latin America knew us better than the Cubans. But that did not prevent a catastrophic breakdown in relations between the two countries.

Ironically, the Chinese have had closer relations than any other Asian people with us. Most Americans who have spent long periods in various parts of Asia find the Chinese more congenial, feel that they have more understanding on a personal basis with the Chinese, than with any other Asians. Yet, the two countries are sworn bitter enemies with little prospect that that situation will change radically in the near future.

An equally absurd formulation is the concept of "pro-American" and "anti-American." It seems perfectly clear to me that if an Asian politician is worth his salt, he is that combination known in politics the world over of self-interest and statesmanship employed *for his own country's interests*. If, as is the universally held concept, American interest in Asia lies in the creation of strong, stable, independent states moving toward democratic societies, then it befits us to consider those politicians and writers and thinkers "pro-American" who look to their own problems in a creative fashion.

I think now, for example, of the editor of an Indian weekly journal of opinion who is considered "pro-American" in some circles. But his technique is gutter journalism, outdoing the Communists, catering to petty class interests in the country. I doubt that in the long run he is a valuable "American ally."

One of my journalist friends in Saigon, on the other hand, is often considered "anti-American" because he has been extremely critical of much of American policy in his country since 1963. He is an honest, consistent—given the highly volatile state of Vietnamese politics during these past twenty years—advocate of humanism in his own society. We do not always agree. I would fault him on what I believe to be his naive notions of economic organization (which he calls "socialism," whatever that word means in an underdeveloped economy in Asia), his extreme and often blind bitterness over what he considers American perfidy toward the Diem regime. But in the long run, he is—if we have to use these labels—"pro-American." He would sacrifice a great deal for values which we Americans hold dear and necessary in any society.

SLOPE-HEADS AND MY-VIETNAMESE

THIS American naiveté arises, I believe, out of a tendency to approach Asians with two alternate philosophical views, sometimes compounding the two.

The first is what I call "the slope-head syndrome." It is basically racist, I suppose. But it is often held by people who are unaware of its psychological origins and who may be extremely well intentioned. The American sees the overwhelming physical backwardness of the Asian societies, the poverty, the filth, the disease. He sees the totally alien personal habits—the Indian who eats with his hands, or the Vietnamese who sits on his haunches, the Japanese who breathes through his teeth. And he assumes that mental development, that ability to analyze situations, that understanding of problems, matches this "lack of development" of what the American considers Western social graces.

In one sense at the other end of the spectrum, but sometimes complementary to this approach, is what I call "the my-Vietnamese syndrome." The American, thrown into a totally alien environment, as often as not in mid-crisis, with a highly detailed and demanding job to perform, finds a local member of the society with whom he can communicate. The particular Asian proves intelligent, friendly, forthcoming, and above all else, perhaps because he can speak one of the European languages or because he has learned to "pitch" his thought toward an American audience, communicates. He soon becomes the American's authority on everything—from the informed guide to local eating places to an expert on the economic history of Asia.

Ironically, he very often belongs to a pro-Communist milieu. For the Communists have learned, as disciples of an essentially European philosophy, to translate their information into terms the Westerner (and the American) can understand. There is no country in Asia where the U.S. resident community does not have intimate contact locally with a special kind of cocktail party radical, spouting Communist-line analyses of the local situation.

The nationalist, the non-Communist nationalist, tends, of course, to hold to traditional values. He, therefore, may not be able to speak English well—or French or Dutch. He finds it difficult to put his values into terms the American can understand. And his own very personal life—perhaps he is a vegetarian or does not wish to eat with foreigners in India; he does not drink if he is a devout Moslem Pakistani; he cannot entertain in his home and may not be able to afford a bar or restaurant if he is a Japanese— often makes social intercourse more difficult than it would be for one of his more "Westernized" fellow citizens.

Furthermore, much of what the American sees and does in Asia is refracted through special lenses, ground in a totally different society in the West. I think of examples on various levels of importance:

Take the question of dress. Some American women, in a gesture of admiration and in an effort to break through to Indian society, wear the *sari* in that country. I believe that most Indians find it either ludicrous or, worse, positively resent it. A well-known Indian editor, a man proud of his own heritage, thinks that Western women dressed in *sari* look ridiculous. I couldn't agree more. The *sari*, a very simple but cumbersome garment, takes a certain amount of skill in draping and an Indian woman moves in it as gracefully as she can after years of practice. Most Western women look like they are at a masquerade party when they wear it. My friend considers it a kind of condescension to Indians that they attempt it, an aspect of the colonial mentality of "understanding the natives."

I am still not sure that the retiring American ambassador, Henry Cabot Lodge, leaving Saigon, understood that the mandarin robe which some Vietnamese officials had him put on at Tan San Nhout airport before his departure was a mischievous practical joke. My Vietnamese friends either laughed or were outraged that the young officers who persuaded him to wear it had trafficked with one of the vestiges of the old Confucianist culture.

All of this kind of failure to understand what is involved in local custom is based on a misreading of Asian attitudes: Asians perceive, perhaps even more clearly than we, that our societies *are* different, that we are different peoples. More understanding can be reached on the basis of living up to the highest standards of our own culture, while trying to understand theirs, than in making superficial gestures to take on their ways and attitudes, or attempting to make our way theirs.

A few years ago I happened to be in Saigon during the Vietnamese "Tet"—the lunar New Year. In a foolish fashion of trying to identify myself with my Vietnamese friends, perhaps because at that moment I felt they were under a barrage of unfair criticism from my colleagues in the U.S. press, I sent the traditional gift of flowers around to several homes. One of my old friends—granted something of a cynic as Vietnamese have a right to be after all they have gone through during these past twenty years—said, "What's the matter? Are you going 'native' or something?"

It was a joke. But it was also a reproach; he had thought, I am sure, that our understanding did not necessitate that kind of naive gesture. It was a gaffe. It would have been equally distasteful had he, a Vietnamese, sent me a Jewish New Year's card.

When a very successful young American radio and television personality, John Chancellor, became the director of the Voice of America, the U.S. overseas propaganda radio, in the mid-1960s, he instituted a new program policy. A series of programs for Asian overseas audiences modeled on the disc jockeys in the U.S. was begun.

The program included very contemporary music, the standard patter of the disc jockey, and some news. But it was wholly inappropriate for his audience, which is largely Overseas Chinese (for the English-language programs) in Southeast Asia. They are very serious-minded people who turn to the Voice (but more often to the British Broadcasting Company's overseas services) for information, not entertainment. And even in the critical morning hours, the news was so scarce on the program that it would have been difficult for a storekeeper, an engineer, a politician, to arrange to hear it at hour-long intervals.

The small group of sophisticated teen-agers in Asian urban centers, who would have appreciated a breakfast-type program (if they could understand the extremely colloquial English at all), are either not able to buy shortwave radios or would rather listen to local programs. So about the only audience the show had was Americans posted in Asia. Parenthetically, it might be added, most Americans in the U.S. Information Agency in Asia agreed with me, but few dared to tell Washington the truth about the program.

DUTCH NEW GUINEA PROBLEM

INEVITABLY, this naiveté about Asians and their attitudes invades the realm of American policy-making. A case history is the problem of former Dutch New Guinea, a protracted issue that stretches over the period from 1949 to 1962.

After almost five years of faltering U.S. policy, Washington put all the pressure it could exert on the Netherlands government to come to a settlement with the Indonesian nationalists in 1949. By waiting, it had helped to erode the following of the moderate Islamic and social democratic groups in the Indonesian political spectrum. The fact that they survived this period at all—including a Moscow-directed Communist insurrection in 1948 at the moment the Indonesian nationalists were beating off a second Dutch "police action"—was a miracle. But, in part because the Dutch government needed the support of the colonialist elements in the Catholic Party in the Netherlands parliament to push through the final settlement, the U.S. acquiesced to a nebulous arrangement over the western half of New Guinea. The area was to be governed as a "condominium" by the new Netherlands-Indonesia Union established in the agreement transferring powers to the Indonesian nationalists.

It was no more impractical than a good deal of the rest of the settlement. The agreements were to be broken by Soekarno almost before the ink was dry on the articles which came out of the Round Table Conference at The Hague.

West New Guinea immediately became a bone of contention between the two countries. The Indonesians claimed that the territory belonged to them as an integral part of the former Netherlands East Indies—an incontrovertible argument. The Dutch insisted that the Papuan population of New Guinea, or West Irian as Indonesian nationalists dubbed it, was a totally different ethnic group than the rest of Indonesia. And they insisted that turning this primitive people over to the Djakarta administration would be a violation of their role as trustees for a developing society. Both arguments were weak at best: The new Indonesia was composed of any number of ethnic groups, many no more different one from another than the Papuans. And after the record of 350 years of Dutch imperialism, The Hague was on a sticky wicket claiming it wanted to hold on to the New Guinea area on humanitarian grounds.

The argument dragged on. Soekarno used it as a pretext for his seizure of Dutch assets in Indonesia in December 1957. In fact, he needed the issue as a diversion to cover the total bankruptcy of his regime—economically, politically, and psychologically.

Finally, more than ten years too late, in rushed the Americans. The Indonesians had already begun to make a military feint toward seizing the area. It was obvious that the Dutch could repulse a military operation in its initial stages. And, in fact, they sank an Indonesian naval vessel, causing a real crisis in the regime between followers of Foreign Minister Soebandrio and the Indonesian military who felt they were being pushed too fast and too far.

But in the long run, a protracted war would have involved the Dutch in a totally unreal situation. The colony had been a net drain on the Netherlands during the whole period, early discoveries of petroleum had not proved out and the largely stone-age population would be generations developing into a society which would "prove" Dutch good intentions. And "war" between Holland and Indonesia would involve the U.S.

On to the scene entered the late Robert F. Kennedy, special emissary for the President. Soekarno turned on his charm. And Kennedy, the supposed tough young politician, fell for it hook, line, and sinker. It was one thing for me as a naive young journalist to have succumbed to it in the early 1950s. But at this stage of the game, Soekarno was already a proved demagogue and bankrupt leader leaning on the Communists for support.

The agreement to turn New Guinea over to Soekarno simply propped up the staggering regime with one more "victory" cheaply won. The Americans extracted a number of promises, including leaving the U.S. oil companies in Indonesia alone.

Arnold Brackman, one of the best post-World War II chroniclers of events in Indonesia, sums it up this way:

> . . . In Washington, Kennedy Administration officials defended the settlement by asking, "Are you ready to risk nuclear war for Dutch New Guinea?" Of course nobody was. But the import of this assessment was that the single alternative, a settlement on Soekarno's terms, was not a matter of judgment but a fact established beyond any shred of doubt.
>
> Yet post-Irian military studies showed that the 2,000-odd Indonesian troops landed in New Guinea during the campaign fared poorly in jungle terrain and had been easily handled by the meager opposing Dutch forces. The Indonesian troops had neither the will nor the desire to fight. After signing of the New York agreement, the U.S. Air Force—at [U.N. Secretary-General U] Thant's request—was rushed into service from Manila to drop food, tents, and medical supplies to beleaguered, isolated Indonesian Army "pockets" in West Irian. The situation was ludicrous —the U.S.A.F. bailing out Indonesian "guerrillas."
>
> . . . If, indeed, Djakarta had planned a full-scale invasion of West New Guinea, then Washington should have been alarmed not by Indonesia's prowess, but by the failure of the American mediatory effort—the Kennedy-Soekarno correspondence, the uninterrupted flow of American arms and food to Indonesia during the negotiations, the U.S. diplomatic pressure on the Dutch, the assignment of [Ambassador Ellsworth] Bunker as a U.N. agent

and mediator, and the American offer of massive economic assistance to Indonesia after a negotiated settlement.

It might have been argued that nothing more could have been salvaged from the wreckage of a ten-year policy. But, instead, what was argued was that Soekarno "had seen the light," that he was turning over a new leaf. One of the most important American diplomats concerned in the affair told me in what I could only regard as utmost sincerity that Soekarno was a changed man. He would now devote all his energies to "nation-building"—economic development and constructive politics.

Our conversation ended on this note:

DIPLOMAT: I have it on the best authority that Soekarno is really ready to change his approach.

SANDERS: That is certainly possible. But given the history of the past fifteen years what is the evidence that he will?

DIPLOMAT: Soekarno has come to realize that his "role as the George Washington of his country" is now in jeopardy.

I didn't know whether to laugh or weep.

(It is no wonder that that diplomat has for years been called *Merdeka* [the Indonesian word for freedom] behind his back. The story, perhaps apocryphal, is that he once attended a typical Soekarno ceremony where the President gave one of his demagogic speeches punctuated with refrains of slogans from the crowd. After a particularly pithy denunciation of the U.S., the shout of *Merdeka* rang out from the audience and the diplomat, ignorant of what had been said in Indonesian, joined in.)

Brackman, again, puts the case well:

> In Indonesia . . . [the] agreement to turn over West New Guinea after a plebescite to the Indonesians was no sooner placed in the archives of the United Nations than Djakarta began to agitate for its amendment. . . . Soekarno disembarked from a Soviet-built cruiser [in West New Guinea]. . . . His prestige in the islands—and in the Malay world—soared. And his relatively easy acquisition of West Irian exhilarated him and the expansionists in Djakarta. Although Indonesia was wholly dependent

141

on foreign arsenals and silos for arms and food, Soekarno and his aides were intoxicated with their "conquest." They began seriously to believe that Indonesia had attained "great power status" and, therefore, was entitled to a sphere of influence in Southeast Asia.

Of course, this led to the "confrontation" with Malaysia and the British over Borneo, an open alliance between Soekarno and Peking, which only because of the weakness of Soekarno's regime did not present the U.S. with a crisis of the magnitude of Vietnam later. And it laid the groundwork for new and perplexing headaches for American policy-makers.

The history of our relations with Soekarno is a prime example of another aspect of our naiveté: It is the embrace by Americans of a kind of phony anti-colonialism.

A decade ago, in the U.S. on a home leave, I participated in a debate on what was happening in Indonesia. My attack on Soekarno's policies was answered by a young, rising New York City politician. He is the sort of dilettante in foreign affairs who, twenty years ago—when European colonialism was a real issue in Asia—did not know one Asian country from another. Then the weight of U.S. power and prestige thrown behind Asian non-Communist nationalists might have done some good. Unfortunately, Asian anti-Communists had to try to escape the onus of espousing collaboration with the West. And it was a Western world still fighting for colonial aims, in Indochina and Indonesia.

In our debate he upbraided me for refusing to see that Soekarno was "a product of 350 years of Dutch colonialism." I replied, in heat and in pungent language, that Soekarno was a creature of figuratively uncertain parentage, that he would have been such at any time in the world's history, in any society.

THE RITUALISTIC LIBERAL

THE young politician's approach to Asian problems is widespread among the members of the U.S. left. It arises in no small part out of what my friend, Professor Sidney Hook, calls the philosophy of "the ritualistic liberal" in American politics.

I believe American guilt, for our own racist past, plays a big role. This leads many American intellectuals to apply a different standard to the speech and actions of Asians. That is to say, perfect nonsense is accepted—sometimes on technical subjects which is easily refutable—from Asian politicians and intellectuals simply because their skin is a few degrees darker than the average white American.

My own approach is very emphatic: I was never a racist. I opposed racism, and still oppose it, in my own country. I hope, too, that I have made a maximum effort to overcome the effects of being reared in the American environment, admittedly permeated with racist sentiments. And, while I am prepared to try to understand the intellectual environment in which Asian thought is generated, I insist that Asian leadership be the object of the same kind of scrutiny as we would expose leaders of thought to in the West.

This problem is not just an academic one.

It explains, in part, a recurrent myth about Vietnam: The insistence that Ho Chi Minh and other Communist leaders were "forced" into their espousal of Communism. It is true, of course, that French colonial policy, the attempt to re-establish the prewar colonial rule in Vietnam after World War II, and French arrogance in dealing with the Vietnamese pushed many Vietnamese into the arms of the Communists. But Ho had spent twenty-five years in the Communist movement by 1945. He had acted as agent of the Comintern, had participated in the internecine wars among the Communist factions during the period between the two wars.

In 1946-48, I actively participated in a group in the U.S. lobbying for the Vietnamese nationalist cause which then we mistakenly thought was represented by the Viet Minh (the Communist-led nationalist organization negotiating with the French for independence). We were a group of young Vietnamese, most of them political refugees from Indochina, and Americans.

At one point in our activities, we had been able to arrange for Ho's representative to come to Washington to plead for American pressure on the French, perhaps through the United Nations, to compromise with the Vietnamese nationalists. Word came from the Vietnamese—presumably from Ho himself—that we were immediately to desist in all such efforts. It was obvious to my friends that he did not want to be "rescued" from international

Communism, with which he was increasingly identifying the Viet Minh. Ho made Vietnamese "social fascists"—the important Trotskyist movement in the south—and other nationalists his number-one enemies. His tactics were essentially Stalinist—and there is little, even circumstantial, evidence that he "wanted" to do otherwise.

One can, of course, exaggerate the concept of the individual's "free will," in the turbulent events of Asia in the past fifty years. But Ho's identification with Communism, its aspirations, its methods, were only partially the product of his extreme nationalism brought on by French oppression.

Other nationalists facing similar problems did not choose the Communist route. Sjahrir, for example, in Indonesia, was thrown into a pestiferous New Guinea prison colony—even though, unlike some other Indonesian nationalists, he publicly espoused a policy of collaboration with the Dutch in an interim period in order that the Indonesians might gain the intellectual tools they needed for independence. He did not become a Communist.

The argument can, of course, lead to all the complications of the various societies, the differences in the colonial regimes, the individuals themselves. But I simply want to make the point that persecution does not in itself drive Asians into moral positions unacceptable to ourselves and to their own traditional values for which they can be "excused." If liberalism and objectivity in dealing with Asians has meaning for Americans, it must mean understanding coupled with hard-headed analysis of their thought and actions and no special allowances for their ideas because of the color of their skin.

This "double standard" of the ritualistic liberal is compounded of theses based on false premises, developed during the 1930s honeymoon with Soviet totalitarianism by a great part of the American left. (And woe unto us, the so-called New Left may have to go through the same learning process.) Projected into the Asian scene, they have little meaning and no relevance.

Not too long ago, the editorial writer of a very important American newspaper called on an old acquaintance in one of the Southeast Asian foreign ministries. He told the Asian that he and his minister, one of the most outspoken anti-Peking figures in Southeast Asia, must "learn to live with Communist China."

His advice came only a few weeks after the Chinese Communists had announced in radio broadcasts their support for an underground group seeking to subvert the government of the country, to liberate it from "the shackles of American imperialism." He went on to say that the Southeast Asian nations must learn to live with the Chinese and their designs on Southeast Asia just as Latin American nations have learned to live with "American imperialism."

Recovering from his initial shock, my Southeast Asian friend told the learned editorialist—on his first visit to Asia, incidentally—that he thought it might be possible for his country to "live with the Communists" when China began to treat Southeast Asia as well as the U.S. manages its relations with Latin America.

VIOLENCE IN ASIA

THE ritualistic liberal approaches Asia with a set of preconceptions that just are not founded on fact. Take the problem of violence. Moving from the relatively stable cultures of the Western world, he cannot understand the role of violence in what have always been societies controlled by despots, now in the midst of revolutionary changes.

In 1964 the Communists blew up—as they had many times before—a train traveling through central Vietnam. The United States Information Service had a photographer on the scene within a short time after the attack. And they had some of the most graphic photographs of the passengers, most of them women and children, blown out of the cars onto the railroad tracks and strewn along the right-of-way. The horror of the situation was stupefying, and I can appreciate how any American would be tremendously affected by it.

USIS in Saigon rushed the photographs and descriptive material to a printer. And within record time, they had distributed literally hundreds of thousands of leaflets throughout the country. They saw it as proof of the cynicism of the Communists, who

145

waged a campaign against the Saigon regime without regard for the innocent suffering of the Vietnamese people.

But, as I tried to explain to an important USIS official, the whole American approach was not only misdirected, but probably of positive benefit to the Viet Cong. Terror has been an intimate part of the struggle in Indochina since conflict erupted during the Japanese occupation. The Communists first used it against their competition for leadership of the nationalist movement in the 1945-48 period. (For example, in Quang Ngai province alone they murdered some 15,000 people in 1945 in an effort to wipe out the old established anti-Communist Vietnam Quoc Dan Dang, a traditionalist, quasi-secret society, a nationalist organization.)

To spread the word about new effective (from their point of view) terrorist attacks by the Viet Cong in 1964, when the grip of the Saigon government over the countryside was in growing jeopardy, was simply to do the Communists' work for them. And I told the American official: He might better have dropped those leaflets on New York to demonstrate more effectively to American liberals the real nature of the struggle in Vietnam.

That Sunday morning in 1950 when North Korea invaded South Korea I was in Djakarta. Almost in jubilation, I went to see my friend Sjahrir.

Triumphantly I said, "Now, at least, there can no longer be Communist fellow-travelers in Asia. They will either have to acknowledge that they stand with the Communists—who, when they cannot win their way by any kind of legal means, resort to violence and aggression—or quit."

Sjahrir, with that wry sense of humor which won him so many friends over the years, said, "As long as they are winning, they will always have followers who can compromise their ideals."

I have remembered that morning all through the years since. True enough, in all societies, the great part of the population follows the leadership wherever it leads them. In the West, opportunism among intellectuals is, to say the least, not an unknown phenomenon. How much more difficult it is in the East where the intellectual, at best, has a very precarious economic existence. They are not societies like my own country where even "dropout" hippies get a monthly check from home, where relative full employment has for more than two decades given—especially the educated—more economic security than any society has ever known.

Force and violence do play a major role in international politics. And John Foster Dulles perhaps showed more courage than diplomacy in his famous statement on "brinksmanship." But I do not believe that you can deny his thesis: The U.S. must be prepared to use its power if major wars are to be prevented.

In three different crises in Asia in the postwar period, *the announced reluctance of the U.S. to use that force* has played an important role in bringing on the crisis:

Secretary of State Dean Acheson's speech before the National Press Club in Washington in January 1950, placing South Korea outside the "defensive perimeter" of the U.S. in Asia, played a role in convincing Stalin he could take the gamble to unite Korea by force of arms under a Communist regime, resulting in the costly Korean War.

A Congressional debate on whether or not the Offshore Islands were part of our commitment to defend Taiwan helped bring on the 1958 threat to those islands and the defenses of Nationalist China. Only an American display of firmness prevented a Chinese Communist war to take the islands and eventually Taiwan itself.

The constant litany of the 1950s and early '60s by spokesmen for the American military that we would not, *under any conditions,* fight another land war in Asia, helped persuade Hanoi that the North Vietnam Communist leadership could launch a full military invasion in 1964 to destroy the Saigon regime.

It is a generally accepted thesis in government and academic circles studying national strategy that a careful delineation of our national interests *to the enemy* is essential for peace. Yet repeatedly in Asia we have done just the opposite: We have signaled our Communist enemies that we are prepared to accept aggrandizement of their territory and power, then reneged and fought them when the implications of our statements had to be squarely faced.

It is a remarkable evidence of the defects of American ritualistic liberalism that we have not faced up to this truth.

Nor does the American intellectual find in Asia some of his

147

most cherished reactions to classic Western political and social problems.

One of the more amusing examples I can cite is the case of a former Japanese naval officer. He was a Japanese official in the city of Shanghai under the 1940-45 occupation by the Japanese military. In part because he was a naval officer and there is a bitter tradition of rivalry with the Japanese army, in part because he is basically a decent human being, in part because it was not a highly critical decision, he refused the Japanese military junta's order from Tokyo to turn over to the Nazis the stateless Jewish refugees who had taken sanctuary in the International Quarter of Shanghai in the 1930s.

But there was also an important complicated ideological reason behind his decision: He had read the "Protocols of Zion" furnished him by the Nazis and the Japanese military cooperating with them. He accepted "the evidence." But his reaction was that the Jews were an extremely able and powerful group. He saw no reason to antagonize "World Jewry" by precipitate action. Needless to say, when I knew him long after the war, he was convinced the major reason for the defeat of the Axis Powers was that Hitler *had* challenged the Jews and their power—described in epic terms by the German anti-Semites in their propaganda outpourings he had read!

The belief that representative government institutions modeled on the Western tradition can be equated with democratic society in Asia is also a sacred cow of these ritualistic liberals. (Although, in fairness to them, it always seems they apply the criterion of the presence or absence of representative government only to U.S. allies and anti-Communist powers in Asia, rarely to Communist China, North Korea, North Vietnam. The same critics of attempts at parliamentary government in South Vietnam are willing to overlook the despotic nature of Sihanouk's regime in neutralist Cambodia.)

Speaking of this general problem, an Indian historian has put the problem succinctly:

> The Indian intelligentsia, deeply imbued with the ideas of English liberalism, could not think of freedom from foreign rule in any other terms [but the establishment of parliamentarian-

ism]; and even *English opinion, lacking for the most part any real insight into Indian conditions, tended to view with equanimity, if not enthusiasm, the export of parliamentary democracy to India.* [my italics] And so there was introduced into that vast country of illiterate peasants, belonging to diverse races and religions and held together by geography and common subjugation to British rule, a system of government which, while it has served English and some closely kindred people well enough, has elsewhere been—and doubtless will continue to be —a constant source of strife, disunity and disruption.

NGO DINH DIEM

PENDEREL MOON might well have been writing about Americans and their attitudes two decades later toward the problems of Vietnam. Nowhere has American naiveté expressed itself in such flamboyant terms as during the crisis of the Vietnamese regime in 1963—a crisis that ended in the fall of the legitimate Saigon regime and the murder of Ngo Dinh Diem.

I would not argue that had Diem remained in power, the situation might not have degenerated, that the U.S. might not have had to send large-scale military forces to Southeast Asia. Those are the "ifs" of history that are imponderable.

But I think it is important to put into perspective how the tensions grew between the Saigon regime and the U.S. government to the point where an American effort to subvert and overthrow it became inevitable. And it is an epic tale of how the American Establishment—military, civilian, officialdom, and nonofficial—failed to cope with a challenge to American foreign policy in Asia.

The central character is Diem himself. I met him first in 1951 in the U.S. Earlier, during my stay in Hanoi, I had heard his name often. Vietnamese anti-Communist nationalists—caught between the Communists leading the guerrillas against the French and the Paris refusal to concede the new era of Asian independence—had told me that he was the only man who might offer alternative leadership to Ho Chi Minh.

His reputation arose out of his refusal to collaborate with any government which did not concede real Vietnamese independence. In 1933 he had quit the French Indochina bureaucracy for which he had been trained, refusing to perform the role of puppet for the French administration. When the Japanese formed a puppet government in Hanoi in April 1945, after overthrowing the rapidly disintegrating government of the Vichyites in Indochina, he had refused to join other Vietnamese nationalists in creating the first "independent" regime.

Ho Chi Minh offered to make him vice-president of the so-called "national" government opposing the French in 1945. Diem refused; he was steadfastly opposed to the Communists who, he knew, dominated the government. His older brother had already been assassinated by the Communists, as had many other anti-Communist nationalists.

He fled with young, dethroned Emperor Bao Dai to Hong Kong where he counseled this descendant of the still prestigious Nguyen dynasty to refuse collaboration with the French except on terms of real independence. But Bao Dai agreed in 1949 to return to Vietnam within the framework of a series of partial concessions from the French toward creating a Vietnamese state, still far from the independence Diem hoped for and for which the Communists fought. Diem refused to return with Bao Dai, instead drifted to the U.S.

Diem had read my pessimistic dispatches in the *Christian Science Monitor* on the progress of the war. My estimate was that a Communist victory was certain if Paris was not willing to concede real independence to a non-Communist regime while, at the same time, upholding it militarily against the Communist-led Viet Minh. He was then staying in New Jersey with the Maryknoll Fathers, a Roman Catholic order long concerned with Chinese problems.

Our first meeting came on my invitation that he come to tea. It was the summer of 1951. I was living in a tiny apartment in Greenwich Village, grimly aware that whatever expertise I had accumulated in a few years of living and reporting in Southeast Asia had no market value. I couldn't find a job that would take me back to South Asia as a correspondent.

Diem was equally depressed. He had not been able to talk to anyone of importance in the State Department or other agencies of the U.S. government to try to make his point: American pressure should be exerted on the French to grant real independence to the Saigon regime of Bao Dai if it were to be meaningful in the fight against the Communists. (It is amusing to read the new "discoveries" by those opposed to the U.S. Asian commitment of elaborate contact between the CIA and Diem in this period.)

Diem was appalled—it is ironic to think of that now—at the enormous destruction of the war, the killing of innocent civilians by the use of what was then considered far superior French firepower (he mentioned napalm) supplied by the Americans.

We sat and commiserated with each other over what we saw as the inevitable defeat of the non-Communist forces in Indochina —it did not come until three years later at Dien Bien Phu. We then thought it could culminate only in Communist rule over all Indochina. And Diem was equally pessimistic about the possibilities of his country maintaining its identity in the long term so long as China was ruled by an aggressive Communist regime.

I saw Diem only once or twice after that in the U.S. There seemed to be little he (or I, in my small way) could do to reverse the course of history in Vietnam.

I wrote a few scripts for the Voice of America, more labors of love than anything else, trying to point out that there was something between the devil and the deep blue sea in Vietnam, between Communism and colonialism, if only American policy would recognize it. I wrote an article in *The New Republic* which they entitled "There *Is* a Third Force in Vietnam." (I even spent an agonizing Saturday evening with Jawaharlal Nehru in New Delhi in 1951, en route back to New York from Hanoi, arguing the same thing. But Nehru's answer was that he could do nothing to help; as the Indonesians had found out much earlier, Nehru's anti-colonial assistance to other Asians was more rhetoric than substance.)

Even that feeble effort soon evaporated: The McCarthy era was entering its hysterical climax. Somewhere—I could never find out just where for my immediate boss at the Voice was a brother of one of McCarthy's most famous victims—a dossier had been compiled proving I was less than reliable. My "socialist past," the fact that both of my parents were born in Eastern Eu-

151

rope, membership in a notoriously Communist-infiltrated anti-segregationist organization in the South (perhaps that was enough in itself) were three strikes against me. I had brazenly told a "security officer" in Paris, when I had unsuccessfully applied for a job in the Marshall Plan there, that I would join the southern organization again, if I had it to do over; that I thought the issue of segregation was that important. And I was again on the pavement job-searching—this time convinced that neither the press nor politics were my *métier* and that I should seek fame and fortune in public relations.

My relatively successful infatuation with huckstering wore thin at about the time the French Indochina War reached its climax. I returned to journalism. And, suddenly, Diem appeared in the headlines.

In the complex of compromises at the Geneva Conference of 1954 fixing an armistice for the war, Diem emerged as the prime minister of the newly truncated non-Communist half of the country below the seventeenth parallel. Diem accepted, for although few at that time gave the Saigon regime more than six months before it would be gobbled up by the new Communist regime installed in Hanoi, he at last got what he wanted—the French were, seemingly, prepared to permit a truly independent non-Communist regime under Bao Dai, however long it might last.

What followed is well-known history. Diem accomplished, as it was proclaimed far and wide, a miracle. He divested the South of the so-called religious sects' private armies—the Binh Xuyen, a collection of pirates and Trotskyist renegades, the Cao Dai and the Hoa Hao, local warlord groups the French had armed in their desperate fight against the Communist-led nationalists.

An attempted coup d'état by Vietnamese army forces directed by the French failed (the leader, an ethnic Vietnamese, is today in one of the top planning positions in the Paris military command). Within a few months, Diem relieved his regime of the albatross of Bao Dai. A nationwide "referendum" was held, in which the voters chose between Diem and Bao Dai as chief of state (it was the kind of charade of Western-style elections that we Americans approve of, when the end seems to justify the means).

During this period, he had less than wholehearted American

support. The Eurocentrists in the Department of State still leaned toward the French interpretation of events; General J. Lawton Collins, the American ambassador in Saigon, cautioned Diem against moving against the sects (while he was egged on by Colonel Edward Lansdale, local Central Intelligence Agency representative).

By 1957 Diem had stabilized the regime and went to the U.S. as a conquering hero. (I wrote a speech for him, setting forth his economic policy of private enterprise—even to the point of protecting the former French holdings.) By 1957 rice exports— the best index of stability and contentment of the peasantry in the vast granary of the Mekhong River Delta south of Saigon— had risen to 340 thousand tons, one-third the pre-war figure.

But behind the scenes, the refusal of the U.S. to accept Diem's analysis of the broad strategic stiuation planted the seeds of what was to become the crisis of 1963. Diem was convinced that Ho would have no choice but to begin to subvert the regime in the South. Diem had refused to hold national elections for a unified regime in both North and South—certain that no true elections could be held in the Communist North. He warned of the inevitability of a Communist effort to subvert his regime.

He asked the U.S. to arm and train a militia force of half a million men in the villages, a force to fight guerrilla warfare such as the French had faced. Two stock American replies came back: From the military, the U.S would arm a force to resist an across-the-frontier aggression by North Vietnam "until American troops could arrive." (That was based on the Korean War experience.) From the civilians—and particularly the American liberals— how could the regime destroy itself more quickly than by putting so much of its economic wherewithal into a military force of such dimensions?

Diem warned the Laos corridor would be an avenue of infiltration into the South, as it had been during the French war. He asked for a massive program to resettle peasants from the plain of central Vietnam to the highlands facing Laos, relieving the population pressure in the poorest parts of the country and building a barrier of loyal settlements against infiltration. Washington's reply: It won't work; there is no threat; it is too costly.

I do not wish to exaggerate Diem's case. But it was significant in the context of the extremely complex problems of the regime that he could at least identify the issues. In 1959, after a trip to Vietnam at Diem's invitation, I wrote in *Business Week*:

> . . . The decision on apportioning U.S. aid depends on political strategy—how to keep South Vietnam strong enough to withstand any Communist threat from the north. Both Vietnamese and Americans in Saigon agree that to reduce armed defense would simply invite another Korea-type attack.
>
> This problem of security tends to conflict with the development of democratic institutions in South Vietnam, another aim the U.S. has tried to promote. The country can hardly boast Western-style representative democracy. Its national assembly is something of a rubber-stamp, taking the president's dictates. The government blocks almost all political opposition, and censors the press.
>
> . . . Terrorism is one reason why Pres. Diem's government feels it has to take a tough-minded stand.
>
> If the U.S. applied enough pressure, it might [for example] force Diem to loosen his restrictions on the South Vietnamese press. But that might bolster the Communists' pet charge against the Diem government—that one way or another it is under the thumb of Western powers. The Vietnamese themselves remember too well the 80 years of French colonial rule, and don't want more of it from the U.S.
>
> Diem, for his part, believes his country is moving slowly toward representative democracy, with benevolent authoritarianism as a middle stage between French rule and the ultimate goal of free institutions. He interprets the failure of parliamentary systems in neighboring Thailand and Indonesia as proof that Western institutions won't succeed overnight in Vietnam. As things stand now, any political group that replaced Diem would probably bear down on its opposition as hard as the present government does.
>
> . . . Diem believes that only strong government can make a go of large-scale land reform—the kind the U.S. occupation forced through in Japan and Gen. Chiang Kai-shek successfully imposed in Formosa. Now Diem hopes to complete by the year-end a land reform program that will hand over 2.1 million acres to 250,000 families. He also hopes to boost average productivity

on Vietnamese farms, where it is something like one-third of that in Japan or Formosa.

Corruption within the Vietnamese government is a headache. But it seems to be a minor one—compared, for instance, to the reported squandering of U.S. aid funds on nearby Laos.

NON-IDEOLOGICAL CONFLICT

LOOKING back now, some of the faults that were to take over the regime were implicit; i.e., Diem's preoccupation with detail. But the working relationship between Washington and Saigon deteriorated for other, less ideological, reasons. In 1959, one of the American press lords (Roy Howard of the Scripps-Howard newspapers) decided that foreign aid was costing the U.S. too much. Inflation, he argued, was the greatest menace to "the American way of life." The U.S. aid program overseas seemed to represent the best target for cuts. But the two largest recipients, Nationalist China and South Korea, were sacrosanct. So a reporter was dispatched to South Vietnam, the third largest program, to investigate corruption and waste of American aid funds (they were running at about $180 million a year then).

The reporter found little or no evidence, but the stories were written anyway. That brought on a Congressional investigation. And the investigating committee sent a subcommittee to Saigon to look into the whole matter. It investigated. But it also met *in* Saigon, and *on* Vietnamese territory made its announcement of a clean bill of health for the Diem regime. The old Vietnamese nationalist, Diem, was humiliated and bitter over what he considered this expression of a new kind of colonialism.

One of my most trusted informants in the American bureaucracy in Saigon at the time has told me of a mission of Pentagon brass and civilian military advisers who came to Saigon to look into the problem of building the Vietnamese army during this period. The then U.S. ambassador, acting as his own interpreter, briefly summarized a long monologue by Diem of his problems by saying, "He's giving you the same old line about the French again." Diem preferred not to speak English. But he understood it, of course. Relations between him and this patricular ambassador degenerated into both of them doing dinner-table imitations of each other—Diem's of the ambassador was considered a classic.

There is little doubt that when an attempted coup d'état against his government came in 1960, the U.S. Embassy was largely aware, prior to its outbreak, of its origins and nature. Yet Diem and his government were not informed. Even if there were no U.S. complicity—and there appears to have been none at any policy-making level—it put into question the relationship of Washington to the regime.

Much has been made of Diem's personal characteristics. Because of the events since 1963, I believe the general newspaper reader is now aware that much of what he was reading in the headlines then was the stuff of the peculiar personality and nature of the Vietnamese people. Their politics were developed in the long struggle against Chinese domination, then the French, in the fierce civil war fought during a twenty-year period, particularly of 1945-48 in Hanoi.

William Henderson and Wesley R. Fishel, two students of Vietnam during these past two decades and well acquainted with Diem, have put the case well:

> Conditioned by more than two decades of underground activity against the French and the Communists, during which he learned that even close working associates could not always be depended upon, Diem tended to rely heavily on members of his family and close personal friends. The persons in this cluster shifted from time to time as foreigners withdrew or were withdrawn from Saigon and, in the process, from positions of immediate and continuing influence.

Diem was shocked to find several members of the American Establishment in Saigon who had stood with him during 1954 and 1955, when the very existence of the regime was in jeopardy, withdrawn by Washington. In some cases, it was the simple process of the U.S. bureaucracy's routine shift of officers. In others, they were withdrawn for precisely the reason that they sympathized with Diem and had won the approbation of being accused of becoming afflicted with "localitis."

Much has been made of what are called Diem's endless monologues to visitors. He is said to have talked without substance about Vietnamese affairs. (Too often his American interlocutor spoke no French; the interpretation was often poor and exceedingly tiresome.)

I know little of what he talked about with others. But our long conversations were neither monologues, nor were they inconsequential.

In 1959, during a visit, I posed the question why some of the more important non-Communist political figures—friends of mine from Hanoi days, in part—had not been encouraged to come into his government. He spoke eloquently on the subject. And he went into great detail to defend his position. One could argue that it was not necessary for him to do so—to a noninfluential reporter. But it was certainly a logical and balanced presentation, even though I did not agree with it—and told him so.

Again, much later, I remember an instance in the spring of 1963. I spent a week in one of the provinces in the Delta near the Cambodian border. I came back to see him and reported on what I saw. I was astounded at his detailed information about the situation. He knew, for example, all the specifics of a small bridge which the Communists had blown up and which was causing severe economic dislocation in the province.

Later that summer, only a few weeks before the coup d'état was to bring down his government, he discussed in great detail with me a cable to my magazine alleging that his brother, a Roman Catholic bishop, had been running important business enterprises in Saigon. It was anything but a monologue. He explained that profits of the enterprises were going into Catholic charities. I argued that while I was convinced that was true, could he not see that whatever the purpose of the profit-taking, it was destroying his image as a figure above such mundane pursuits?—and I used the old cliché of Caesar's wife.

PHONEY "RELIGIOUS WAR"

NOWHERE was the gullibility of an American audience so exploited as in the reporting on the question of the Buddhists in 1963. The picture given American newspaper readers was that a

157

Buddhist majority, "80 per cent of the population," was being persecuted by a minority Catholic regime.

Most Vietnamese are not believers in the sense we know the concept in the West. Certainly 80 per cent are not Buddhists. Most are Confucianists, believers in ancestor worship. So ingrained is the concept, in fact, that many Catholic families in central Vietnam, Christian for more than two hundred years, have eldest sons who are not formally Catholic because they must do the ancestor worship ceremonies—rites prohibited by the more orthodox Catholic priests. (Yet in 1967—perhaps another sign of the changing times in Rome—when a famous Vietnamese Catholic bishop died, the one hundredth-day-after-death ceremony, a purely Confucian concept, was performed—and performed in the Catholic cathedral in Saigon.)

It is certainly true that Catholicism is a minority religion in Vietnam. But, paradoxically, although the persecution of French missionaries in the late nineteenth century provided the pretext for expansion of French domination, Vietnamese Catholics are as much a part of the national life of their country as other religious entities. They have been part and parcel of the highly complex struggle among so many social, historical, and "ethnic" groups. It is true that some 800,000 Catholics migrated to the South when the Communists took over the northern part of the country. But it is also true that an important Communist-front group in North Vietnam has been, since the mid-1940s, the so-called "Catholic Resistance."

I remember in 1951 visiting a Catholic seminary in Hanoi in search of an interview with a particular priest. I wandered about the building for some time and finally abandoned my project, unable to find a seminarian who could speak French. I doubt that a similar experience is possible anywhere else in Asia; in almost every other Asian nation, Christians are so identified with the former occupying power that they are among the first in their proficiency in the former colonial masters' language—English, Dutch, French, Spanish, or Portuguese.

Nor was it true that Diem's fate was identical to the Catholics'. He had had a major row with Rome early in the regime over control of Catholic schools in Vietnam. In fact, leaders of the northern Catholic refugees—extremely antagonistic to Diem, who was originally from central Vietnam—were anti-Diem. And there was close collaboration between some of their priests and the Buddhist political monks in the movement to overthrow the regime.

The Buddhists, themselves, while they had a mass following—particularly among women, who are the main communicants of Mahayana (Chinese and North Asian) Buddhism in Vietnam—were led by politicians. There are a dozen sects—some of them Hinayana, or the Buddhism of Ceylon, Thailand, and Cambodia, more different from northern Asian Buddhism than Mediterranean Catholicism is from North Europe Protestantism.

During all the reporting on the so-called Buddhist crisis that summer, rarely did one see in the dispatches of American newsmen identification of the primarily political nature of this "Buddhist" leadership. Nowhere was it reported that Thich Tri Quang, the leader of the radical Buddhists, had been brought into the pagoda by the chief figure of the Communist-front Buddhist organization in North Vietnam. Nor was it reported that for a long period after 1945 he had also been the head of a Communist-front Buddhist organization in central Vietnam. Nor that his organization in central Vietnam had been financed by Ngo Dinh Can—Diem's brother and representative in Hue—ironically, in an effort to prevent Communist infiltration of the Buddhist pagodas.

The press reports were an excellent example of that greatest failing of the American newsman: History begins at the moment of crisis. And since most reporting for the American press in Asia is crisis reporting, more and more by jet-hoisted correspondents moving into areas they have not known intimately before, the distortions are incredible. Events and facts are torn out of their context to describe the situations of the moment.

THE JOURNALISTS AND DIEM

ONE of the most flagrant examples of what was going on was demonstrated to me in the spring of 1963. A group of journalists, I among them, were waiting at the door of the main Saigon hospital. A famous Vietnamese writer and political figure had committed suicide. He left behind a note accusing the Diem regime of persecution of the Buddhists, of failure to meet its obligations.

We were waiting with friends and relatives and a group of political figures to accompany the cortège from the hospital to one of the Buddhist pagodas, then to burial. (Permission for the funeral procession through the heart of Saigon, which had been granted by Diem himself, gives some idea of the nature of the regime. It has been described as a ruthless dictatorship, thoroughly merciless in its persecution of its opponents, yet this display of political opposition was permitted by Diem, even though the so-called Buddhist crisis was already moving toward fever pitch.)

We stood talking in the courtyard. I saw some old Hanoi acquaintances among the politicians. One came over to me and I introduced him to some of the other journalists. And after the Vietnamese had broken away, I murmured, almost to myself, "This is a real Dai Viet 'do.'" The Dai Viet is one of the traditionalist political associations of North and central Vietnam, organized originally under Japanese auspices, one of the many Vietnamese political organizations which draw much of their inspiration and method from the old Chinese revolutionary secret societies.

I overheard one of the reporters turn to another who had been standing near me and say, "What is the Dai Viet?" It was a little like a New York reporter asking, "What is Tammany Hall?"

Yet the young American reporter who posed the question was the representative of one of the most prestigious newspapers in the U.S. and had for many weeks been writing highly critical and "learned" interpretive articles about the Vietnamese political situation.

We still do not have all the details of how the decision to "dump" Diem was made in Washington. Even the most superficial survey of the literature of the Kennedy advisers who have broken into print with their evaluations of that administration show considerable conflict. But whatever the rationalization advanced in official quarters, in Saigon and Asia the fall of Diem is laid to overwhelming American pressure.

One can sympathize with the harried policy-makers in Washington during that long, hot summer of 1963. The American press was painting a picture of persecution of Buddhists, Buddhist monks were committing suicide in fiery flames. The reporting was replete with television and still photos of women and children being beaten by police in Saigon's streets. The press never failed to call the Saigon government "the South Vietnamese regime of Roman Catholic Ngo Dinh Diem," emphasizing the critical problem for Kennedy, the first Catholic U.S. President. There was the growing conflict between the press reports and the U.S. military and civilian executives over the power of the Communist insurgents.

Failures since the winter of 1962-63 have "proved" for some observers that the news reporting was more correct than the official accounts of progress in putting down the insurgency.

I think it is significant, though, that there is a general admission in Communist writings on the period that 1962—the year when the Diem regime and its military came under heaviest criticism for its failures in the war—was a very bad year for the Communists. The Australian Communist journalist, Wilfred Burchett, has written that the guerrillas were so hard pressed that they considered withdrawing to the mountains of the Vietnamese-Laos border region.

Again, we are dealing with the "ifs" of history.

My own analysis is that the failures of the regime were rampant during this period. But just as many of the most influential newsmen were wrong in calling the Communist-led insurgency primarily a revolt against Diem's "dictatorial" policies, rather than a conspiracy dictated from Hanoi against South Vietnam's regime, they were wrong on other aspects. I believe they exaggerated the failings of the Vietnamese military at that time.

What is inconceivable is the decision in Washington to push Diem out *without a full realization of what would be needed to replace him* in the growing crisis. The substitution of a *junta* of army generals under American auspices paid little attention to the historic situation of the country.

In Korea, a military regime replaced—eventually—the Rhee regime. But while American officialdom has often taken credit for the relative success of that regime in the past dozen years, it ignores the two most fundamental facts in that situation which did not parallel Vietnam:

The members of the Korean *junta* were a group of Japanese-trained officers with wide experience in military command, tested in the bitter campaigns of the Korean War. They had an *esprit de corps* totally different from the heritage of defeat, corruption, and lack of idealism which the French had left among the skeletal Vietnamese officer corps after 1954.

Secondly, and one of those footnotes of history neatly forgotten at Foggy Bottom, the Korean *junta* took power *in spite* of American demands and protests that it let civilian government continue. For months, the U.S. Embassy in Seoul did everything it could to force the Korean colonels to back down and return the government to a weak civilian leadership.

AMERICAN NAIVETÉ IN 1963-64

IT would be hard to exaggerate the naiveté of the Americans in Saigon dealing with the situation in the winter of 1963-64.

After an extended trip to the Mekhong Delta, I had a long conversation with Ambassador Henry Cabot Lodge, head of the U.S. mission. I can only believe that he was speaking to me in relative frankness.

I asked: What are we trying to do here? Are we looking for another "in-group" like the Ngo family to take over? Or do we want a military dictator? Or do we want a parliamentary system, even risking all its defects in a civil war atmosphere, in order to gain popularity and widespread support of the population?

Lodge said: Those are all political considerations. We want to leave all that aside. What we need now are military victories.

This "solution" was put forward at a time when we had just seen a political crisis tear the Diem regime to shreds. It was put forth at a time when the U.S. was paying lip service, and had been for years, to the thesis that the war was as much political as purely military in Vietnam. And it was, in fact, after we had faulted the Diem regime for its inability to make "political" decisions to aid in the fight against the Communists.

162

It took no account of the actual situation: I had just returned from a Delta province adjoining Saigon-Cholon's suburbs, where the local province chief had received five visitors from Saigon in one week. Three were members of the *junta*. All were military figures who had given him totally contradictory orders on very specific military problems.

The local American adviser told me plaintively, "I don't think it makes much difference which plan we adopt here as long as we stick with one. We have had three province chiefs and four local military commanders in six months. And we have had five pacification plans in less than a year and a half."

Yet, Lodge—a veteran American politician and diplomat— was refusing to concern himself with the "political" situation under which any kind of military decisions, and therefore progress, would have to be made! A few weeks later, of course, all that changed and the U.S. had to throw its weight behind another coup d'état to rescue the country from paralysis. With each turnover in government, the prestige of the regime, its legitimacy —as high and firm as any in Southeast Asia in 1959—took a beating at home and abroad. And, given the nature of bureaucracies in the underdeveloped countries of Asia, its efficiency fell again spectacularly.

Historians—and not the politicians-*manqué* at Harvard and Columbia—will have to sift the evidence in the coming years. But I believe it is abundantly clear that however difficult the problem of halting Communist subversion and guerrilla warfare was before the death of Diem in 1963, those final months of the year and the first part of 1964 gave them enormous gains in building the infrastructure of clandestine support which was the essence of their later successes.

Former Ambassador Frederick E. Nolting, Jr., Lodge's predecessor, has put it well:

> For years, the number one tactical objective of the Viet Cong and Hanoi had been the overthrow of the Diem government. By that, they calculated to bring about political chaos in South Viet Nam. They were handed that objective by the military coup d'état of November 1, 1963. For different reasons, Buddhist agitators, large segments of the American press, and our own

Department of State all played important supporting roles in that fateful tragedy. . . .

The coup d'état of November 1, 1963, destroyed the legitimacy of the Vietnamese government as well as its established structure. It set back the progress of pacification and nation-building by decades. It identified the United States with an illegal military *junta* and thrust upon us the responsibility for its failures. It forced us into the role of major combatant—to prevent collapse in Saigon. Our present [1966] predicament stems more, in my judgment, from the chaos and disillusionment in South Viet Nam following the overthrow of the constitutional government than it does from any other factor, including infiltration from North Viet Nam.

If the realities of Vietnam and Asia have often eluded us because of our naiveté, we have equally been the victims of a false kind of sophistication. It is to that problem that I next want to direct our attention.

7 ✤

Pseudo-Sciences and the Professors

THE PROFESSOR: Sit down and I will give you a twenty-minute political science lecture.

I had asked what he thought of the forthcoming Indian general elections.

There are two kinds of representative government in the world, he said. One is the type that we have in the Anglo-Saxon countries, Scandinavia, and a few other countries around the world. There are two parties, not differing very much one from the other. They present their program to the electorate. One wins, gets into office, succeeds or fails to carry out its program, and the electorate makes a new decision.

But there is another type of representative government—"and I am not sure that it isn't a better system," the Professor said. You have one party which represents the widest possible range of views in the country. Ideas and methods of governments are argued inside the party. After an election, one group gets ascendancy. If its program fails, that automatically sets up a movement to achieve a new balance within the party. That is the kind of system they have in Mexico, in Italy and, of course, here in India.

That's very interesting, I said. But I thought that the one "constant" in Mexican politics since the revolution of 1910 was the rule that no president can succeed himself. That has led to dramatic changes from one president to another. And the main political fact of life in India has been, of course, the overwhelming domination of one man—Nehru—since independence in 1948 (the time was 1962). As far as Italy goes, hasn't the whole history of the postwar period in Italian politics revolved around the fact that the Christian Democrats did not have an absolute majority and had to go either to the right or the left to patch up its majority?

The Professor, losing interest rapidly: Those are details.

Allowing for the whimsy of a great man, the irresistible possibility of playing cat-and-mouse polemics with a reporter, the incident is a serious reflection of one of the prevailing attitudes of part of the American community in Asia. For the Professor was not just a schoolteacher in a standard "bull session" with a student, but Ambassador John Kenneth Galbraith, representing the U.S. in the second-largest country (in population) in the world.

Americans like to believe that they carry with them into their enormously important role in Asia three standard qualifications as native as T-bone steak and apple pie: Pragmatism, great capacity for detail and systematic approaches to problems, and a lack of cant, realism about how the world moves.

My own experience is that we are far too often bogged down with "theological" attitudes, unable to carry through on concepts, and hypocrites about how our systems work.

These may be simply human characteristics common to all men. But they are being exaggerated by a new kind of American "neo-neo-positivism"—a belief that all problems are solvable, and that solutions can be found through methods of inquiry that rely on the use of statistical data, new formulations of old social problems in a pseudo-scientific gobbledegook.

Computers are too often being substituted for common sense. One famous example that went the rounds in Saigon was a meticulous and highly complex statistical study of attacks of guerrillas against Vietnamese villages. Thousands of words were lavished on the report, prepared at considerable expense in one of the "think tanks." Net result: The Viet Cong guerrilla attacks reached a high density during those periods of the month when the moon was in eclipse.

Pseudo-Sciences and the Professors

In mid-summer 1967, my home office referred to me a study made in Vietnam. It was supposedly a guide to a more effective American-aided agricultural policy by the South Vietnamese government.

The interviewers had chosen a sample of forty-seven farmers in the country to interview during a short visit by a group of American agricultural experts. I am not sure how the sample was chosen. But you can see how farcical it was, no matter the method, when you consider the difficulties.

Farming varies tremendously from one region to another in South Vietnam, often from one province to another (and there are fifty-one provinces). Much of the rural area was not under government control. Interviewing was extremely difficult —not only because the whole concept is alien to the Asian peasant, but also because of language problems. (A few years ago a Saigon prime minister, who is native to a portion of central Vietnam under Communist administration, Ho Chi Minh's birthplace, had to be accompanied by a South Vietnamese politician as interpreter when he went to visit and speak to villagers in the Delta below Saigon.) Any foreign visitor, of course, brings up all sorts of other special problems when he arrives on the scene in villages harried by twenty years of civil conflict.

Old hands in Saigon could only laugh bitterly when they reached the section of the report stating the surprise of the visitors that the peasant-owners did not know how much paddy they raised on their fields. It's obvious that no Vietnamese farmer is going to tell a foreigner—accompanied by the district official who collects taxes and makes other kinds of "squeeze" on any number of local activities—how "rich" he is. Nor would any farmer in the world. In my home state of North Carolina, the visitor might be thrown right out of the cornfield!

Yet this "study," as many other pseudo-scientific inquiries into Asian problems, was being used as the basis of policy in highly critical areas. Methods of research developed in the American social sciences are being used in totally alien Asian environments, methods which at best have only been partially successful in the U.S. (Do we really know that much about the psychological attitudes and sociology of the black ghettos in our own large northern cities?)

Clifton R. Wharton, Jr., an agricultural economist who has worked in Asia and is one of that small but remarkable band fighting the good fight against the "pseudo-sciences," put it this way:

> . . . The U.S. agricultural economist who visits Southeast Asia under a Fulbright, Smith-Mundt or Ford Fellowship is a common sight. He goes to the region for a year or two and then returns home well laden with government reports, statistics, and notebooks replete with his "brain-pickings" of key Southeast Asians. Somewhere in his first tour there are one or two garden-variety research projects, but once home he quickly turns to the easier task of theoretical model-building. This can give fuller reign to his display of the traditional tools of the profession and his artistry with mathematical symbols, equations and graphs, but not with too many hard facts to test the model, only "impressions." For the next five to ten years his professional reputation is built by the skillful exploitation of his brief "overseas tour"—frequent university seminars, conference papers, journal articles, all designed to exploit his brief experience to the fullest and to establish his professional domestic image as an "expert." Every two years or so he may secure a fortunate supplementary travel grant from some foundation to re-visit his area and freshen his fading materials and refurbish his professional expertise.

ABANDONING COMMON SENSE

My contention is that often in the process of using these methods, we abandon ordinary "common sense" in using factual detail easily at hand. And this whole process is a considerable factor in our failure to understand and deal with what is happening in Asia.

The whole attempt to "quantify" social problems is virtually useless in Asia. Like all peoples living in pre-industrial societies, most Asians are extremely vague about figures. In many cases the most elementary statistical information is not available.

Take the question of population. Indian government planners for years used 2.2. per cent as a figure for annual population increase. A few intensive U.S.-Pakistani projects by joint academics in East Pakistan, however, indicate that at least in some areas the annual increase may be running at more than 3.5 per cent. (These areas are very similar to neighboring states in India.) More recently, the Indians have begun to use a figure of 2.6 per cent. But even that probably falls well behind the actual increase, which must be nearing 3 per cent a year.

The immensity of the subcontinent, the diversity of the patterns of social behavior in the population, the varieties of health problems, make any approach to this problem monumental. Faced with the effort necessary to get valid figures competing for the scarce bureaucratic talents that are needed for the programs to intensify food production and initiate birth control, it is highly unlikely that anything much better can be produced soon.

I do not argue against attempts to improve these statistics, nor against using what is available. What I am arguing is that the use of statistical elements as *the main basis* for Indian planning, as was done in the 1950s, or any other Asian policy is bound to bring on disaster.

When I visited India in 1956 to report on the formulation of the Second Five-Year Plan, I was horror-struck by this approach. Thousands of figures on population, resources, village "inputs" and "outputs"—largely based on guess and hearsay—were being churned out. These were being incorporated into a huge central plan for economic development, with hard targets and mathematical goals.

I wrote then in *The New Leader*:

> Take the argument of a Western journalist, typical of the rationalizations given in defending Indian foreign policy: "You can't expect Nehru to be a Western European Socialist, like [the then British Prime Minister Clement] Attlee, for example. You can't expect him to be so clearheaded on the Communist issue."
>
> With this foundation laid, then, it's no wonder that the country accepts a Second Five-Year Plan starting this spring [1956] which at best is a bumbling mess and at worst a Soviet plot. Its chief philosopher is a former physicist, Professor P. C. Mahalanobis, a prominent member of several Indian-Soviet friendship or-

ganizations and Red China groups. Mahalanobis' chief collaborator has been Oskar Lange, the former University of Chicago professor, who went over to the Polish Communist government after World War II.

Mahalanobis has sold the country—but most especially Nehru —a "heavy industry" program. Percentagewise, the heavy-industry component doesn't look big in the [Second Five-Year] Plan. But if you stop to consider that there is general agreement outside planning circles that the Plan won't be fulfilled as it stands and will have to be pared down, then the question of priorities becomes all important.

Mahalanobis is building up a psychological atmosphere which will dictate steel first, consumer goods second. Making a bow in the direction of the Gandhi-ites, he has asked for restriction on machine production of consumer goods in favor of village production. These handicraft industries cannot possibly meet the increasing demand created by vast "deficit financing" [a misnomer in India's primitive economy], which totals well over a third of the Plan.

The over-all theoretical approach to the problem—whether one was talking of "socialism" or "capitalism"—was largely irrelevant, but what was important was the realities of the situation.

I remember at the time teasing the well-known Swedish economist, Dr. Gunnar Myrdahl, whom I met several times during a long trip through the country. I told Myrdahl that his opposition —in India—to much of the planning techniques then being used would get back to his social democratic colleagues in Western Europe, that he would be accused of promoting "free enterprise." His reply was to the point: "Brother, I am in favor of any kind of enterprise—as long as it is enterprising." Unfortunately, Myrdahl was not prepared to take a public stand on these issues for another decade.

Yet, because of the Indian planners' ability to couch their plans in excellent English with "statistical" affirmation, many U.S. academicians and government officials were willing to accept proposals which in their very nature were outrageously improbable of fulfillment.

I will cite only one example: It was proposed that the Indians embark on a major program to produce steel. The country has vast reservoirs of limestone, coal, and iron ore. And the statisticians "calculated" that India would be the second most efficient producer of steel in the world, after the Australians. Where would the steel be used? An expanding economy needed unlimited quantities of steel, it was argued, and—and here is where statistics took wings—if surpluses developed, India could always export them.

The Indian steel muddle in the 1960s is, of course, the classic example of how an underdeveloped society should not use its resources. Vast amounts of capital have been invested in mills which, far from being efficient producers, are among the most inefficient industrial enterprises in the world. Food production and other more basic problems have been neglected.

It is fashionable now in the U.S. to pin the blame on the Indians. But U.S. observers and commentators—and those in the American aid program who permitted U.S. funds to be indirectly used to promote the whole heavy industrialization program—bear equal responsibility.

THE NEO-RENAISSANCE MAN

It seems to me that much of what has happened comes out of the great new American theory that developed in academe after World War II and reached its apotheosis in the Kennedy administration—the concept of the Neo-Renaissance Man.

The rationale goes something like this: A well-educated, flexible, intelligent, and highly motivated American intellectual, put down into any complex situation, can effectively "de-fog" himself, as the French say.

Therefore, a Harvard professor can become a first-rate ambassador, or a government bureaucrat charged with sensitive political missions in Asia, or an authority on the problems of underdeveloped societies. There is, runs the argument, a systematic way of approaching social and political problems wherever they may be, and the modern American intellectual, with the great mechanical skills of his society at his disposal, can cope with whatever problem he encounters.

Alas, it is not true. And Vietnam was the graveyard of this theory if only we will face up to it.

The problems of Asia are the problems of layers upon layers of culture accumulated through the centuries. There is a vast body of detail involved in understanding even the simplest of them, much less achieving any "solutions." And no matter how ambitious, how intelligent, and how adept we are at "information retrieval," it takes a particular kind of expertise.

Essentially, of course, many of the problems of Asia cannot be couched in ideological terms. It makes much less difference whether an Asian calls himself a Communist, a democrat, or an intellectual, than it does whether he is an Eta, a Brahmin, a Haka, a Menangkebauer, or a Kachin.

I have seen one of my Vietnamese friends through at least six "incarnations"—although he is still a relatively young man. I first encountered him as a bodyguard of Bao Dai. The next time we met he was a protégé of Ngo Dinh Diem, "an adopted son." Not too long after that, he was a refugee in Phnom Penh after participating in an unsuccessful coup d'état. On next encounter he was a very good line officer. Then I saw him as a warlord in the Saigon regime. And most recently he was a political refugee in the U.S. What is most important about him is that he is a typical product of the centuries of mandarin society of Hue in central Vietnam.

Nor is the more "determinist" Communist side of the political spectrum so very different. The poet-politician who wrote the words of the national anthem of the anti-Communist Saigon regime was Mai Van Bo, the ambassador of Ho Chi Minh to Paris for most of the 1960s.

I used to be puzzled by the fact that one Southeast Asian foreign affairs chancellery was so well informed about minutiae of the situation in Saigon. The foreign minister of the country was extremely able and so were his assistants. But they knew too much detail about situations which were hardly known to people on the ground in South Vietnam. By accident, I learned why finally: The "uncle"—an all-inclusive Asian term for almost any male relative outside the immediate family—of the wife of the foreign minister was a member of the Chinese Nationalist intelligence operation in Saigon.

One of India's leading economists has for the past decade and a half taken a consistently pro-Communist political line. It is baffling in that it often leads him into illogical intellectual stands. He espouses the heavy industrial program of centralized Indian planning, but he has been a foremost exponent of liberalization, of using market mechanisms in government-owned industry, a seemingly contradictory position.

I think the key to the mystery is obvious: He was born into one of the depressed communities of South India, one which until very recently was a victim of the most vicious Hindu caste rejection. As a student, he was pro-British during the 1930s when most other young Indian students were nationalists and anti-British agitation was part and parcel of all students' makeup. That was because the entrenched castes, the local Indian power structure of his area, were pro-Congress and anti-British. Before independence his caste community saw British power as the only block to total domination of his community that had existed before their coming to the Indian subcontinent.

And today, when the same Congress rules India and much of the time his state, his caste has swung over to the Communists as the most effective weapon for redressing their still inferior social and economic situation. Whatever his ideological rationalizations and his intelligence dictate on economic issues, I believe this strong emotional attachment to the problem of his own people is the main motivation for his political line.

My old friend, Ram Lohia, used to say, "If you cannot find an obvious explanation for something in our country, remember: Caste, caste, caste! It is an explanation for much of what goes on."

One is well advised in Asia to keep in mind what one astute American official's wife calls "the brother-in-law theory." When in doubt about why a particular phenomenon has developed, look carefully for the family relationship which dictates it. In the pre-independence period, even under colonial domination, the family was the only unit that held up in most of the deteriorating Asian societies. And in the revolutionary period through which

Asian societies are now going, in which issues and sides constantly change, family ties still offer one of the more enduring bonds.

NO REAL PRAGMATISM

IF Americans in Asia have tended to turn their backs on real pragmatism, to ignore the vast body of detail about a problem, and adopt preconceived, ideological approaches to problems of the area, we have also fallen far short of the use of our highly vaunted systems.

Again, Vietnam is an excellent example. In the summer of 1967, some thirteen years after our military advisory teams had taken on the problem of trying to develop an efficient Vietnamese fighting force, I found tremendous and depressing evidence.

Our military advisory teams with the Vietnamese units in the field had a tour of one year. In practice, of course, they remained for even shorter periods with the particular unit to which they were assigned. Some weeks were needed to get in and out of the country. Shifts in personnel may have meant that a man would spend less than the year with the particular Vietnamese unit, or in the same job.

In the field, the problem of the Vietnamese unit—and, in turn, of American advice—came down to a very particularized situation. The abilities and motivation of the commanding Vietnamese officer, the local strengths and weaknesses of the Communist forces, the terrain and demographic peculiarities of the area dictated what the Vietnamese command must do and what the Americans must do to help them. Most American officers were frank to admit that it took months, sometimes as long as half the tour, to learn what the job was and how to get on with it.

Yet in more than a decade, the U.S. army had still not found the means and a system by which rotation of American officers would avoid a "turnover gap." I visited in July 1967 the advisory group in Quang Ngai province in central Vietnam where all the American officers of the unit had changed within one month. Most—including the intelligence adviser!—had not had sufficient time with the man they replaced to "debrief" him, and in several instances they had not even seen the man. Much of the important information on how to do the job could not, in the nature of things, be written down. And certainly "the feel" for dealing with individual Vietnamese officers could not be "quantified."

To go on with this example, it was still not "S.O.P." (standard operating procedure) for an American officer to have a dossier on his Vietnamese counterpart. Lest this sound too much like secret police activities, I mean that the American officer often was not told whether his Vietnamese "counterpart" was from the North or the South, to whom he was related in the Saigon bureaucracy, whether he had served in other areas, some evaluation of his abilities, etcetera. These criteria had been discussed, and the system was supposed to be in operation. But, in fact, it rarely was.

For the most part, young American officers were fending for themselves—the more intelligent able to get some material or be helped out by other members of the bureaucracy who saw the need. But there was no system.

Or take an entirely different problem of the so-called leadership exchange programs. Under this program, U.S. embassies in Asian countries pay the cost of sending foreign nationals—businessmen, newsmen, intellectuals, teachers, government officials —to the United States. The effort is aimed at acquainting these people with the realities of American life. Only the richest Asians can afford to come to this country on their own. And no amount of propaganda can possibly tell the story of the vast bounties which American life has given to its people, the freedom of life in the U.S., and our intellectual resources.

Although the program has been in effect for almost two decades, it is less than a great success. I personally have encountered tens of Asians who came back from their trip embittered by their experiences. They were almost cast adrift in the hurly-burly of U.S. life, or they were guided into programs for simple-minded tourists. Aside from the difficulties of choosing the proper persons —those best equipped to learn something from the visit and to make an impact on their own societies when they return—the program is vastly mismanaged in the U.S.

Granted that there are difficulties; most American professionals with whom the Asians would like to talk about common problems and considerations are extremely busy. But the essence of the problem is that there is no system for particularizing the individual program. And I believe that many Asians return to their own countries with their Hollywood movie ideas of America reinforced.

HYPOCRISY IN U.S.-ASIAN DIFFERENCES

THE third element in our refusal to face up to application of American techniques to the underdeveloped countries of Asia is a widespread hypocrisy.

Americans—especially my colleagues in the news business—are always waxing eloquent about "corruption," a catchall phrase for the legal and illegal methods of public officials' enhancing their incomes at the public's expense. Many of the Americans who talk about this problem seem oblivious to it in U.S. life or, in fact, in their own livelihood. I have known more than one American correspondent in Asia who writes of corruption of public officials, who at the same time was making a small "killing" from the difference between the official rate of exchange of the local currency to the U.S. dollar and his purchase of local currency on the black market listed on his expense account.

Nor do many Americans seem to be aware of the "legalized" kinds of peddling of influence that exist in our society; e.g., the former military officers and civilian officials who get jobs based on their "contacts" in the U.S. procurement establishment. One of the least publicized aspects of scandal in Vietnam, for example, was the "pushing" of products on the U.S. military and the Vietnamese by American manufacturers. Cases of the resale of American pharmaceuticals by Vietnamese officials to Communist agents have received maximum publicity. But it was a less publicized but widely known fact in Saigon that U.S. pharmaceutical firms were paying bonuses in dollars to local importers, those dollars deposited in foreign banks, in order to sell more drugs. The inevitable result was that there were ample surpluses to pour into waiting Communist hands.

When South Vietnam was holding elections for a national assembly in the fall of 1967, I heard a young American newspaperman, writing for an extremely influential U.S. paper, insist that the elections were not being conducted fairly. When I asked if he thought the tenor of the elections held by the Saigon regime was worse than some of those in the U.S.—in Alabama or Mississippi or Chicago, for example—and whether there was not some excuse for intimidation in a country with no experience in representative government and in the midst of a civil war, his answer was that the elections in South Vietnam "had" to be fairer than in the U.S.! Needless to say, his reporting of the whole electoral process in that critical period reflected this kind of double standard of morality.

This hypocritical evaluation of our own institutions and motives often blinds us to realities of Asia. One aspect is what I call "the table of organization fallacy." The Americans come out to Asia, look at a problem in one of the aid recipient countries, and then set about creating a new table of organization in a government, a ministry, or a company, expecting that it will automatically work the miracle of introducing new entrepreneurial abilities and techniques.

It doesn't work. Nor does it work, in reality, in the U.S. I have never been associated with an American company or government institution in which the table of organization actually functioned according to its outline on paper. Relationships between individual officials of the organization, informal arrangements among sections of a large bureaucracy, "shortcuts" which are not prescribed but tolerated are usually the essence of effective operations.

I watched all this at work in Saigon during the period of 1964-65, when the U.S. was trying to funnel an enormous amount of materiel and men into South Vietnam through totally inadequate ports and harbors. Over and over again, the U.S. insisted —and the Vietnamese went along—on reorganizations of the organizational structure of the Ministry of Public Works and the Port of Saigon. But the situation got only marginally better.

One American AID official, a port expert brought out to streamline the harbor operations, told me a little desperately one morning after more than a year in Vietnam, "We still don't know, somehow, how the decisions are made on the Vietnamese side for the port."

One important aspect that I knew, simply from longer acquaintance with the problems of the functioning of the Vietnamese bureaucracy, was that a daily informal breakfast conference was held at the home of an old South Vietnamese (Cochin Chinese) bureaucrat. He was a member of that "aristocracy," the French-trained bureaucracy, which had grown up over the seventy-five years of French rule. The group had, and still had under changing Vietnamese administrations, contacts in each of the important ministries of the government. And little happened without their knowledge, or without their approval. They formed a kind of informal but extremely influential organization. They had a great deal to do with wrecking the government of one post-Diem minister, Dr. Phan Huy Quat, a central Vietnamese whom they disliked and distrusted.

Earlier an American political scientist, a university educator, on a contract to write a diagnosis for the U.S. bureaucracy of the functioning of the Vietnamese government and where changes might be made which would produce quick results in efficiency and method, had come to me for advice. I suggested that the beginning of any kind of study would have to be an investigation of the old French Indochina bureaucracy. I was sure, I told her, that French academic studies of the old Doc Phu Su (the highest rank in the old Cochin Chinese bureaucracy) were available. But it was obvious that what was wanted was "instant reform." And, again, in that all-too-familiar American manner, that meant only looking at the superficial evidence thrown up by current events.

The combination of these three facets of American exposure in Asia—the attempt to ideologize without reference to a body of detail, the failure to carry through on our own concept of systemization, and our hypocrisy about the differences between our society and those of the Asian countries—produces monstrous and totally irrelevant theories.

No better example exists than the whole fanfare surrounding the concept of "counter-insurgency." Members of the military establishment, the "think tanks," a whole bevy of authors have become famous in the past decade for their long treatises on "counter-insurgency" as a new scientific treatment of "limited" war.

The facts are starkly eloquent: Very little connects the insurgency by peasant nationalists led by the Communists in Vietnam, by middle-class university students bred on Latin romanticism in Venezuela, and by the sophisticated anti-Nazi underground of Western Europe under German occupation from 1940 to 1945. What generalizations that are applicable from one of these situations to another are so vapid as to be virtually meaningless; i.e., the government's army and police force should be "good" to the population to win them away from the insurgents.

Economic factors are important. But they are not decisive. The peasant of Vietnam may fight for social justice against landlordism, but many of the provinces with the best Communist infrastructure do not have a land tenancy problem and some of the strongest anti-Communist movements are among the country's poorest peasantry. Burma's Kachins are fighting the central government in Rangoon over political, not economic, issues; furthermore, they and the Karens, engaged in "bourgeois" movements predominantly Christian-led, have made common cause with the Communists.

A good case can be made for the thesis that the insurgency which developed in the 1960s in Northeast Thailand *was in large part brought on by economic development.* An essentially static society of peasants living on subsistence agriculture suddenly began to grow cash crops—abaca and corn—for market. A major highway built by the U.S. for the Thais for *military purposes,* to connect Bangkok with the Laotian capital of Vientiane, had opened communications and economic prospects never before known. The revolution of the automobile was beginning. There were other important reasons—Communist infiltration across the Mekhong River from Laos and an extremely capable pro-Communist structure among the Vietnamese minority in the area—but the standard American liberal theory of poverty producing Communist agitation was as irrelevant here as it is often elsewhere in Asia.

In this infinitely complicated pattern of patterns, six-week

179

courses for American officers in "counter-insurgency" are pretty meaningless.

NO AMERICAN OMNIPOTENCE

NOR is the idea valid that some Americans carry with them to Asia, about their omnipotence in dealing with problems. The truth is that American "advisers" can do only two things under the best conditions: They can help a Vietnamese or Burmese or Indonesian official to get attention for his particular problems at a local level by reaching up and around the local bureaucracy and through the American mission to call attention to his problem. Secondly, they can, of course, sometimes bring technical assistance to bear on specific problems, out of their access to American wealth and advanced technology.

But the average local official knows more about the so-called "insurgency" than the American will learn in many months or years on the job. The average local official has grown up in the environment which produced the insurgency. If he cannot function, it may not be his fault; it may be simply that the whole weight of backwardness of the government setup, of which he forms a part, is an easy victim to a rebellion dedicated to doing in the military or civilian areas of organization whatever is necessary to tear it apart.

After 1965, when the U.S military forces moved into Vietnam in force—following a long period of relatively small numbers "advising" the Vietnamese on what they should do—we saw over and over again many of the same problems redevelop without solution. For example: Forces were spread thin throughout the country. The problem arose repeatedly of relieving a military outpost under attack. It was perhaps the only government "presence" in an area. Relief forces faced almost inevitable ambush along the usually limited routes which those forces could take. It was as difficult a problem for American forces as it had been for the Vietnamese. Unfortunately, many of the reporters and military critics of the Vietnamese, who had been around to describe the difficulties in 1962-63, 1963-64 as peculiar to the Vietnamese

ASIA IS VILLAGES

Although Asia's metropoli are among t
largest in the world—Tokyo, Calcutta, Sha
hai, Hong Kong, Bombay—most Asians s
live in villages. There they follow the tra
tions of their ancestors, in many areas of t
East largely cut off from monetized soc
ties, living largely as they have for centuri

village chief

village belles

evening meal cooks

ese Lao villagers were living only a few
'es from fighting between Communists
d anti-Communists in 1961. But their life
s hardly affected by what was happening
he country as a whole, a crisis that brought
"civilized" world close to war.

gossip time

elder sister's care

next generation

Dawn starts in a Burmese village as it has fo
centuries with the Buddhist monks arriv
ing to receive their food. The villager earn
"merit" by feeding the monk, the monk ha
more time for contemplation to find a wa
out of this life of sorrows.

making merit

morning soup

to the fields

abundant rice

old methods

The Malabar Coast of the Indian state of Kerala is one of the most densely populated regions in the world, a long village that stretches for hundreds of miles. Everyone has passed this way—Chinese and Arab traders, the Portuguese, the Dutch, the British, the Indian nationalists, and now it is a breeding ground for one of the most virulent Communist movements in India.

bulging schools

ancient Christianity

primitive fishing

bright-eyed children *Communist posters*

market day

handicraft
barter

impoverished agriculture

"only an anna"

untouchable

How much has Communism changed the village life of North Vietnam, a product of some 2,000 years in the development of that culture? These photos (1950) show what it was like less than two decades ago. Much that has been written by the occasional visitor, most of whom did not know the area before "liberation" and who have not been allowed to travel widely, indicate far less change than Communist propaganda would allow.

street bazaar

village elders

to see Bao Dai

Hanoi's lakes

Haiphong troubadour

tribal children

ASIA IS POVERTY

More people are living under worse conditions in Asia, by far, than in any other region of the world. Human degradation in some parts of the continent defies the imagination of Westerners from the industrialized societies. It is the beginning and the end of the explanation of everything that happens.

Calcutta. Nehru called it "the nightmare city". I was threatened when I first tried to take pictures in one of the slums; succeeded only when a Communist trade unionist accompanied me. Even the visitor to the city rarely sees the fenced off "bustees", the stagnant pools, the huts where smallpox, cholera, and typhoid are endemic.

holy man

refugees

Hooghly River water

man as beast of burden

"bustee" family

student surveyors

prayer at dawn

Calcutta's Edwardian landscape

Famine struck again in 1967 in India, in Bihar state, the first major failure of the food supply since independence came in 1948. An internationally supported program of food donations and other assistance in the field prevented mass death. But many observers feared it was only the prelude to a continuing breakdown as population explodes and food production does not keep pace.

famine works

mission step kitchen

starvation in village

soup line

vigil for gruel

"*job*, sahib?"

first sip pains

seeking ground water

sowing prayerfully
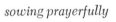

Twenty years of failure to move ahead economically in South Asia is best seen in Indonesia. A visit to President Soekarno's hometown of Blitar shows the steady deterioration of a once prosperous East Javanese village. Even Bali, once an island with a balanced economy not yet broken down by the contact with Western industrialization and a decaying social structure, is moulding away. All this while Soekarno built his prestigious monuments in Djakarta.

village candy shop

ladies of the town

Bali Communist office

sweets stall

distributing imported rice

ox-speed economy

Djakarta slums

Soekarno's Djakarta showpieces

THE AMERICAN EFFORT

Often haltingly, often misplaced, the Americans are in Asia with their enormous energies and resources. With their organized programs of aid and defense, they try to win time as floundering Asian governments seek answers to their problems. Perhaps more important in the long run will be the Americans' "left-hand" influences, their simple unpremeditated contact with Asians and the taste for a new life they bring with them.

The Americans got their first taste of the difficulties of fighting a war against guerrillas in South Asia in Laos after 1954. By 1961, we had experienced small teams operating with the Royal Laos Army in the jungles between the Mekhong River and the Annamite Alps which separate— but only on the maps—Communist North Vietnam from Laos. At Geneva, we negotiated an end to the conflict for a promised neutral Laos. The Communists never honored the agreements.

*training
Lao guerrillas*

Lao command post

sick call

first aid

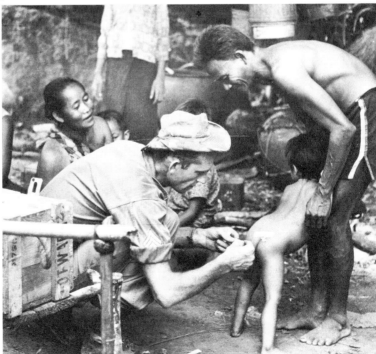

Peace Corps and A.I.D. officials a
trying to help revolutionize Indian a
riculture. The Peace Corps kids showe
villagers how to drill wells in Bih
during the famine of 1967. Georg
Knierim, a veteran of the droughts
the 1930s in our own Southwest, trie
to show Indian farmers methods use
in winning the west by the Mormon
Both had minimal success.

surveying for terracing

tractor maintenanc

basic farm techniques

well drilling

John Norvelle, a U.S. army officer in a South Vietnamese delta province in 1963, was trying to help a province chief defeat the guerrillas. It was part of a skeletal U.S. advisory effort throughout the country to buck up the South Vietnamese government of Ngo Dinh Diem, an effort that failed. And by 1965, massive American troops had to try to do the same job, after it had become even more difficult.

militia training

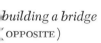

building a bridge
(OPPOSITE)

visiting outpost

supplies for hospital

conference with province chief

Mangla Dam, one of the huge irrigation and power projects in the Indus Waters System in Pakistan and India, was built by U.S. construction engineers. The contractors had total disregard for any political or social program. They simply wanted to get the job done—and did more than a year ahead of schedule. But they left behind a model American town and awakened new aspirations among tribal peoples where they had lived.

modern
construction methods

building housing

equipment handling

new folkways

army and military, were no longer there to report the same thing happening to the Americans.

Americans are prone to take credit often for those successes we have had in Asia which are as much a result of the accomplishments of the Asians as the American "advisers," in spite of American policy. I have referred earlier to the case of the Korean colonels in South Korea.

An even more dramatic example is the Japanese Occupation. Much of the U.S. program had long been proposed by the Japanese themselves. For example, a detailed program for land reform had been initiated in Japan during World War II. The final law pushed through by the U.S. Occupation authorities was in fact virtually those same Japanese proposals. It can be argued that it would never have been accomplished except by an outside force, but the analysis of the problem and the solution in a theoretical sense were Japanese. Historically, of course, the whole Japanese "revolution" since 1868 had been imposed from the top—just as the MacArthur administration functioned. On the negative side, the Japanese economic comeback after the war was largely based on the Japanese forms of economic organization which the *Occupation had not been able to destroy.* The program to break the *zaibatsu* conglomerates finally had to be abandoned when the U.S. faced the choice between the continued dependence of the Japanese on American bounty or allowing them to take their own course to become economically self-sufficient again.

Perhaps the most insidious—and what could turn out in the long run to be the most damaging—of the effects of what I call the "pseudo-sciences" is their intellectual corruption of the Asians, themselves. This "feedback" from the inadequate American social science research methods is everywhere in evidence.

A few years ago on a trip through Northeast Thailand, where I was investigating the budding insurgency there, I visited one of the Thai army units. It was a special command aimed at helping to build the local civilian structure of government and public services as a counter to Communist propaganda. The whole thing was a sham. It was undermanned, the most important technicians for agriculture and health were missing. The demonstration television for adult education was not functioning. Yet, on very short notice, I was given an American-style briefing with Pentagon and "think tank" flourishes that came off with great dash. There were elaborate four-color charts, a lecture hall, slides, and statistical material—even though we were miles from Bangkok or a town of any size.

I could not help but feel that by learning these techniques of internal propaganda, internal to officialdom running the project, the young officers were obscuring the real failures of their program.

Or take the School of Economics at Delhi University in India. It was probably the best economics faculty in Asia, with the possible exception of Hitoshibashi University in Tokyo. Yet most of my Indian friends are agreed that it has been steadily going down hill. There are many reasons, of course. But a principal one appears to be the encroachment of the American system of foundation grants and peripheral jobs for faculty members. At a given time, few of the experienced faculty members are in residence teaching. Too often, they are on one of the various American or international agency grants taking them abroad for seminars, for study, and for participation in government or semi-government economic inquiries. In a country which desperately needs not only a school turning out a growing cadre of young economic technicians but also an independent source of criticism of governmental policy, the Delhi School has been sucked into the vortex of often superficial make-work studies.

While the U.S. academic community has no monopoly on the kind of idealization of Asian politics that has produced much of our mistaken policy emphasis in the post-World War II period, the American academics have epitomized it.

LOST OPPORTUNITIES

JOHN KENNETH GALBRAITH's support for the Nehru government in 1962 against pressures *inside* India for an accommodation with Pakistan may, in the long run, be one of the worst decisions in the period. The Chinese Communist attacks on the border area in northern India showed up the bankruptcy of the Indian regime.

It revealed the ineptitude of Nehru's policy of camouflaging the nature of Communist regimes. It showed the total inefficiency of the administrative bureaucracy, of how Nehru's political manipulations of the Indian Army—aided and abetted by Defense Minister V. K. Krishna Menon—had left the country totally unprepared.

It forced Nehru, for the first time since the early days of his rule which began in 1948, to face up to internal criticism. Not only moderate elements, but such ultra-Hindu-revivalist organizations as the Jan Sangh political party were prepared to compromise with Pakistan for a settlement of the Kashmir and other problems in order to build a common defense against China.

Galbraith threw all the weight of the U.S. into the breach. He urged Washington to commit itself to a massive—in the subcontinent's terms—arms program to the Indians. And it was given without a *quid pro quo.*

I remember going to see a veteran Indian anti-Communist political figure who told me at the time: "Don't you know what you are doing? You are arming Chinese divisions as they come across the Himalayas. This regime cannot meet the challenge unless policies are changed. And you Americans are making it possible for Nehru to continue not to face up to it."

Another important Indian political leader, today holding very high office, told me that he had been promised by the American ambassador "unlimited support" without a basic change in Indian foreign or domestic policy. He has since repeatedly conceded his mistake in accepting Galbraith's assurances.

Luckily for the moment, the Chinese pulled back. The immediate crisis evaporated. The American aircraft carriers ordered into the Bay of Bengal did not have to use air strikes against the Chinese. And, thanks to the Chinese Communists, we did not get into a major war as the ally of an Indian government riddled with ineptitude and corruption.

But the golden opportunity was lost. No accommodation was made between India and Pakistan. And less than three years later, an embittered Pakistani regime, now certain that only by playing power politics among the major powers could it get a settlement with India, launched its "Algerian-type" operation

183

in Kashmir, bringing on the disastrous if short-lived Indo-Pakistan war of 1965. Both India and Pakistan upped their expenditures for defense, with increased pressure on their resources. And the Russians mediated.

(Ironically, it was Galbraith who was arguing five years later that the U.S. was fighting the wrong war in the wrong place in Vietnam. It's a Hobson's choice, but I know no American military or civilian strategist who would have preferred to stop Chinese Communist aggression in the subcontinent in 1962—with a hostile Pakistan at India's back—as Galbraith's policies would have inevitably meant rather than to take up the challenge of the North Vietnamese in Indochina.)

That India is important to American foreign policy in Asia is unquestionable. That the U.S. prefers Indian forms of representative government to military *juntas* and inherited royal houses is also clear. But the paramount fact is that some accommodation between the two countries in the subcontinent must be a cornerstone of American foreign policy in the subcontinent. And that went out the window in 1962 when a purely parochial view of the situation dominated the American Embassy in New Delhi.

The romanticization of real problems in Asia is less an Asian affair than an American problem. One evening in Tokyo, I heard Japanese intellectuals give American Ambassador Edward C. Reischauer a bitter debate. Reischauer, an academic with strong credentials in Japanese history, contended that Japan had a democratic tradition. One Japanese professor replied that if Ambassador Reischauer meant that there was a certain tradition of equalitarianism—that Prime Minister Ikeda spoke to his barber—yes. But if democracy meant representative government, and that was the only definition acceptable to him, then Japan had little tradition in democracy. To Reischauer's insistence that Japan had been moving slowly but steadily toward democratic institutions since the Restoration in 1868, the professor said: Perhaps. But would the ambassador not agree that if Japan had another interregnum in the movement like 1937-45 (the wartime military dictatorship), she might not survive?

Obviously, the Joseph McCarthy theory that China was "sold" to the Communists by a conspiracy in the State Department and the academic community in America has no validity. But it is true that many academics (and many more newsmen) did equate the Chinese Communists' sincerity of purpose with American interests. They were not Communists, but "agrarian reformers," it was said, and were the only hope for a revitalized China cooperating with the U.S. In fact, of course, once launched on the Communist road, the dogma of their philosophy took over.

Almost the same rationalization was working among the students of Indonesian Communism at Cornell University in the 1950s and 1960s. For years, Cornell students of modern Indonesian history had been building for the Indonesian Communists the same kind of case that had been built for the Chinese party earlier—that they were primarily a reformist movement. The whole theory blew up with the attempted Communist coup d'état in 1965 against the Indonesian regime. One of the Cornell scholars on the ground chose to see it as an answer to the plotting of the Indonesian military. (How it was that almost the entire leadership of the Indonesian military plotting to take over the country was cut down by terrorist assassins in their homes with virtually no resistance was never quite explained!)

In a famous memorandum prepared by some members of the Cornell team in Indonesia—which the university's Southeast Asian studies center has officially disclaimed but which does, in fact, continue a consistent line of thinking by them preceding the unsuccessful coup—the following incredible statement is made:

> Though both [the Indonesian Communist Party and Soekarno] were deeply involved, it was after the coup plans were well under way. They were more the victims than the initiators of events.

The whole thread of this explanation of the Indonesian events of 1965 has been picked up and spread through academic and pseudo-academic circles. An article endorsing the theory, for example, appeared in the *New Left Review*, a British publication published in London in the spring of 1966.

My argument is not anti-intellectual. Academic studies of Asian politics, social structure, and economy are essential for the backgrounding of American policy there. But we have been particularly afflicted by a mushroom growth of new Asian "experts." Their studies are largely based on the above-the-water part of the iceberg—documents, statements of public figures, and naive understanding of the differences between European and Asian societies. It has been compounded by a mechanistic, computerized approach to sociological investigation. All this goes hand in hand with another American problem of understanding in the East: The question of time.

8 *

Asian Standard Time

I was called on as mediator. Two of my closest Indian friends, husband and wife, were having the kind of unimportant, domestic, bantering argument that can turn households upside down anywhere in the world.

Was it or was it not true, asked the husband, that he drives too slow?

Isn't it so, his wife said, doesn't he drive too slow?

I thought about the problem. It was an indicator of how far I had come over the years to falling in with Indian attitudes when living or visiting there, rather than "fighting" them constantly. Yes, it was true, he drove too slow.

My friend's wife, more attuned than he to "Western" concepts, was irritated by something I experienced only occasionally. When my friend meets me at Delhi airport, drives me the five miles or so into Delhi, along good roads and streets which rarely have any traffic except an occasional diplomat's car, taxi, army vehicle, or a bullock cart, we do creep. And why not? We usually have not seen each other for months and we have a thousand subjects—personal, political, professional—to discuss.

But, when pointed out, I do see that he drives at a snail's pace. If my brother or sister-in-law meets me on similar occasions at Boston airport, you can be sure that, whoever is driving, we make a harried exit from the parking lot, race along the highway the forty minutes "home" to New Hampshire. And as often as not, there is no immediate, logical explanation for our rush.

My Indian friend, even though he has driven a car for many years, even though he is a professional working for an American organization in the U.S., is simply expressing that most common of phenomena—the unhurried East. And it is only a more modern version of the ghostly bullock carts one meets in the night *en route* into Delhi or Bombay or Calcutta, piled high with produce for market, the driver invisible and asleep on top, the oxen slowly plodding along the road, using their own sense of direction. New Delhi is perhaps the only city in the world where one must ask the taxi drivers to speed up.

For the American, time is equated with change. For the Asian, time means the seemingly changeless pattern of life viewed through the centuries. The American sees "the inevitability" of the emergence of new forms and new concepts. The Asian accepts and only rarely questions the time-honored traditions of his ancestors.

Much has been made in the past two decades of the phrase, "the revolution of rising expectations." It is the idea that most Asians want and expect great changes ushered in by the newly independent regimes, spurred by Asian nationalism. Much of American policy and thinking has been based on this assumption.

My own experience is that the concept is so nearly false as to be of little use in analyzing events of the current Asian scene.

A few years ago I visited a Burmese village north of Mandalay. It is, ironically, the scene of the first Christian mission in Upper Burma—the first contact on a continual basis with the cloistered Burmese kingdom before the British conquest extended to all Burma in 1886.

The Burmese government, like the British colonial regime before it, was trying to persuade the peasant farmers to grow two rice crops a year. Even without new methods of cultivation, new seeds, fertilizer, and machinery, such double-cropping is possible in Burma because of the climate.

Yet the Burmese farmer has generally refused to do it. You can explain his reluctance in many ways. But basically, it is a psychological attitude. He just does not see why he should raise more food than his own needs demand and beyond what he needs to buy a few commodities of life that come to him from outside the village.

It is true, of course, the post-independence Burmese government policy has further removed any incentive. Surplus capital has been squeezed out of the rural areas to fund inefficient industrial projects and to pay the increasing load of the new bureaucracy. Consumer goods, even of the primitive variety that might spur the peasant's appetite, are not available.

Hla Myint, a Burmese economist writing on the problem of economic development, puts it this way:

> . . . [many of the newly independent countries of Southeast Asia and Africa] tend to divert the larger part of proceeds from peasant exports obtained through marketing boards and other forms of taxation to industrial development, so starving the peasant export sector of capital and technical assistance.
>
> An extreme case of this tendency was found until recently in the policy of the Burmese government, which, like the Ghanaian government, obtained on the average some 40 per cent of its total revenue from the profits of the marketing board and other taxation on exports. Yet the only direct benefit which the Burmese peasants obtained from the earlier development plans was the subsidized agricultural loans which covered only about 16 per cent of their total short-term credit requirements.

But I thought the quintessence of the problem lay in the new tractor that had been given to the village by government officials. It was being used, when I was there, to give rides to the children of the village.

The fatalism of the Asian peasant has been commented on for centuries by Westerners. But somewhere in the past two decades, this basic fact—a problem in the sense of being a barrier to economic development—has gotten lost in the learned literature about raising standards of living in Asia. A lengthy dialogue has been going on over the heads of the Asian villagers by American officials and academics and their Westernized Asian colleagues without much recourse to the realities of village life.

The basic impediment to economic advance in Asia is not the absence of capital, not the absence of technology—although both of these increments are essential to progress. The basic problem is the attitudes of the great mass of the people in the continent.

Maurice Zinkin, a Briton, who has combined a career as colonial administrator and successful Western-style businessman in the East and in the West, has summed up the problem extremely well:

> The Westerner tends to miss the point. He is accustomed to see only poverty and dirt in the East. He goes into a village and imagines that its people could go Communist tomorrow; yet the only foundation for his so imagining is that that is what he would do in their place. He does not realize that he is looking at a community, most of whose people still today have the deepest of all satisfactions: they have a place in the community: in the East unlike the West a man knows where he stands with his neighbors. He may not like them or they him; still they have to accept him and he them.
>
> The Eastern peasant, where he has had enough land, was, and is, right to be contented. He lives in a community which is largely self-governed. Village affairs are still considerably left to the village council, or the village elders. He is master of his time, and his own labor. He can, if he is fair-minded, and capable, attain to a position of authority and consideration amongst his neighbors, a position which may appear of no great importance to the district officials in the great world outside but usually is all that he or his family wants. In most areas he has above him neither squire nor parson; in many areas he does not have below him any large section of society so visibly poor—on his standards—that it burdens his conscience. His position is of course far from perfect. His officials are corrupt, his moneylender usually extortionate, his landlord's agent (if he is a tenant) normally quite unconscionable; and, wherever there is war, in the present as in the past, he is looted by every side. But, nevertheless, he is the backbone of society; and he knows it.
>
> . . . Until perhaps the nineteenth century everywhere, and today still in such places as Thailand, this old life gives complete satisfaction to its adherents. The Hindu division of life into student, householder, service to society, and the attempt to obtain salvation, was one which covered every aspect of man's nature. . . .

REVOLUTION OF FRUSTRATIONS

WHAT the American academic and bureaucrat has mistaken for the "revolution of rising expectations" is what I would say can more aptly be called the "revolution of rising frustrations." It is the frustration, the increasing embitteredness, of members of that small group of Asian elite—with the exception of Japan and the relatively small progressive areas of South Asia, such as Thailand, Singapore, and Malaysia—who do not see the road open to material progress. A member of this elite wants rapid increases in material well being—for his people if he is a humanitarian, for power if he is an aspiring politician, for revenge if, like so many members of the Asian elite, he suffers from a kind of inverse racism, the product of the colonial period.

Yet all of us who have worked and lived in Asia have had repeatedly the experience of seeing even these members of the elite turn passive. One of the greatest frustrations of the American, government or nongovernment, working in Asia is to watch a dedicated Asian friend or collaborator become a totally defeated man. More than anything else it explains the ability of the small Communist minorities in many of the countries to push through their programs.

How is it explained? We are no longer talking of the villager, the villager who, Zinkin has said, has had, at least until recently, something of an idyllic psychological situation whatever our reservations as materialists from the West. We are talking of the members of the elite. Why have they in so many instances not been able to pursue a program of action and dynamism?

I turn again to my old friend, Sjahrir, who has said it so eloquently. Writing about the prisoners he encountered in a pre-World War II Dutch political penal colony, some of them Communists, he muses on why there have not been suicides, given the enormous psychological and physical suffering of the prisoners; why he himself has accepted his existence as a convict in a Dutch jail, not to be rescued until the Japanese arrive as conquerors in 1942:

. . . The Westerner makes demands upon life and shuns death. The contrast between death and life dominates everything for him, and is delineated as sharply as possible in his thinking. If life can give him nothing, and if it only signifies a total failure, then there is only death, *non*-living, *non*-existence. And thereby he is still dynamic and active. He still chooses, and he prefers, as it were, death in place of life.

On the other hand, the Easterner accepts a life of suffering, and in fact shuns death. His shunning is not conscious, but he comes to the same result by never making a sharp distinction between life and death, and by not asking anything from life. He never comes to a choice between life and death, and never undertakes an action from which he predicates choice. He does not act, and he does not struggle. . . .

So, faced with the overwhelming problems for which neither he nor anyone else has answers, certainly not easy answers, even the most dedicated Asian leader can so easily fall victim to a lapse into this traditional passiveness which marks his society. And that passiveness is marked by the Asian's obliviousness to time.

DIFFERENCES IN VALUES

THE American finds constantly in Asia that time has a different value than he puts on it. The hour, clocks, appointments, of course, are an accoutrement of industrial societies. In the pre-industrial world of most of Asia, sunrise and sunset are the only fixed times for villagers.

And even today among most sophisticated urban Asians there is a strange ambivalence about time. English-speaking Indian friends in New Delhi would say to me that they would drop by "in the evening at six or nine o'clock"—and you could expect them to appear at just such an ambiguous hour. Curiously enough, the Japanese—exaggerating as they often do other "imports" since their industrialization—often show up before the appointed hour. I learned fairly quickly in Tokyo always to be prepared for the one or two Japanese guests who would show up either a half hour before an invitation to my house indicated or exactly as the clock struck the hour. In Thailand, an American learns just not to expect guests. They may come or they may not, even though they have accepted or not responded at all to an invitation.

The abrasion of this difference in time concept for the American working in an Asian environment is incalculable. But I believe it is an extremely important factor working in all situations involving American cooperation with local people and organizations. And it is one that is rarely noted for several reasons—embarrassment, ambiguity, lack of recognition.

Picture to yourself the typical American member of a bureaucracy—whether it be his own government, a private company, or some nonprofit organization—trying to get a job done. At his back, in the U.S., is a home office working on Western time. They make demands on him for information, for profit, for "results," on their own time schedule. But he is working at a totally different pace.

Setting up an office and apartment in New Delhi a few years ago, myself, I often ran into an American friend who was trying to establish the Indian office of a nonprofit American organization. From time to time we compared notes on the problem of getting a phone, an import license for a car, a lease, furniture, etcetera. And one day he said, only half in jest, "I am not sure which irritates me more when you go into an office to do business: The Indian official who says, 'Sit down, Mr. X, and have a cup of tea,' or the one who tells you for the tenth time, 'Just write me a letter telling me what you want, with as many copies as possible, asking that we do the necessary; I can assure you we are seized of the problem!'"

Nor is the irritation limited to the American side of the confrontation over time. A Westernized Indian friend of mine gave me a lecture a few months ago about the "sharp edges" of the Americans.

We want everything delineated in such concrete detail, he complained. And he told me about an American Embassy officer who had asked a friend for coffee, then insisted that they "go Dutch" in paying the very small check. I am sure that the American wanted to make sure that his Indian acquaintance didn't think he was being "bought." But the Indian had long since concluded that he was being asked for information, that his very appearance at the rendezvous had already compromised him if compromise was possible, and that the American was simply being "sharp edged."

Or take the case of "the screaming American." Mild, temperate, well-mannered, intelligent Americans have more often than not been turned into absolute howling monsters by the frustrations of working in the ambivalence of Asian time.

An incident twenty years ago in Indonesia illustrates my point. I was riding with an American colleague from the local office of his news agency to the cable office. We were halted by an Indonesian sentry. The sentry pointed his bayoneted rifle at us through the car window, insisting that we take a longer route around the main Djakarta square to get to the wireless office in the center of it. My friend was desperately trying to get a three- or four-minute jump on his competition. Simply putting the message into the telegraph office first might have made considerable difference—in the American time-span reference—in its arriving in New York. The sentry couldn't and wouldn't understand it. My friend turned livid, began to scream at the soldier, and I wondered if we both wouldn't get shot before the incident was over.

Two decades later, I was helping two friends through customs at the New Delhi airport. Their plane was about to leave, or so I thought. A sentry was prohibiting me from talking to a customs official whom I hoped to convince to rush them through so that they would not miss their plane. And the same kind of altercation arose. I became the same kind of raving lunatic—at least for a few minutes—that I had seen my friend turn into so many years before. I am afraid the phenomenon is fairly common.

The Asian reaction to this temporary hysteria of the individual American is a complicated affair. Among the Japanese, with their exaggerated sense of decorum, a deep freeze sets in. Or, to use a metaphor I like best to describe what happens: The Japanese drops a venetian blind, turns the slats closed, and you get a polished, bland, but absolutely impenetrable exterior. The Korean—that most un-Eastern of the Oriental peoples—replies in kind: An insulting statement to a Korean will bring much the same kind of reaction it would bring in the West—violence or a counter-insult. The Indian turns apologetic, switches on his verbal barrage in an effort with words to turn your anger.

Yet I am not simply talking about a problem of social responses. This time element plays an enormous role in the technical dealings of an American with the Asians.

In my own profession, the journalist encounters new problems. Interviewing in Asia is an art which bears only a casual resemblance to the same kind of method of investigation in the West.

One may not ask direct questions—and expect to get answers. In the West, the reporter tries, usually, to put the interviewee "on the spot," to challenge him with such a simple, forthright query that he must make a response in substance. In the East, one never asks the direct question. You approach your subject and your immediate quest for information by indirection. You ask a dozen questions around the central theme until you can extrapolate your subject's attitude on the particular issue about which you want to know. It takes time.

If he is a North Asian (again excluding our Korean friends), he wants to talk in elaborate metaphors. (One could feel for Nikita Khrushchev during the early period of the Sino-Soviet feud, when the Russians complained so bitterly about their Chinese "comrades" using non-Marxian language with allusions to flowers, numbers, and literary references.) If he is an Indian, a Javanese, or a Cambodian, you must prepare yourself for a torrent of words from which the essence must be culled in an almost intuitive fashion by simply "soaking" yourself in it and by osmosis absorbing the essence. It takes time.

A Japanese friend and scholar of Chinese affairs comes to mind: He is probably the most well-informed Japanese on China. And his particular field of interest is the most specific; he is an economist and a close watcher of the Communists' efforts to build the Chinese economy. Yet a conversation with him about this particular subject must be of at least three or four hours' duration if one is to glean significance.

When I introduced him some time ago to a news colleague who was not prepared to wait out that kind of conversation, it was a disaster—for both parties. There just was no communication.

A few years ago one of the worldwide aluminum companies, an industrial giant, was negotiating for a plant to be built in India with local partners. The Indians were extremely anxious to have the investment, representing as it did $34 million alone from the U.S. and an important factor in the whole industrial development scheme. An American expert, one of a small staff of the international company whose specialty was moving from one place to another on five continents to carry out a longe-range expansion program, ran into obstacle after obstacle. But in the end, I believe, he left because Far East Standard Time got him. He had spent eighteen months in India on the project, and other proposals all over the world were being held up. He or his company could no longer take the attrition.

But, as I have indicated, this failure to synchronize watches of Asians and Americans produces more than a harassing and time-consuming daily lowering of efficiency for the American. I believe it leads Americans away from the whole timing and history of Asian societies which dictate and explain so much of what is happening today.

Milton Sacks, a well-known academic student of Asian politics, likes to tell this story, perhaps apocryphal:

At a meeting of the Berlin Allied Control Council, the U.S. representative makes a proposal. The British member opposes the action. But, in the interests of Anglo-Saxon solidarity, he does not press his point. The debate is largely carried on between the American delegate and the Frenchman. At a crucial moment, the Russian joins the discussion, and throws his weight to the U.S. official and the proposition carries.

On the way out of the meeting, the American, upset by the fact that he has received Russian support, turns to the Frenchman and says, "I was right, wasn't I, General, to push for that?"

The Frenchman shrugs his shoulders. But the American insists, "No, really, wasn't my position correct? What do you really think?"

The Frenchman replies, "*Mon cher*, I think that Americans *think* that history begins when they take a job."

It has become a favorite in my repertory for explaining much of what goes on with American policy in Asia. It throws light on one whole aspect of our current experiences: The young reporter who arrives in a crisis and believes that it has all begun when he gets

196

there. The young foreign service officer who, unquestioningly accepting the *bona fides* of an Asian politician, is rarely aware of his position on the same issues at an earlier time. The American foundation representative who discounts the weight of experience through the last century, believing that his proposals for backing scholarship or reform have never been tried before.

IMPORTANCE OF HISTORY

THIS American lack of a sense of history contrasts sharply with the Asian's. He lives his.

On my last trip to Kerala, the state on the southwest coast of India, my driver was a Brahmin. But he was not of the local priestly caste. His ancestors were clerics of the Hindu community in what was until 1961 the Portuguese colony of Goa.

When the Inquisition began to function in Goa in the sixteenth century (actually preceding its activities in Europe), forcing local people to convert to Christianity, his family fled. Today—some four hundred years later—among members of his family he still speaks Kokani, the local dialect of the Goan coast. Marriages are still only among the thirty thousand members of the caste-community spread all over India. The history of the group is not an uncommon story in the Indo-Pakistan subcontinent. It is typical, too, of a continent in which time frames are hundreds of years, not decades.

As I discussed the failures of Burma's postwar governments a few years ago with a brilliant Burmese politician, a socialist intellectual, he admitted his earlier mistakes in economic planning as a minister in successive governments. I asked how he would describe the then current policy of the Ne Win dictatorship. He answered, laughing, "You want a definition of the Burmese road to Socialism? It is a full-blown retreat from the twentieth century!"

The expulsion in 1963 of almost all foreigners—including the American academics, foundation representatives, our aid program, etcetera—was usually attributed by observers in the Western press to anti-Americanism. But a better explanation was the

197

age-old Burmese xenophobia which preceded the British conquest. (I thought it was an ironic twist that the most important hotel in downtown Rangoon, where the rare foreign visitors spend their short stay, was run by an Armenian, one of the few foreigners left in the country. In the eighteenth century, Burmese kings, not wanting their subjects to be contaminated by their exposure to foreign parts, hired members of Calcutta's old Armenian trading community to represent them in foreign lands.)

This is the stuff of Asian history, the continuity which we Americans so often seem to lose track of in our calculations of what is happening.

American observers saw the Vietnam War as a new manifestation of the Communist ability to subvert and to wage "total war," the use of political methods as well as purely soldierly prowess, against an enemy with superior military hardware. That is, of course, a considerable part of the Vietnam War's historical importance.

But it is equally significant to reread Chinese accounts of their attempts to subdue Tonking (North Vietnam) in the Mongol and Ming dynasties. Substitute a few names and figures and you get a vivid description of the same kind of strategy and tactics used by the Vietnamese Communist leadership against the French and the Americans.

When the 1965 attempted coup d'état by Communist leadership in Indonesia failed, Americans were quick to see the whole episode as climactic and unique. It was not. So-called "left wing" elements of the Communist movement in Indonesia had tried to take power by force and failed in 1926-27 under the Dutch. And they had tried again in 1948 when the Indonesian Republic was battling the Dutch for independence.

The violence during the affair came as a shock to outsiders. And it was reported as unique by many commentators in the U.S. But the same kind of violence had occurred in both the earlier two convulsions (if to a lesser degree). If, as many Indonesian anti-Communists believe, a revulsion against the Communists' use of violence was the main reason why in the end the Communists failed to get their objectives, that, too, was not new.

Suripno, one of the leaders of the 1948 revolt, wrote in his memoirs later:

The most regrettable thing in connection with the Madium affair [the 1948 revolt] was the killing and other atrocities which happened in some places. We [Communists] did not feel responsible for these happenings. . . . It was a great pity our organization was less perfect and that we were continually pursued, so that this [Communist] Council [of Justice] would not be asked its advice about prisoners [killed by the Communists].

Only history will tell, but I predict that the American observers who have written the Indonesian Communist party off, destroyed by the counter-terror which followed the failure of the coup in 1965-66, will be wrong again. Those forces in central and eastern Java society which have been the source of Communist strength still exist. And the Communist movement has no more disappeared than it was wished away by its opponents and observers outside the country after the 1926-27 and 1948 outbursts. (It is significant, for example, that while thousands, perhaps tens of thousands, of Communists were killed in the 1965-66 aftermath of the Communist failure to take power, dozens of party members have taken refuge in Moscow, Peking, and Hanoi. It was "returnees" of the 1926-27 revolt who led the 1948 attempt at a power play.)

In part, it involves the whole history of Islamic and Hindu cultural strains in Java and their fight for dominance over the past five hundred years. In our day, this struggle has been "phrased" in the conflicting movements for an Islamic basis for Indonesian nationalism against a secular philosophy for independence, reflected again in the anti-Communism and Communism of the Indonesian radicals. And while history may not repeat itself, Asians have proof over and over again that patterns in their part of the world are repeated and must be studied to account for the events of today.

The American in Asia expects changes to occur, sometimes with a wave of a wand. When the Vietnamese regime in Saigon was trying to reconstitute itself on some sort of legal basis in 1965, after a rule by a military *junta* from the fall of Diem in 1963, the U.S. sent a political scientist from an American university to advise the Vietnamese constituent assembly on writing a constitution. The concept was ridiculous. The old-line Vietnamese politicians in the constituent assembly had been reared on Confucian legalism and French Cartesian logic. They could have cooked up a half dozen constitutions in as many days.

But implementation was something else. There is little in Vietnamese tradition to foster representative government; nor is there much encouragement to be taken from their French colonial heritage. Nor did the Americans who wrote about the whole electoral process in Vietnam appear to remember its slow evolvement in Britain, or even in the U.S. (Our Senate was, after all, a "club" with its seats bought and sold in the state legislatures as late as the turn of this century. Direct election of senators did not come until 1913.)

Too often we seem to take the concept of "next year's model" of our industrial assembly lines into our relations with underdeveloped Asian economies and political institutions. We seem to believe that it is possible, simply by rewriting a constitution, setting up a new ministry, or creating some elaborate structure of administrative cooperation with the U.S., to overcome the centuries of difficulties which have precluded the development of that particular institution.

One vivid example was in our attempt to create in Vietnam a cadre of dedicated young rural workers that would match the Communists' efforts. In central Vietnam, in Quang Ngai province, such a group had been developed. But it was based—and the Americans who ran it did not know that for some time—on the youth organization of one of the old Vietnamese secret societies-political parties. The Americans assumed that its *esprit de corps* and dedication was created whole cloth when the organization was named and put into government uniforms.

When an attempt to "mass produce" such cadres on a national scale at a government school was tried, it floundered. And it failed for the simple reason that the conditions which had obtained in Quang Ngai, one province, were not nationwide.

If we Americans believe in "next year's model," we are also

always looking for a "gimmick." I remember breakfasting with an American ambassador in a neighboring Asian country after leaving a long reporting stint in Vietnam in 1964. The situation was already bad, if not so critical as it was to become for American policy-makers later on. At his urging, I explained what I believed were some of the difficulties. And after a long recitation of our problems—those of ourselves and the anti-Communist Vietnamese—my host asked, "Isn't there one thing we can do that would help things?" I carefully went over the ground again, pointing out the incredibly intricate problems that we had. And, again, the same question, "But isn't there one thing we could do?"

I finally answered in some heat, "That's exactly why we are in the mess we are in now, because we have been looking for simple answers to a very complex problem."

Perhaps this comes out of the American experience. We live in a society where, whatever our social and political problems, our physical world is cataclysmically changing year by year. Next year's model of whatever-it-is will be better than this year's. A society which produced a 25 per cent increase in the average income from 1961 to 1965—even allowing for the 10 per cent of the population which has not found its livelihood improved—produces an intellectual climate in which time is considered a factor for solving everything. A society in which more than 50 per cent of its youth who go to college have parents who only went to grade school, has a "fatalistic" notion of progress with time.

For the Asian, time is neutral; not necessarily on anyone's side in the battle with age-old problems. And therefore he cannot equate the passage of time with progress as the American in Asia tends to do.

PART THREE ❋

THE
FUTURE

9 ✢

Twenty Lost Years

WERE it independent, India's Uttar Pradesh would rank among the ten largest countries in the world—a huge area more than twice as big as our state of New York, a population of eighty million, bigger than most states in the United Nations.

Yet since independence in 1948, "all systems" in the U.P. are "stop."

Population is growing beyond any reasonable expectation to feed, clothe, and educate it. Per acre food yields are down. Literacy is diminishing—probably in absolute numbers as well as percentagewise.

The state's elite, which once led the Indian movement for regeneration, is demoralized. Caste tensions, racial conflicts, religious prejudice are stronger than ever. The educated youth is frustrated and nihilistic.

The promise of political independence after World War II has turned sour and bitter. Two decades of neglect of the basic issues of food production and population control, of imitation Soviet-style planning, of punishing any assertion of private initiative are leading to catastrophe.

Many so-called reforms not only have not accomplished their purposes, but they have turned out to be essentially regressive. The land reform or abolishment of *zemindari*—tax farming by local officials—has not worked. Peasants oppressed by centuries of near servitude have no initiative, no ability to control their

205

own affairs. The amount of acreage under irrigation—by systems formerly maintained under the *zemindar* system—is now less than in the 1880s. (The peasants have told investigators that they do not want to maintain the irrigation ditches; the government did away with *zemindari,* who kept up the system by using the most brutal methods. Now the responsibility for the irrigation is the government's.)

An attempt for nearly twenty years to bring about reforms in the villages through so-called community development has failed spectacularly. Village workers have not been found with either the dedication or the training to cope with inherited problems, plus the vast array of new jobs handed to them—irrigation, fertilizer, and seed programs, literacy, health, birth control, and surreptitiously, organization work for the political party in power.

LAND REFORM BACKFIRES

Kusum Nair, in her intensive investigation of the community development program, tells of a visit to the area:

> . . . Take a village in the district of Ballia, in eastern Uttar Pradesh. It has had six years of "Community Development," and the Rasra Block in which it is situated has been retired into the "post-intensive" stage.

> . . . The children—mostly naked, with hair matted and faces caked with dirt—stand around chewing on sticks of sugar cane and spitting the remnants. The women are thin—their tattered sarees barely cover the body. Being of a lower caste than *Rajputs,* they do not observe strict *purdah* and they talk freely. Holding me by the wrist, they take me into their homes saying: "Come and see the tasteful dishes we have prepared for our mid-day meal," and lifting up their utensils they shake them upside down.

> . . . Every peasant in this hamlet in Rasra Block grows some sugar cane, no matter how small a fragment of the earth he owns. Apart from its juice, which he must drink in the winter, he converts the surplus into *jaggery,* which he sells for cash to pay taxes or to purchase his extra requirements of grain. Even so, with only one meal a day and despite the various loan facili-

ties offered by the official agencies, every family in the village is in debt to the moneylender.

In six years of "Community Development" one drinking water well has been made sanitary in the village, and one lane has been paved with bricks. Half a dozen *ambar charkhas* have been introduced in an attempt to set up a cottage industry to supplement their meagre incomes, but the women find them too heavy to operate. "It is equivalent to grinding ten *maunds* of wheat," they say, "and even then what we earn is not worth mentioning."

Of the 85 families, 81 have land, though less than three acres. Of the four landless families, some members go as far as Assam to seek work. Those with land are finding life more difficult with the abolition of *zemindari*. As Shiv Saran, who has to feed a family of 18 members on five *bighas* [1½ *bigha* equals one acre], put it: "Previously at least we could get some additional land to cultivate on lease, even the landless could get some. Now we cannot get an inch." Very few of them could assume their *bhoomida* [tenant's] rights, because they could not afford to pay the price, or more often, they say, because the *zemindar* compelled them to give up their rights on the land "voluntarily."

Ironically, only the ex-*zemindar*—he owns land in the village though he does not live there—seems to be happy with the abolition of his *zemindari*. His *baithak* is the only structure of brick in the whole village, with empty stables where his elephants used to stay in the good old days. He still owns 200 acres of land but is happy to have been relieved of the responsibility of administration, rent collection and so on which *zemindari* involved.
"There used to be too much trouble before. Now we have peace. We have received our compensation and we have more than sufficient land for our own needs," he tells me.
"What will happen when a ceiling [Editor's note: A maximum land holding for one owner] is imposed?" I ask.
He is not worried. "We have sufficient people within the family to divide up the property."
Shiv Charan, on the other hand, who is landless at present, refuses even to consider investment in land. "I would like to own my own land, but where is the guarantee any more? Today it is one government and it has abolished *zemindari*. To-

207

morrow there may be another and that may take away all land. What would I do then? No. I would not purchase any land now even if I could find the money."

For the rest also, they repeat with minor variations the same experiences, views, attitudes and apprehensions as those of the peasants in Mahewa Block.

Universal suffrage has turned into a divisive force, pitting caste against caste, religious groups against each other. Voting is largely on the basis of caste blocs. And some Indian sociologists are afraid that increasing communications, added to the one vote-one man principle, have strengthened the whole hierarchical system, rather than it dissolving under the impact of modernism.

The state government has become an uneasy, constantly shuffling, game of musical chairs between the majority Congress Party, its bitter in-fighting groups, and a wide array of minor parties whose coalitions combine everything from pro-Peking Communists to right-wing Hindu extremists. The elected government is constantly at odds with the entrenched bureaucrats who, in the continual political intrigue, take on an autonomous life all their own. It's a measure of the whole impotence of the government structure that a strike of all government employees for ninety days in 1965 did not bring a breakdown of the whole political system; most of the people of the state simply do not feel any effect of government on a day-to-day basis.

The situation in the U.P. is classic of the frustrations and lack of progress since independence in South Asia. But it is by no means unique. The failures it exemplifies dominate most of northern India, large areas of the south, much of neighboring Pakistan, and Indonesia and Java. Burma, much more richly endowed by nature, is moving toward the same future. (There were rice riots in one of Burma's pre-World War II surplus areas in 1967.) So is Ceylon. The Philippines has thrown up a more responsive —in relative terms—governmental structure since independence. But if there is cause for optimism there, given her more rapid increase in population, it is only because of a kind of tradition of freedom (tending toward irresponsibility) left by U.S. concepts.

Except for "the prosperity belt" that runs through Taiwan

(Nationalist China), Thailand, Malaysia, and Singapore, the last twenty years in Southeast Asia have been lost. In these two decades these countries might have begun the long road toward rebuilding their societies. Instead, not only has the distance between them and the industrial nations of the world lengthened, but their problems have become infinitely harder to overcome.

Why? What happened?

I have tried to describe some of the historical and cultural elements of the Asian societies, of the Americans in Asia, and their effects. But if we turn to the specific issue of the lack of material and cultural progress, there are a series of detailed, complex reasons:

At independence, throughout the underdeveloped world in Asia there was a false note of optimism. There was almost no awareness of a basic shift in the terms of trade—the value of Asian produce exchanged with the products of the West—which occurred in the last century and which has been accelerating at a frightening pace. The program of forced industrialization undertaken by most of the new governments further blighted their economies. This program was part and parcel of a totally unreal system of priorities set up by the new leadership. And, finally, the so-called aid programs of the industrialized nations contributed to the mismanagement of their economies.

THE NON-ECONOMIC FACTORS

It is, of course, a distortion to separate out the economic elements of the present situation. Nowhere in the whole realm of human activity in the modern world is there such a wealth of self-deceit as surrounds our study of economics. Whatever the particular school—capitalist, socialist, Marxian, Keynesian—propped up with arithmetic and evidence of "hard fact" that, in truth, does not exist, we only have to look at the daily evidence in the affairs of the industrialized nations, with their massive access to data and their at least nominal ability to control economic movement, to see how far is the distance between reality and myth, between economics as a science and an "art form." Ultimately the functioning of any economy relies on individual choices of millions of people, psychological factors, which even now our computers cannot calculate.

For much of the early post-World War II period, the whole literature of the problem of development in the backward countries was talk of capital and resources. Authors like the British publicist, Barbara Ward, banged away at the concept that a prescribed portion of the gross national product of the industrialized countries had to be devoted to the problems of underdevelopment as a solution to the problem. Such proposals flew in the face of the common-sense observation that development was not primarily a question of capital and resources. Had it been, the Japanese would be starving on their little rocky islands in the North Pacific and Brazil would be a super-superpower! (In fact, Indonesia was an example of how wrong investment patterns could be. As Indonesia *dis*invested year after year, decade after decade, in the post-independence period, it was abundantly clear that the previous Netherlands Indies government, long considered the most efficient, if the most rapacious, of the colonial economies run by Europeans, had been overcapitalized. How else to explain the fact that it continued to exist without a total breakdown even though the Indonesians were taking more out than they were putting in?)

In the underdeveloped economies of Asia, all this "systematizing" of "economic" factors has been compounded since World War II. There is almost total absence of real information on a large part of the economy. Yet intensive and extensive mechanistic programs of development have been undertaken, based on so-called hard economic evidence. It is sometimes argued that the 85 per cent of most of the Asian countries' population which lives in the rural area is outside the money economy, that it is subsistence agriculture and, therefore, of little impact on the modernized section which functions much like modern economies in the industrialized countries and which must be the base for advancement. That may be true. But the moment one of the new countries undertakes to change the traditional pattern of centuries, to move toward higher levels of efficiency, it must take account of this great inert mass in the countryside.

"The importance of non-economic elements in economic behaviour has influenced the U.S. agricultural economist and the rural sociologist, especially in such areas as innovation, diffusion, and adoption," Dr. Clifton R. Wharton, Jr., writes. "But empirical research on these problems has been largely limited to the United States, where undoubtedly the relative importance of such factors upon the economic process is far less than in developing nations. . . . Yet, though we all admit the centrality of human factors in economic and agricultural development, we rarely make it central in our research. . . ."

Into this void of information and research at independence plunged two types of Asian leaders dominant in the formulation of economic policy: One was the intense nationalist, often obscurantist, sure that the history of the decline and fall of former high levels of Asian civilization—idealized beyond all recognition, of course—was simply a product of the colonial period and European domination.

Even such realists as Ngo Dinh Diem, for example, were subject to this kind of romanticism about the pre-colonial past. Diem maintained in talking with many of us that Vietnam had had almost universal literacy at an earlier period in the country's history. That seems a totally false premise when you consider that the Romanized Vietnamese was widely used only in relatively recent times, that prior to that Vietnamese was written in Chinese characters. And while one can make all kinds of arguments for the efficacy of the Chinese ideographs, they present an enormous problem for the student that can be overcome only with long hours of memorization that historically only the leisure class in the Sino-ized societies of East Asia, with their emphasis on using great masses of people for huge nonmachine-built tasks, have been able to afford.

There was still another type of Asian leader, particularly in the former British areas of South Asia. He was a graduate of Western universities in the East or in the West, the archtype being the London School of Economics. A smattering of Marxian economics had taught him that the way toward progress was essentially one of harnessing raw materials and coupling them with manpower. Progress had not been made in the past, he argued, not only because of exploitation in favor of the dominant European countries, but also because there had been no planning on a grand scale.

Both of these Asian types were intensely aware of the role that the colonies in the East had played in building up the capital structure of the West European countries, in helping to finance their industrialization. They naturally assumed that these resources would now be devoted to building an industrial plant in Asia.

ECONOMIC ILLITERACY

SINCE rarely did one of these Asian economic philosophers come from origins in the Asian trading communities, his knowledge of the whole process of how business is done, how capital grows, how trade flows, was at best totally theoretical, at worst totally irrelevant.

One of my Indian friends, intimate with Nehru, tells of a dinner party with the prime minister in the mid-1950s, when India was about to launch its Second Five-Year Plan. My friend suggested to Nehru that the plan was overly ambitious, that resources would not be available for it at the level at which it was drawn, that it would run out of money. Nehru, with one of the outbursts of temper that was so typical of him, turned on my friend and shouted that he was one of those people who constantly worried about money. He shouted that he, Nehru, had never worried about money in his life, and it had not held him back in pursuit of his goals.

That was the London School ethos. At the other extreme was an Indian politician, a minister of agriculture in a government in the 1960s, who clung to the notion, of which no one on his technical staff was ever able to disabuse him, that water could not be used for both power and irrigation. If, he insisted, it was put through penstocks to produce electricity, all its "vitality" was gone and it would do no good to use it on crops.

Both the Asian nationalist-obscurantist and his London School-ed compatriot were victims of the legend of "The Wealth of the Indies." That the wealth existed was certainly once true. In the pre-industrial ages, the bountiful natural resources of Asia were the envy of the Western world. Much of the material splendor of the late Hellenic world developed out of its contact with the essentially Oriental Persian empires. The Romans early became habituated to the use of Chinese silks. Later, they needed pepper from the East—not only to supply their own demands, but, along with gold, to buy off the barbarian hordes as the empire degenerated under their successive blows from the north.

"All these articles, it is interesting to note," the historian, Sir G. B. Sansom, writes, "played an important if not an essential part in the life of the urban population of the Roman Empire, and they have been since then in urgent demand by European peoples until our own day. . . . The urgency of demand was not equal on both sides because, as we have seen, the Asiatic economies were in general independent and conservative, whereas the European economies tended to expansion and diversity, largely no doubt because of their greater development of urban life and their greater spread of purchasing power.

"It resulted from these differences that the balance of trade was against Europe. The West being unable to furnish the Asiatic peoples in quantity any commodities that they urgently needed or desired, the Asiatic trade was for the most part an exchange of Asiatic products against European treasure.

". . . the Western empire was unable to redress the balance of trade with Asia; and this was a condition that persisted until modern times, when at length the trading peoples of the West were able to create a demand for their products and to reverse the eastward flow of gold and silver."

This redress which Sansom speaks of happened in our own era. As late as the 1830s and 1840s, the British were still not able to pay the Chinese in goods for the products they wanted. And the introduction of opium from South Asia to China by British and American traders, the Chinese Empire's resistance, and the so-called Opium Wars—ineffective Chinese resistance to the opium trade—which established Western hegemony in China and the East, were the result.

Only the products of the late Industrial Revolution changed the nature of the trade. Cheap textiles and other products of the West—with the help of colonial conquest and trade policies—pushed out Indian and other Asian handicrafts. And the East became the economic dependent of the West for the first time in history.

The whole history of the textile industry in the West, particularly in Britain, was in large part the imitation and cheaper manufacture of the great cloths of the East. Carried down to our day are the names: "muslin," the beautifully woven thin cotton of Bengal; "calico" and "madras," bright-colored prints of South India; "shantung," the rough silken "domestic" cloth of China. These products were cheaper, and often superior to the "originals."

"It is easy to observe how in most underdeveloped countries the trading contacts with the outside world have actually impoverished them culturally," Raúl Prebisch, the Latin American economist and one of the chief polemicists for a better deal for the industrially backward regions of the world, writes:

> Skills in many crafts inherited from centuries back have been lost. A city like Baghdad, with whose name such glorious associations are connected, today does not harbour any of the old crafts, except some silver smithies, and they are adapting patterns from abroad requiring less craftsmanship; similarly, it is only with the greatest difficulties that one can buy a book of Arabic literature, while cheap magazines in English or Arabic are in abundance.

I remember discovering a curious instance of the postwar change that had come about in the relations between Asian and Western produce. In 1948, in Bangkok, I went out into the marketplace looking for chopsticks for my household. I could not find the traditional Chinese ivory or wood utensils. But I did find some made of plastic, not to realize until I returned home and examined them carefully that they were made in the U.S.A.—a product of the vast development of plastics that took place during World War II.

On the eve of World War II, Asia appeared still to have a bargaining position. Look at the list of exports of the Netherlands East Indies in 1939: Java was the world's second largest sugar producer. Quinine alone, used in medicine, valued at $1.3 million, was exported to the Netherlands and the world. Rubber, petroleum, tin, all seemed to insure the endurance of the relationship of the Indies as a powerful trading partner. Yet by the end of World War II, quinine's value had almost disappeared, replaced by synthetics, and the other exports, too, had been, for the most part, adversely affected.

It was perhaps natural enough that the Indonesian nationalists should continue to live with their illusion of "The Wealth of the Indies." They believed that with their own control over these resources, they might begin the process, and accelerate it rapidly, of industrialization which had brought power and relative abundance to the West.

In a sense, the two great "civil wars" of the Western world— World War I and World War II—seemed to add strength to the argument. At the end of World War II, independent India held more than $3 billion in sterling balances—in effect, debts which Britain had incurred against her former colony (despite trading rigged in her favor) in order to survive against the Axis Powers.

TECHNOLOGICAL CHANGES

YET several things had already happened before 1939 and would happen in the next three decades to make this hope illusory. The isolation from most of Southeast Asia under Japanese occupation during World War II had forced the industrial producers to look elsewhere for raw materials. In part, they simply moved through research and substitution away from traditional exports from Southeast Asia—from natural to synthetic rubber, from fibers to wood-pulp papers, from Southeast Asian petroleum sources to development of the Middle East and Latin American fields.

The dynamism of technology in the developed areas of the world speeded up the trend that had been developing throughout the nineteenth and early twentieth centuries, and in which manufactured articles were worth more than raw materials. (The estimate is that commodities in 1876-80 which would buy 100 units of manufactured goods could buy only 68.7 units in 1946-47.) And the incredible growth of the U.S. economy, in agriculture and mining as well as in manufacturing, made it a major competitor in world markets for many of the kinds of products which the Asian underdeveloped economies could produce—food grains, soya beans, cotton, edible oils and fats.

All this meant that the Asian economies (always excepting Japan, of course) found that their raw materials and commodities bought another 5 per cent less between 1952 and 1964 in manufactured goods from the industrial powers. The economist John Pincus estimates that, during this thirteen-year period, all the underdeveloped nations (including Latin America and Africa, as well as Asia) increased the value of their commodity exports by 2.75 per cent a year. I believe it likely that Asia probably got less than this rate because its share was declining in relation to both Africa and Latin America. (For, as political unrest shook Asia in the 1940s and 1950s, African producers also began to displace the traditional Asian suppliers.)

That means that the growth of these exports was no more, and probably less, than the population increase in most of the Southeast Asian countries. They were, of course, overwhelmingly dependent on commodity trading as their principal source of income to pay for imports, including capital equipment which could work the revolution of industrialization.

The answer of the new regimes in South Asia to this problem was to throw their whole effort into breaking this chain reaction by trying to limit their reliance on the production of raw materials as soon as possible by industrialization. The industrialization, in theory, would permit the substitution of goods produced at home for imports.

Largely based on a misreading of Russian history (i.e., that the Soviet Union had come from the ranks of *a backward country on a par with the post-World War II independent Asian regimes* to a position of a superpower in forty years), programs were directed at putting the emphasis on building heavy-industry capability and relegating production of raw materials and agriculture to second place.

The Indian planners of the mid-1950s hoped to build a modern industrial economy in urban centers. They hoped that they could continue the dual economy in the country until that modernized sector was producing efficiently, then "go back and rescue" the backward rural areas—as one of them explained the program to me in 1956.

But their hopes were based on two false assumptions: That separation between the two elements in the economy could be maintained; and that traditional agricultural production would provide sufficient food without revolutionary changes and major investment. The population increase and the innate failure of an unrealistic industrial program swamped the cities and are now forcing attention to largely stagnant food production.

ACCEPTANCE OF SOVIET PLANNING

THERE was a total lack of realism in such countries as India and Burma on the needs of an industrial society. The leadership would not face the fact that the lack of entrepreneurial talent could not automatically be solved by calling the program "socialist" and putting investment policies in the hands of government.

Few Asian leaders were willing to face the awful truth: The new states had come of age with a bureaucracy barely able to keep its head above water in simply administering justice, maintaining law and order, and beginning the social welfare schemes that had been wanting under the colonial regimes.

Every modern society plans, of course. But "planning" for the underdeveloped countries of South Asia became synonymous with an attempt at the highly centralized allocations of raw materials and production quotas that had grown up in the 1930s in the Soviet Union under its forced industrialization.

Asian intellectuals were prone to misunderstand two aspects of Soviet planning: They discounted, as they so easily could, living with their own misery, the enormous price that the Russians had paid for the mistakes of their system.

Manya Gordon, an economist on the left who made intensive research in the true nature of Soviet progress, writes:

> In the second half of the first [Soviet] Five Year Plan, 1931-33, the workers were actually starving. Famine and the catastrophic destruction of live stock were the result of Stalin's policy of forced farm collectivization. Hunger was not the only outcome of Communist war on the tillers of the soil. For that

matter the loss of eight or ten million people by famine would not in itself have disturbed the Soviet government. In the words of one Communist, "Of people, that bounty, we have plenty." Stalin was fully aware of the eventual cost in human life, but he was determined to achieve the subjugation of the peasantry. The greater the loss of life the more effectual the lesson.

. . . Of course, the Czars also exported grain at a time of scarcity, in 1891-93, but their inhumanity was condemned by everybody, including the future Communists. Furthermore, the Czar was not a Marxist. He did not confuse his loyalties. Exporting foodstuffs during a national shortage did not conflict with his class interests. His immediate entourage of landowners, bureaucrats and capitalists did not suffer. Stalin's agrarian policy weighed down on the very people who had a right to expect protection from the Soviet government. The exportation of food while the industrial workers were starving was proof that the Soviet government was more interested in its industrialization formulas than in the proletariat. It revealed a capitalist-employer attitude towards production.

The Plan was the thing, and not the life of the workers. To be sure, it was all done for the good of future generations and in the name of the Socialist state. The exploitation of the Congo by Leopold II, J. D. Rockefeller's early Standard Oil activities and other capitalist aggressions have been defended with the same kind of cant. During the Czarist regime Leo Tolstoy and other great-hearted Russians, with a majority of Russia's "bourgeois capitalists," came to the aid of the starving masses. The Communists, on the other hand, insisted that the Russian people were not starving while the all-powerful OGPU stifled every protest. Instead of appealing for foreign aid as in 1921-23 when the American people came to the rescue, every effort was made to conceal the catastrophic situation. Foreign correspondents were forbidden to enter the famine stricken areas and the censors deleted all "undesirable" information from their dispatches. "The greater the toll, the more effective the lesson."

Asians bought "whole hog" the Communist fiction that the Soviet Union had come from the ranks of an underdeveloped country in 1914 to a major industrial power competitive with the U.S. in a half century. (Few Asians are aware that Imperial Russia in the three decades preceding the Revolution had one of the highest rates of economic growth of any country in any period. Nor do they see that comparisons between their countries now and Russia at the Revolution are not valid. In 1913 Imperial Russia had 4.36 million metric tons of steel as against 31.8 million tons of steel in the U.S.—a large margin, but by no means the enormous distance between India or China, with their much vaster populations, and the developed countries in 1945. Further, agricultural surpluses, which both Imperial and Soviet Russia swapped to the West for capital goods, are not only unavailable in the underdeveloped countries, but no longer salable in the West.)

So, on their already heavy bureaucratic burden, they loaded an enormous planning operation and government responsibility for operating major industrial enterprises.

Often virtually illiterate clerks have been shoved into positions where they were administering the increasingly burdensome paper work of the new governments. Once, a few years ago, I crossed the Indo-Pakistan border near Lahore by land, something few foreigners do except those who are known locally. I had a complicated multiple-entry Indian immigration visa. The clerk at the border could not make head or tail of it, obviously because he read English poorly and had never seen a visa like it before. I explained to him the procedure of my surrendering my police authorization to him and his stamping the visa with the proper notation. He was grateful, and made no pretense of the kind of expertise that I would have been sure to encounter with one of his superiors in a New Delhi office under similar circumstances.

During the most bitter anti-American period in Indonesia, preceding the attempted Communist coup d'état in 1965, I used a U.S. Department of Defense correspondent's accreditation card to get past Indonesian security police to enter a ministry. I was testing just how far I might go out of a perverse sense of adventure. It was obvious that the reception clerk could not read and thought the U.S. eagle emblem was the *garuda* (a mythical Hindu animal, part bird, part man) on the Indonesian national seal.

It is no wonder that many of the new projects in India turned into industrial nightmares.

219

THE FUTURE

"TEMPLES OF THE FUTURE"

NEHRU often spoke of the new industrial enterprises as India's temples of the future, suggesting that they represented the new faith of his people as her religious structures had in the past. Ironically, he was right, but for another reason than his romantic philosophical concept. Their efficiency was so low that in fact they did represent the same kind of "economic waste" as the enormous temples of worship built throughout India's history.

I spent two weeks investigating the operation of a German-built Indian government steel mill in 1962. I found evidences of incredible waste. The German builders had originally intended simply to build the mill and turn it over to an Indian government agency. Then they found it necessary to run it themselves for an initial period. But they found that the whole psychology of the Indian government management and the worker was totally incompatible with industrial management techniques.

Much of what went wrong was not at the level of conceptual planning, or even the arithmetic of the economic proposals. The Germans complained, for example, that workers operating a steel rolling mill had no sense of discipline. An operator would leave a hot ingot on the bed, go out for a cigarette or to relieve himself, then return and start up the operation with a cold ingot. The rollers would break. And the mill would be shut down until a new roller could be flown at enormous expense from Germany. This purchase was possible only after long delays in getting the approval of several ministries in New Delhi for import licenses, foreign exchange, and tariff waivers. This single kind of incident happened so often in the first few years of the mill's operation that it became classic. It did not help that left-wing newspapers ballyhooed the difficulties, attributing them all to the "capitalist" mentality of the West German government and engineers on the project.

The nadir of the whole project came during the Hindu-Moslem riots of 1964. The German management found that weapons used in a brutal three-way slaughter among Moslems, Hindus, and tribal peoples in the area of the project had been made inside the plant, using its steel and machines.

The Russians were more "successful" with a plant built earlier; they simply insisted on total control over its operation. Then they maintained high levels of production by virtually abandoning quality standards, refusing to produce anything but steel rails— giving high tonnage statistics—which had to be dumped on the world market at below cost.

In Indonesia, the Russians began building a steel mill which was totally unfeasible from the start. The ore was to be brought from the island of Kalimantan (Borneo), along roads through the jungle that proved impossible for the Indonesians to build and on shipping that did not exist. The plant itself was placed at a point on the island of Java where there was no water, no labor supply, and no communications. But even that didn't equal the East German sugar mill—designed for beet sugar instead of Indonesian cane!

The Pakistanis (ostensibly in an effort to break "the monopoly of the Anglo-American petroleum cartel") built an uneconomic oil refinery in East Pakistan, financed by short-term French credits at a cost which appeared to be some 50 per cent higher than world prices. The Indians, contracting for a long-term supply of crude at better than world-market prices, set up a refinery in Kerala where they quickly found that there was an insufficient market. Also, since it was automated, the refinery provided few jobs—the original purpose of the project in a region of high unemployment even by Indian standards.

I have watched with morbid fascination for over more than a decade the compounding of errors on one particular project, the Rihand Dam in eastern U.P. in North India.

The dam was built—on original projections for it dating back to pre-World War II British surveys—in the First Five-Year Plan in the 1950s. It was a high-priority project because a maximum water storage capacity could be achieved with a minimum construction. The water was to be used for surface irrigation in the eastern U.P., one of the poorest regions of India, and in the neighboring state of Bihar. The electricity produced by the project would be used to fuel tubewells for irrigation in other parts of the two states where underground water sources were available.

But when Planning in India took a turn for the worse in the mid-1950s, when Mahalanobis sold Nehru the heavy industry emphasis, the whole approach was changed. It was argued that the best way to help the people of the eastern U.P. was by rapid industrialization. An aluminum mill was projected to use the dam's electricity. And the plant was started near the dam site—despite the fact that the bauxite raw material had to be brought some two hundred miles over an area which then had no roads or railway (instead of carrying the more easily handled electricity to the ore).

Meanwhile, the neighboring state of Bihar did nothing about the irrigation system that was to have used the dam's water (in part this was the explanation of the great famine in Bihar in 1966).

American investors—using the subsidized aid program loans —and Indian developers built the aluminum plant, under extreme difficulties. When I visited the area in 1962, the plant was about to go into operation, far behind schedule. Workers (only a few, for aluminum plants are not "labor intensive," in the economists' jargon) had been employed from the Punjab, for the eastern U.P. *wallahs* had neither the stamina nor the interest in becoming industrial labor. (The tribal peoples in the area had been displaced to make way for the reservoir.)

The Planners in New Delhi had not taken into account the problem of fabricating the aluminum. Proper allocation had not been made for funds to finance rolling mills. So the Indian management was sending aluminum ingots through the expensive and incredibly congested port of Calcutta to Taiwan to be drawn into wire. Since the Indian government by this time had no foreign exchange, payment was made to the Taiwanese "in kind"— aluminum ingots. But the cost of manufacture of the aluminum at Rihand was well above world market prices and the aluminum had to be sold to the Chinese at below cost. The wire was then brought back to India, to be sold again at extremely high costs, adding another increment to the already high costs of the whole nationwide electrification plan.

Nor does the story end here. Since the whole dam was originally envisaged as primarily an irrigation rather than a power scheme, the aluminum plant soon found that it did not have enough power. So additional electrical-producing units in the area—operating on coal—were purchased from the Soviet Union. But the railway system in the area—the main line between Calcutta and northern India—could not haul coal for these power stations and at the same time supply coal-driven steam locomotives. It was decided to electrify the state-owned railways in the area with the Russian power plants. The Russians could not meet their delivery dates on the heavy electrical equipment, and production at the plant had to be curtailed.

I don't know where the whole mess stands as I write. But I am sure that the morass into which these harebrained decisions led deepens. And it would take a Solomon to unravel the whole knot of inconsistencies now.

UNECONOMIC INVESTMENT DECISIONS

THAT is the main difficulty at this stage of the Indian economic development: Vast sums have been put into uneconomic plants. In many cases there is no market for their high-cost products. Enormous capacity lies idle. But there is tremendous pressure to continue to build more capacity, for the whole network of preferences for government-financed heavy industrial investment has become an ogre which the planners cannot control and which they dare not halt.

A director of one of the biggest Indian privately owned financial and industrial empires told me during a recent visit, "I am certainly in theory against our building another steel mill (the fourth government-owned plant, to be built by the Russians at astronomical costs). But what can I do? The only customer we had for products from our construction equipment manufacturing subsidiary this year was the steel mill project."

The investment of tremendous sums in these enterprises exhausted the reserves which had piled up during the war in India, exhausted international credit in other countries. They were high in capital, low in producing jobs badly needed in the light of huge underemployment and unemployment. But more important, the investment policies which dictated putting huge sums into heavy

223

manufacturing bled the rural sector of the economy. That has meant that as populations have exploded, capital has not been available to the farmers to keep up with the increasing demand— or to raise the abysmally low consumption and improve the diet.

Even in Pakistan, where at least the first decade of planning was more rational, the problem of markets for high-cost manufactured goods was apparent. The Pakistanis, largely because at independence they had no economic theoreticians to speak of, because they were committed to a policy of following Western economic example and advice, put a larger portion of capital into agriculture. They expanded their cotton acreage and textile industry. But there soon was overproduction. A half-naked Pakistan countryside could not buy the textiles (though there was no question of foreign exchange) because the increase in food production and, therefore, rural income, was little better than the galloping population growth.

Common-sense priorities for development were simply thrown out the window. A former Indian Civil Service officer who was asked to write the basic memorandum for economic policy just after independence told me that he wrote a simple policy paper pointing up that India must do something about two things: Population control and food. It was filed and forgotten.

Gandhi's emphasis on the village nature of India went by the boards. While the New Delhi Planners talked and wrote of steel mills, no program to put decent drinking water into India's 600,000 villages was formalized, much less carried into practice. While they helped the Russians set up a demonstration farm for mechanized agriculture (the Russians! those great theoreticians on agriculture who had to import $367.5 million in wheat in 1964 to meet their own demands, and in 1961-64 imported as much wheat as India!), no effective plan was made to introduce a simple iron-shod plow to replace the traditional Indian wooden stick. While the Indians invested $22 million in a heavy machine-tool plant built by the Russians which, after seven years, has produced only $1 million in goods, virtually nothing was done to halt the increase in population.

(In fact, the total bankruptcy of the government's industrialization program was revealed in these figures: An official Indian government publication estimates that as of the fiscal year ended March 31, 1967, government-owned enterprises with an investment of $6 billion suffered losses in excess of $10 million for the operating year.)

AID-GIVERS' RESPONSIBILITY

BUT if the Asians have put the wrong emphasis on their plans, the aid-giving countries have encouraged them in their follies. Manufacturers in the U.S. and Europe have been anxious to sell the Asians machinery. While this has been extended on low-interest, long-term loans (at least from the Americans), it has called forth large expenditures of "brainpower" and capital from the Asians to finance local costs of the projects.

Professor B. R. Shenoy, of Gujerat University in India, a bitter opponent of past policies, says the aid-givers are equally culpable with the Indian Planners.

> I would place the blame [for the failures] no less on the aid-giving countries than on the government of India. The reason is this: It is not as if foreign aid provides but marginal aid for Plan finances. If you look into the statistics, foreign aid funds represent as much as 60 per cent of Indian national savings, in recent years. Provision of the bulk of finance is implied endorsement of the policies of centralized planning. On top of this, American experts, including academicians of distinction, until recently have conferred their blessings on Indian economic policies.
>
> With this record of financial and moral support, how can the aid-giving countries and the aid-giving agencies, like the World Bank, wish to disown responsibility for the multiple economic crises, which are now upon the Indian economy, and which are the direct outcome of the policies of the past one and a half decades?

The cynicism of some of the aid-giving mechanism is virulent. After the incredible failures of the German steel project in India, I was appalled in 1965 to learn that the Germans were pressing for an expansion of the project. I asked one of the German officials involved in the proposal for an explanation.

225

"I'll tell you very simply," he said, "why we are pushing for an extension. The machinery producers in Germany want to sell their equipment. They are not concerned with whether the Indians will be able to pay for it in the long run or not. That's the Bundesbank's problem. The Bundesbank says it has its direction from the economic ministry. The economic ministry says that the 'loans' to India are a form of subsidy to the West German steel equipment producers, to give them capacity for production for markets that will some day again open in Eastern Europe. The foreign ministry believes the steel mill project is a small price to pay to keep India from flirting with the Pandow regime (in East Germany). Whether the project is what the Indians need or can use . . . well, that's their problem."

If short-term, high-cost financing of machinery they may not really need at this stage of their development is the price that Asians pay for European aid, the price for what they get from the East Bloc is still higher. The East Bloc sold to these countries for payment in "local currency." In fact, however, these local currencies—unlike the U.S. receipts for food and some other goods which are turned back to the host governments for developmental projects—are used by the Communist powers to buy local products for export to their own countries and to other industrialized countries.

In many cases, these products are simply diverted and sold into Western markets. In India, much of the cashew nuts (not consumed anywhere in the East Bloc), tea, jute, hides, all go eventually to the U.S. and Western Europe. India loses the foreign exchange, the Communists earn badly needed dollars and West European currencies.

But there were additional problems in dealing with the Communist Bloc. The Indians, the Indonesians until 1966, the Burmese, the Pakistanis (again, only to a limited extent), and others had no adequate way to fix prices for what they get. Since the Communists are willing to pay exorbitant prices for local commodities they buy with their local earnings, it appears certain that the capital goods they sell are heavily overpriced.

In addition, the Asians—whose whole effort is to try to boost their efficiency—increasingly tied themselves to the most inefficient producers in the industrialized world, an admission that Russian and East European economists constantly make. There are hundreds of examples told by members of the Indian business community. Take the case of hides and shoes. The Agra shoe manufacturer does not make shoes for Western Europe and the U.S. because of higher quality standards (and tariff restrictions that keep his product out). But because consumer goods are of such abominable standards in the East Bloc, he finds that almost anything he makes can be sold to the Russians. There is no incentive for him to make a better product. *And Indian-style footwear designed for the American market* must be made in Italy and France!

My own estimate is that this diversion of Indian goods to the Russians and the East Europeans in 1966 alone ran at about $300 million a year. The trade is run by the Communists on principles laid down by the Nazi financial wizard, Hjalmar Schacht, who perfected it in the 1930s in order to finance the Hitler regime. And, in essence, the U.S. helps to pick up the bill by financing purchases the underdeveloped country could not otherwise make in the U.S. and the West.

I have written here primarily of India. The Indian experience is the arch-example of the failures of the two decades. But this is in large part because of her enormous size (her population is more than all the rest of non-Communist Asia, excluding Pakistan, combined) and the relatively strong drive and superior capability of her bureaucracy and leadership. Nor is it to be forgotten that through much of this period in the United States and Britain, India's example was touted as a primary test of non-Communist economic development in the underdeveloped countries of Asia.

Her failures are, then, paramount to our whole view of the problem. Furthermore, much of what happened in India was repeated on a minor scale in the other countries of the area.

The blunders of the past two decades in trying to bring an economic revolution to non-Communist Asia—a responsibility equally shared by Asian leadership and ourselves—have brought us to a grim situation in the late 1960s. Heaped on to the already monumental problems of its people and the distortions of the three and a half centuries of colonialism, what is the outlook?

227

10 ✦

The Onrushing Catastrophe

THE story is an all-too-common newspaper item:

A model citizen lives in one of our vast modern cities. He works hard. He pays his taxes. He educates his children, tries to care for his family in the increasingly complex world of the industrial societies.

But one day, on his way to a downtown office, he is waylaid in the street. A young thug from the slums attacks him, perhaps not even to rob him, but only out of frustration and bitterness. The young delinquent has become a monster, created by the failure of modern society to find him a place, to give him a rewarding role.

Our model citizen must fight for his life. No matter how he comes out of the brawl, things will never be the same again. For his whole moral and social existence has been thrown into question.

We are well on our way, through the failures of Asian and American leadership in the past two decades, to creating in Asia whole societies with a "slum mentality." If present trends continue, I do not see how we, as a society, will escape the inevitable lashing out that is bound to come from the underdeveloped regions of Asia.

The evidence for the continuing deterioration is everywhere apparent. But it is obscured in part by the phenomenal success of the Japanese, by relatively great economic strides in a few "enclaves" (Hong Kong, Thailand, Malaysia, Singapore, Taiwan, perhaps South Korea). And in other areas the visitor is likely to equate new tourist hotels, a few efficient factories, some glib talk by a few politicians as representative of the whole.

DEMORALIZATION OF THE ELITE

THERE are four important forces bringing on the coming disaster: The population explosion, which drowns what little progress that is made in increasing numbers, about which little or nothing has been done; the growing food shortage, which dictates more and more any economic activity; the failures of education to meet the needs of a revolutionary approach to old problems, or even to "stand still" in the face of the multiplying numbers. These three lead into the most crucial, if the hardest to define and substantiate, the growing demoralization of the elites of Asian societies.

A few months before he died in 1966, I asked Ram oh dar Lohia, one of the most brilliant of the Indian politicians who participated in the fight for independence, to explain his political program. Lohia was a flamboyant, individualistic leader of the modernist wing of the Congress movement that had, after independence, broken off—with Nehru's blessing—to form the Socialist Party. He was well educated, not only with a wide acquaintance of his own vast Indian society but also a product of the old-style German university system. He had an insatiable curiosity about his own country and the world. And if he was charged by many of his enemies and former friends with being too egotistical and melodramatic, he was never insincere or an opportunist looking for a quick and easy road to power.

I asked Lohia, in one of our last conversations, why he was making common cause with any and all elements opposing the present power complex. He and his party, the left wing of the remnant social democratic movement, had joined hands with the Hindu revivalists on the right and Moscow-oriented Communists on the left. In fact, the only common denominator, I told him, seemed to be an effort to break up the *status quo*, presided over by the Congress Party.

He told me that my appraisal was correct, that his only guiding

229

principle was the destruction of the current setup in India. And he explained that his reasoning was extremely simple: "If we do not destroy the *status quo*, if we cannot break out of the miasma of present conditions in India, then there is no hope. We would become an anthropological museum, a kind of curiosity in the human race, a species set apart and out of the mainstream of human development."

Even allowing for the bombast and ambitions of a politician, I believe Lohia's statement is a true expression of much of the thinking of the India elite today.

It is, of course, the formulation of an activist. The great passive quality of India still dominates most of the elite. But the underlying sense of pessimism is the same.

There is another face to this demoralization which is as prevalent and as important. It is the slipping into the shoes left empty by departing Europeans by members of the elite. It is this phenomenon which explains, in the face of the overwhelming tragedy of lack of progress of most of South Asia in the past two decades, why leaders have demonstrated so little real revolutionary zeal. Many members of the new governing class have reached positions in the society—government, business, political parties—that they did not anticipate before independence. They are, in a certain measure, satisfied—even if the society, as a whole, is not moving ahead.

Another version of this acceptance of defeat was expressed by a Javanese friend. We met at a U.S. embassy Fourth of July party in 1965 in Djakarta. I had come back to Indonesia for the first time in several years for the tenth anniversary celebration of the Afro-Asian Conference at Bandung, the high-water mark of expectations in the newly independent underdeveloped nations' fight for freedom from European colonialization after World War II.

Apparently something in my whole demeanor expressed my disillusionment with what I was seeing in Indonesia. The party, itself, was a fitting demonstration of what I felt was wrong: Old acquaintances from the Indonesian Revolution against the Dutch were participating in the same old round of cocktail-party conversation and attitudes. Outside on the streets of Djakarta, the

Indonesian capital, there were more signs of poverty and igno-
rance than even the four years of Japanese occupation during
World War II and the five-year struggle with the Dutch had produced. At the party, there was little in the conduct or the conversation of the Indonesian guests to show they appreciated the
fact.

My friend walked over to me and said, "I know what you are
thinking. I see what you see. It happened to me when I first got
back (he had returned a few weeks before from a year's study in
the U.S.). But very quickly you get back into the atmosphere, you
forget how it looks to an outsider. And you accommodate yourself
to what is happening."

On that same visit to Indonesia, I visited another old friend, the
wife of one of Soekarno's political prisoners. She was an extremely
brave woman who had to maintain her family and her husband's
political honor at enormous cost. While he was locked away, the
problems of feeding and caring for their children, and the constant intimidation, had made life a nightmare for almost a decade.
Suddenly, in the midst of our conversation, her stoic calm broke
for the first time in my presence and in a burst of tears she cried
out, "Did you think we would make such a mess of it? Did you
think it would all turn out so badly?"

Even the language of reform, revolution, renewal, has been so
debased in these two decades that very little is left to express such
concepts—even when the spokesman is sincere. For some reason
I have not been able to identify, the arts of the poster, the demonstration, the pamphleteer develop in the new Asian countries
faster than any other manifestation of a modern society. Committees, political parties, commissions, agitational groups prolif-
erate at a rate almost comparable to the birthrate. But they no
longer have any meaning. Many of these politicians who now call
on their sainted revolutionary figures who fought the good fight
against European colonialism, either sat it out or are too young to
have even known the complications of the struggle. (Much of the
reality has vanished in a totally idealistic rewriting of the history
of the period. A few years ago in East Java, I visited the site of
"one of the great battles" of the Indonesian fight for independ-

231

ence against the Dutch. A total of seven persons on both sides had been killed in it.)

This whole counterfeiting of the language of reform and revolt was epitomized by one poster I saw in Indonesia shortly after the unsuccessful Communist coup d'état against the Republic in 1965. For months, the pro-Communist regime of Soekarno had warned the people of the terrors of the U.S. Central Intelligence Agency. But, as it became clearer that Peking had had at least a hand in the Communist attempt to take power, anti-Communist students from Djakarta University had put up a banner reading: "Remember! C.I.A. means Chinese Intelligence Agency!"

On a more sophisticated plane, this disenchantment with political independence and the problems that have developed affect all decisions. One of the most powerful Burmese leaders since independence told an Israeli diplomat acquaintance of mine in the mid-1950s his basic *realpolitik* for Burma: The Chinese Communists, he said, will inevitably take over all of South Asia. It will inevitably lead to an atomic war between the Chinese and the Americans. We Burmese, who suffered bitterly under one occupation (by the Japanese between 1942 and 1945), want to be under the Chinese for the shortest time possible. So we will make whatever concessions are necessary to stave it off.

Cambodia's Prince Sihanouk, despite his great show of confidence and determination, has told French reporters that "if there is only someone in this part of the world speaking Khmer (Cambodian) five hundred years from now, I shall have been a success."

Concepts which would have been rejected out of hand twenty-five years ago by these same people during the fight for independence are now accepted, however reluctantly, with resignation. I remember the shock I had in 1966 when the wife of an Indian friend, a "modern" Indian housewife with a university education, told me that starvation was inevitable in India. It was her reaction to the failures to meet the food crisis and the then current famine in the state of Bihar.

POPULATION EXPLOSION

UNDERPINNING much of the pessimism is the simple fact of population explosion. The statisticians take some meager satisfaction in the fact that most Asian rates of increase are lower than in Latin America. Yet even that may be false.

Constant inquiries to Indian authorities over the years have indicated a steady reappraisal of population growth rates—always upward. My own guess is that it is considerably higher than the official 2.6 per cent annually. For in neighboring Pakistan, the generally accepted figure of "tending toward 3 per cent" in 1965 has now gone to 3.2 per cent. (It is true that, in general, Moslem populations in the subcontinent tend to grow at a rate higher than Hindu and non-Moslem populations in the same region or language grouping. But it seems to me unlikely that the difference between Moslem and Hindu rates of growth are larger than the differences among the various ethnic and regional groupings in the subcontinent.) The truth is that so little is known about peasant life among the more than 80 per cent of the people who live in the villages in the continent that such figures are only educated guesses. And there are all kinds of pressure to make government estimates as low as possible.

In fact, most of this is a quibble. The size of the problem is so monumental that even a difference of as much as a half of 1 per cent may not be very important to the over-all argument of what is happening.

Here are some basic statistical facts that apply all over Asia: A population growth rate of 2.5 per cent per year means that total population will double in twenty-eight years. It has already been proved in several places that the most rudimentary health services for the local population can produce a growth rate of 3.5 per cent, or a doubling in twenty years. That would mean that by the end of this century many Asian countries will face the problem of dealing with a population twice its present size.

The argument against the possibility for economic development in this kind of situation comes out of European experience. At the time when Europe was developing industrially, her population growth rate was probably about 1 per cent a year.

The vast differences do not come only from the large birthrate in most Asian countries. But it also arises out of a lower death rate in most of the new nations of Southeast Asia than existed in eighteenth- and nineteenth-century Europe. The vicious circle of higher birthrates produces a lower median age in the population and that means lower death rates. The introduction of new medical science pulls it down even more. Taiwan, for example, has a lower death rate than the U.S.; and even Ceylon, where health facilities are only beginning to be widespread, has a lower death rate than Britain.

NIP-AND-TUCK BATTLE FOR FOOD

Now fit these figures in casually with economic development and you see the grim spectacle of what is happening. Few countries in the world have ever maintained a food production increase of 5 per cent annually over any significant period. That means if a country were galloping along at 3.5 per cent increase annually in population, it would be a nip and tuck contest at best to keep up with food for the population increase, much less raise nutrition standards.

A further complicating factor, of course, is that increased production in industry, certainly, and probably in agriculture does not require in most Asian countries large numbers of additional labor force. Even if the countries of South Asia were to put the accent on "garden agriculture"—the maximum use of hand labor, as was done at an earlier stage in Japan—the number of new members of the labor force appearing each year could not be absorbed. (And, in passing, it might be pointed out that this has been exactly the opposite tack taken by most of the agricultural development planners, Asian and American, in many of the programs already undertaken in South Asia.)

The demographer, Frank W. Notestein, in a relatively optimistic discussion of the problem, warns:

> In an era of rising expectations how long can political coherence be maintained in the presence of unemployment on a possibly unprecedented scale?

If political coherence cannot be maintained, the risks change
—from those of growth to those of a catastrophic loss of life.
The margins of safety are pathetically thin. It would not take
much disorganization to block transportation and public health
activities so that famine and epidemic disease would stalk the
land. To anyone inclined to point out that this would at least be
one solution to the problem of population pressure, the reply
must be that massive upheavals also jeopardize every aspect of
the development process and every hope of representative government in unregimented societies. The risks of this kind are
real in such densely settled areas as India, Pakistan, Indonesia
and Egypt.

Those of us who have traveled widely in Asia during the past
twenty years have seen exactly this process begin. I think now of
the once exclusive residential section in Bombay—Malabar Hill.
At the end of World War II, this was an area of large homes and
huge, old-style apartment houses inhabited either by wealthy
British and foreign residents or by the old Parsi and Gujerati families.

Today, if you visit Bombay, you see superficial signs of great
prosperity. The "hill" has been dotted with huge, new apartment
houses, what pass for "skyscrapers" in the Indo-Pakistan subcontinent.

But, in the streets below you see something else: Everywhere
there are stray people at any hour of the day, wandering vaguely
about with little if anything to do. They—like those who live in the
acres of improvised huts in sewage-soaked swamps along the new
road from Bombay to its airport—are part of the overflowing
population of the city. And joining them are the offspring of
landless laborers in southern India, pushed off the land and
fleeing toward some kind of marginal survival around India's
second largest city.

Indonesia's Soerabaja, once a neat if impoverished colonial city
and port, is today almost drowning in the increasing indigents
pouring in from the countryside of Java. The banks of canals,
former park areas, now are covered with improvised woven
bamboo lean-tos. And this is only the most obvious manifestation of the enormous growth in the villages of central and east

Java—one of the most densely populated areas of the world even twenty-five years ago.

Can something be done? Will something be done to halt the catastrophic increase in population which, at best, dilutes any program of progress, and promises to overwhelm any efforts if it cannot be brought into check?

I am not optimistic.

FAMILY PLANNING PROGRAMS

THERE are three basic reasons why I do not think that a realistic appraisal of the problem leads to optimism: The slowness with which the Asian governments and ourselves have come to grips with the problem, even in a casual way; the technical difficulties that prevent any family planning program from becoming effective; and the still enormous amount of cant that surrounds the subject.

Again, take the Indians. In part because of the opposition of the followers of Gandhi, no population control effort beyond the government espousal of the so-called rhythm method was undertaken in the first decade of independence. Finally, the first realistic effort to reach any significant part of the population began in 1965—eighteen years after independence, during which period the population must have grown by at least 80 million people, or the equivalent of the population separated from former British India to form Pakistan.

Today the only effective programs, however small they may be, that exist in Asia are in South Korea, Taiwan, India, and Pakistan. In the other countries—and the same criteria might be applied to these four nations, too—the thrust of any present program is largely among the upper and middle classes who either have already understood and are implementing their own scheme and who, in the nature of the problem, are not the target if something really effective is to be accomplished.

Pakistan, despite its lower administrative capacity than India, probably presents the most optimistic picture of an effective plan. (Taiwan's birth-control program owes a great deal to Japanese influences, dating back to pre-World War II. And in any case, its total concern is relatively small compared to other countries like India, Pakistan, and Indonesia.)

Although there, too, it started late, family planning has had the full backing of President Ayub Khan against the incipient opposition of orthodox Islamic influences. Ayub has personally addressed thousands of large and small meetings on birth control. At one point, he carried in his pocket one of the plastic loop contraceptive devices, which he took out and displayed to various audiences—including ultraconservative tribal meetings. During the short but bitter Indo-Pakistan war of 1965, he made personal telephone calls to administrators of the new national population control program in West Pakistan, informing them that whatever the demands of the war, the high priorities given it by the government should be maintained. It was crucial, for family planning had just been launched as the fighting began.

On the American side, while there were hints beginning in the Kennedy administration that the U.S. was prepared, through the mechanism of the aid program, to help finance and lend technical assistance to population control programs, the whole effort did not get high priority. The first forthright public statement came from President Johnson in 1965 that "the U.S. would extend such help [on national birth-control schemes] to countries which requested it."

Yet, even today, there is no American policy which demands as a *quid pro quo* for massive economic aid that such a program be undertaken. Nor is there a growing political atmosphere in which that may be possible. Already some of the more extreme Black Nationalist movements in the U.S. have suggested that any kind of population control is based on an attempt to continue white domination of the world.

The history of birth control in Asia, such as exists, has been one of moving from one highly touted method of control to another. The most recent was the I.U.D., inter-uterine devices. Theoretically, the insertion in the vagina of a plastic device offers "permanent" contraception. Experimentation in the U.S. and West Europe has shown a possibility of "acceptance" physiologically by some 80 per cent of fertile females. The device is inexpensive and simple to produce and could be manufactured even in the underdeveloped economies of the Asian countries.

But the I.U.D.'s have not proved out as the cure-all they originally suggested. Millions of Asian females suffering from malnutrition are less able to host the devices than had been thought from Western research. There appears to be more bleeding than with properly nourished women, and among Moslems particularly, this is a difficult problem relating to the whole concept of the woman as "unclean" during menstrual periods.

The I.U.D., just as the older and more established methods of contraception, are up against a tremendous number of obstacles. None of the new countries has an elaborate bureaucracy needed to carry out any program. Conventional contraceptives—devices, jellies, douches—are beyond the economic means of the vast peasantry which must be touched if any plan is to become really effective. The new oral pills have so far been too expensive. Nor can they be used when a complicated—complicated in the setting of the timelessness of village life—schedule is required.

Above and beyond this are the complex social and psychological and economic factors. For centuries a large family has been a kind of social insurance for a peasant family. Not even with modern health facilities cutting down on the traditional Asian epidemics and endemic diseases, like malaria, does the peasant householder feel he can risk a future as an aged member of his society without sons to care for him. In much of Asia there is a traditional kind of male chauvinism which demands numerous offspring as proof of the virility, the manhood, of the head of the family. This problem, particularly, has weighted the peasant opinion against the relatively simple method of sterilization for males—by far the most effective way to cut into the birthrate if it were applied wholesale.

Much of the literature put out in the West concerning the present programs in Asia is just not realistic. Kingsley Davis, in an article in *Science,* organ of the American Association for the Advancement of Science, makes this point in biting terms:

> With more than thirty nations now trying or planning to reduce population growth and with numerous private and interna-

tional organizations helping, the degree of unanimity as to the kind of measures needed is impressive. The consensus can be summed up in the phrase "family planning."

. . . The actual programs seem to be aiming simply to achieve a reduction in the birth rate. Success is therefore interpreted as the accomplishment of such a reduction, on the assumption that the reduction will lessen population growth. In those rare cases where a specific demographic aim is stated, the goal is said to be a short-run decline within a given period. . . . Under conditions of modern mortality, a crude birth rate of twenty-five to thirty per thousand will represent such a multiplication of people as to make use of the term *population control* ironic. A rate of increase of 1.2 per cent per year would allow South Korea's already dense population to double in less than sixty years.

One can of course defend the programs by saying that the present goals and measures are merely interim ones. A start must be made somewhere. But we do not find this answer in the population-policy literature. Such a defense, if convincing, would require a presentation of the *next* steps, and these are not considered. . . .

It is clear that unless something can be done to halt this proliferation of human beings in Asia, no program for lifting standards of nutrition, of education, of living standards in general will succeed.

Even a country like Thailand, which has had phenomenal economic growth during the past two decades and which appears to be on its way to finding its own synthesis of modernity with traditional values, could get into trouble because of a too-rapid expansion of population. Government estimates are that population is growing at about 3 per cent annually. The estimated growth of the gross national product was 6.1 per cent in the thirteen years 1951-1964. It probably rose dramatically in 1967, in part as a result of the effects of the heavy American spending in the Vietnam war.

But food production increases in Thailand have not kept pace with this expansion of population and living standards. Rice exports, one of the principal sources of Thailand's government revenues and foreign exchange, have fallen dramatically in the past few years. And the total production increases which have occurred have been largely the result of new acreage being brought under cultivation. That virgin land is now virtually exhausted. And the Thais will have to turn to the more difficult task of increasing per acre productivity. (It is true, of course, that the Thais have worked miracles in hybrid corn production and producing abaca, both of which were virtually unknown in the country a decade ago.)

THE FOOD PROBLEM

IT is the problem of food, almost indivisible from the problem of the population explosion, which presents the most horrendous aspect of the Asian scene. Again, statistics are of only marginal use. Measurements of consumption, production, and distribution are at best only educated guesses in such countries as India, Pakistan, and Indonesia.

Much time and books full of statistics have been devoted to the Indian food problem. Yet we have only its vaguest outlines. We know that in the early years after independence Indian production of food grains—rice, wheat, the sorghums, corn—reached a plateau of about 85 million tons. As I write, the Indians hope to harvest a record crop for the 1967-68 crop years. It could reach 100 million tons. It is being hailed in some quarters as an enormous victory, "proof" of the success of the long-term effort to make India self-sufficient in food grains.

Yet the great success of the crop year was based in large part on unusually good rains. And it must be weighed against the probability that the elasticity of Indian consumption—the amount Indians will eat when there is food and that they cannot eat when it is not available—is inconceivable to Western observers. One has to remember that in the 1966-67 failures and resultant famine in the state of Bihar, the estimated shortfall in production may have reached 6 million tons in that state of approximately 50 million people alone!

The casual visitor to India, to Pakistan, to Indonesia can perceive with his own eyes that "hunger" is a relative thing. Even statistics on caloric intake alone become less meaningful when they are put beside the almost total absence of protein foods from many diets in South Asia. Pot-bellied children drifting in and out of the crowd that surrounds a visitor to a village in any of these countries are witness enough to the malnutrition which is rampant even under the best conditions.

Failure to cope with the problem of increasing food production has come at two levels: Initially, the post-independence regimes believed that the simplest encouragement of the dissemination of new and more scientific methods would boost production enormously. Yet in many areas, this was putting the cart before the horse.

The concept that Asian peasants do not produce because of their obstinate loyalties to old methods has been exaggerated. It is not generally known that good wheat farmers in India and Pakistan, for example, produce at about the same level as poor wheat farmers in North America. The reasons are clear: The American and Canadian farmer who produces at marginal rates does so because his land and his methods cannot meet the economics of more water, fertilizer, and the high-yield varieties.

The traditional Indian "good" farmer reached the same yields by the same route. He is producing as much as is possible with his access to water, fertilizer, and with varieties developed over the centuries for those conditions.

If you want to increase his yields, then you must turn to all these factors. And none of them can operate in isolation. It does him no good to have access to the new (and expensive unless the government is willing to subsidize him) high-yield seed varieties unless he has access to water, fertilizer, and insecticides.

That means that two things are necessary: Research and capital. The research has been slow. And the capital, as I have tried to explain earlier, has not been there because of the siphoning off of funds for the program of industrialization in many of the new countries.

The sale (for local currencies) and gift of American foodstuffs to the underdeveloped Asian economies saved millions from starvation. But, ironically, it has played a diabolical role in this equation, economically. Because American foodstuffs were available, without the payment of short foreign exchange, all those tendencies in the bureaucracies of countries like Indonesia,

Pakistan, India, and Ceylon to ignore the food problem have been reinforced. The availability of American surplus food at bargain prices in the great urban centers lessened the ability of the farmer to bargain for the investment capital—through higher prices as well as through government subsidies—that would have led to increased production.

At another level, the whole thinking about agriculture in India, particularly, but also to some extent in the other new countries of Asia, has been falsely attuned to the remarkable results of American agriculture and its "industrialization." Bureaucrats in the capital cities, more often than not with only a theoretical concept of farming and its methods, have tried shortcuts to increased agricultural production. There has been far too much talk about mechanization in countries which have vast untapped sources of hand labor, underemployed and unemployed.

COMMON-SENSE SOLUTION

A FEW years ago I spent some time with an American agricultural technician who had been working in the field on agricultural problems in India. He came with a wealth of experience, not only in subsistence American farming, but also in Iraq and Nepal.

He was considered something of a "nut," not only by the Indians but also by some of his fellow bureaucrats in the American aid program in the American Embassy in New Delhi. And the reason was his fascination with only two aspects of Indian agriculture: He argued, and had proved his theory with some experimental demonstration plots, that a beginning of the solution of the India-wide problem of water was its use on the land. He maintained that a large part, perhaps most, of the water used for irrigation in much of south and central India was in fact wasted. He believed that the introduction of terracing—a simple engineering project which would permit the water to flow slowly over the ground—would dramatically change this situation. Surveying was needed to lay out a farmer's land so that, instead of damming up the water for a period on an inclined piece of land, then letting it flow off, it should be turned through the terracing method slowly across the field.

The surveying necessary was "simple," but simple only in American terms. He trained a few young Indian workers to work with the farmers to lay out their fields along the new lines he prescribed. But almost as soon as these young men were trained, they were removed from that particular job and taken into the bureaucracy. For, obviously, he had chosen bright, young, intelligent workers who were siphoned off into the mushrooming bureaucracy in the state capitals and New Delhi.

His second gambit was the proposal of a set of tools for the Indian peasant. These were six primitive agricultural implements, copies of tools used by the Mormon pioneers in the U.S. West around the middle of the nineteenth century. He argued that the tools could be used by any Indian farmer with only a minimum of instruction. And, more important, they could be made cheaply and repaired in the village workshops anywhere in the country.

His proposal was never seriously considered—even when his own demonstrations won over individual farmers. The reason was primarily that Indian bureaucrats in New Delhi considered the whole proposal an attempt to force "backward methods" on Indian agriculture. And his American superiors were not prepared to do battle on this issue. The road for India, it was argued in New Delhi, was mechanized farming. And a significant portion of the bureaucracy in New Delhi saw a panacea in the Russian method of collectivization and mechanization. One may well ask how this was possible in the 1950s after the total failure of Soviet agriculture to meet its own needs and after the failure of a Russian demonstration farm in India. (U.S. water-drilling equipment was "loaned" to save one Soviet experiment from collapse.) The explanation lies in the whole framework of attitudes toward development which has so largely paralyzed the Indians during this whole period.

The extent of the growing food catastrophe in Asia is told in part by some statistics on the movement of foodstuffs in international trade. Before World War II, the Far East and South Asian countries, as a bloc, were net exporters of food. In the postwar period they became net importers of grain. And in the ten-year period from 1953-55 to 1963-65, imports more than doubled. (The 1963-65 period was particularly bad because of the failure of crops throughout the South Asia area. But the long-term trend was clearly marked by a pattern of about a 6 per cent increase annually in food imports into the area from the West and Australia.) The increasing food prices also posed an additional strain, forcing an increasing drain that food would impose on the ability of the region as a whole to pay for other badly needed imports; i.e., industrial goods and capital equipment to be used to build up an industrial plant.

Famine on a vast scale has been averted until now in the Asian food-deficit countries by the enormously increasing capacity of the North American granary. Since World War II, the U.S. alone has shipped some $14 billion worth of food grains to Asia. (This figure includes the postwar shipments to Japan, now largely self-sufficient in grain but increasingly a larger consumer of higher protein foods.) Canadian sales and gifts have totaled over $3 billion. India alone, since 1951, has received some $4 billion worth of food grains and other foodstuffs from the U.S.

Leaving aside the political question of the American desire to continue to meet this requirement, can it be continued indefinitely?

There is increasing evidence that it cannot on several counts: U.S. technology and the Asian population explosion (together with demands from other underdeveloped parts of the world) are running neck and neck. Some authorities on the subject already see the end in sight. Secondly, the cost of feeding larger and larger groups of people in the Asian food-deficit regions is increasing—not only through the subsidies which must be paid to finance the surpluses over our own needs in the U.S. but also through contributory costs such as hauling and storing the foods. A third problem is that as nutritional standards—and population times consumption—go up in the industrial countries, farmers are turning away from production of cheap food grains (sold or given to Asia) to high-protein, higher profit foods.

CAN THE U.S. CONTINUE TO FEED ASIA?

WILLIAM and Paul Paddock, in their book *Famine—1975!*, predict the U.S. will not be able to meet the growing crisis. They write:

. . . With the supply line from wheat producer to wheat consumer so fragile, as well as harried by weather fluctuations and politics, the establishment of a firm governmental policy to organize adequate charity shipments to the hungry nations will become increasingly chancy as food becomes scarce. Basic to the formulation of such a policy must be the question: Will the United States have in 1975 enough wheat to keep starvation from the hungry nations?

Secretary of Agriculture Freeman says, "Yes—until 1984."

In 1966 he demonstrated his awareness of this problem by having his staff assemble essential figures both for the world food needs in the years ahead and for the capacity of the United States to meet those needs.

. . . The Secretary stated that unless the hungry nations improve their own agricultures their food *shortages* (excluding China) will grow from 18 million tons in 1965 to 25 million in 1970 and 42 million in 1975. By 1970 there will be a need for nearly twice the amount of food aid the United States is now giving. By "turning loose all of our production," he said, we would only postpone the disaster for a few years. [Editor's note: Paddock quotes Secretary Freeman]

The most serious consequence of all would come at that time, probably about 1984, when the total U.S. agricultural productive capacity would no longer be sufficient to meet the food needs of the aid-recipient countries. This would lead to a breakdown of the world food economy with consequences that would range from catastrophic famine in many areas to an elemental struggle for the control of food resources. This pattern of massive food aid, by itself, would be a road to disaster.

In testimony before the House Agriculture Committee, the Secretary said the deficit will reach such a size that "by 1985 there would be no way to fill the gap." Thereupon he read to the Committee President Johnson's statement: "The time is not far off when all the combined production, on all of the acres of all the agriculturally productive nations, will not meet the food needs of the developing nations—unless present trends are changed."

This testimony of the Secretary is extremely important, partly because of his official position and partly because most other world leaders have refused so far to acknowledge such a serious prospect publicly. Nevertheless, I find I must challenge his department's conclusions. The deficit gap with its catastrophes will come upon us, in my opinion, in just half the time projected by the Department of Agriculture, that is, by 1975 instead of 1984.

The inability of the U.S. to avoid a decision in this whole field of food supplied to the underdeveloped world is dramatically posed in the following growing dilemma:

Recent scientific research in human nutrition suggests that the months immediately following weaning may be crucial in forming the brain. Should the child fail to get a minimum nutrition during that period, no amount of "environmental" aid can repair the damage.

In recent years, in such countries as India, the U.S. surplus food shipments have been preventing famine. But they have indirectly also kept hundreds of thousands, perhaps millions, of people just above the starvation line.

Some observers fear that we may be creating a whole new group of people who will not have the basic mental ability to earn their own living, who may not be trainable for even subsistence agriculture.

Yet, on strictly humanitarian grounds, it appears impossible to deny them food to keep them alive.

Is it, then, a problem with which we can refuse to cope? Or one which we can continue to permit to drift?

If we do, I can foresee the possibility in a decade or so of a new dilemma: Whether or not we provide the governments of the underdeveloped countries who cannot meet their food problem with the technical means to exterminate portions of their population? That kind of moral decision might well destroy the whole of our complex of civilized values—as the Nazis' decision to commit genocide almost destroyed the moral fabric of the Western World in the 1930-40s.

Inevitably, any discussion of progress on either the question of population control or of increased food production leads back to education and training methods in the new countries of Asia.

Here, again, the picture is black.

SOMBER EDUCATION PICTURE

EDUCATION in the colonial regimes was the most grievous failing of the European powers. British India, with 350 million people, where perhaps the British made the greatest effort anywhere in the Asian colonies, had only 116,615 students in institutions of higher learning in 1939. British Indian education was totally inadequate in the sense that it ill prepared the Indians, either for independence or for the tremendous task of modernizing their country with technology. It was an education for clerks, reinforcing the pre-industrial prejudices against "dirty-hands" labor needed to bring on the technical revolution.

That hangover is still there. A few years ago I visited an Indian experimental farm, a government institution dedicated to demonstration farming. An American technician and I called on the director of the farm, which was also a teaching institution. He reluctantly agreed to accompany us to look at some experimental plots. But while we walked about in shirt-sleeves, he accompanied us in a waistcoat with an employee who held a parasol over him to protect him from the sun. My American companion jumped down off the path into a field, showed me a plant by tearing it out of the ground. Our Indian host obviously had no interest, and the idea of actually touching the soil was totally abhorrent to him.

In Indonesia, the situation was even worse in Dutch times. There were five institutions of higher education in the country, including the Bandung Technical Institute, a glorified trade school (Soekarno finished there in 1926, one among only three Indonesians). In 1940, with a population of some 65 million, Indonesia had about 1,600 students enrolled in post-secondary schools.

In 1966, 58 per cent of the total enrollment in Indian institutions of higher education were studying law, literature, and the arts. This explains in part the ironic phenomenon that at a time when the underdeveloped nations of Asia desperately need trained technical manpower, tens of thousands of graduates of the universities in India, Pakistan, Indonesia, and other more prosperous Asian societies cannot find jobs.

The gap between what is called a university graduate in these countries and his actual educational attainments is, of course, large. A United States Information Service director in one of the largest university centers in South Asia complained bitterly to me that he could not fill jobs on his staff with qualified applicants, even though the salary scale he paid was better than other local employers and even though there was a large roster of unemployed graduates. He required at least an elementary speaking and writing knowledge of English. And although the university in the city taught *in English,* graduates holding a bachelor's degree in arts could not satisfy even a minimum standard of competence in the language.

In most of the former colonial countries, standards of the universities have deteriorated in large part because of this language problem, as their size has expanded. A friend teaching in a college of Bombay University, one of India's most prestigious faculties, told me he has an impossible job. He is asked to teach Shakespeare to a group of students whose English is not adequate. They are fed into the university system from lower schools which now are largely conducted in the vernacular tongue.

"I could teach them English as a foreign language, if I were permitted," he said. "But instead I am told to teach them Shakespeare and they simply do not have a minimum comprehension of the language."

The language problem poses a dilemma for all the universities in Asia: Should the language of the former colonial power (English, French, or Dutch) be continued as the medium of learning, providing access as it does to the whole historical background of the past three hundred years and the door to the new technological societies? Or must the schools shift to local languages to provide for students in their own tongue, with the concomitant problems of translations of texts and, in many cases, the creation of a whole new vocabulary for the technical learning?

The terrible thing that has happened too often is that a choice has been made which combines the worst of both possibilities. Schools have changed over to the new languages without proper teaching materials and learning has declined as a result. Or they have held on to a totally outmoded syllabus of the old system (grade school children were being taught Macaulay's essays by rote when last I was in Kerala, in a language they progressively understood less well).

In Vietnam, for example, the preparatory schools for the university were conducted not only in the French language, but largely along old French lycée principles. But the university in Saigon was using English for many of its courses. And where English was not used, an American method of teaching was sometimes superimposed on the French language and French curriculum. In Indonesia, the new Bahasa Indonesia often is used for students whose mother tongue is not the Malay basic to the new Indonesian language, which itself is largely artificial and as yet extremely limited in expressing technical or sophisticated concepts.

Faculties have suffered from the shortage of trained personnel throughout the whole society. They have been drained off into the growing government bureaucracy, into the new political machines, into business. Even when they remain with the universities or the schools, they often take on new tasks—moonlighting jobs—that leave little time for teaching. (All during 1966, for example, virtually the whole economics faculties of the Indonesian universities at Djakarta and Djogjakarta were at work on a government economic program for the new regime of General Soeharto. An Indonesian university faculty member was paid less than $20.00 a month.)

BASIC EDUCATION SUFFERS

Basic education has suffered and there is little hope anywhere that it has kept up with a steadily increasing population.

249

The numbers of young people to be educated in even the smallest countries of the region are astronomical. Singapore, for example, with only two million people, has a median age of only twenty-one years.

Illiteracy is on the increase throughout Asia. Statistics again are highly suspect, but it appears certain that the percentage of illiterates in the population has actually increased, as well as the absolute numbers.

The United Nations Economic and Social Council (ECOSOC) has estimated that the target for enrollment for primary education in Southeast Asia was 104 million in 1964. By 1980 it will have more than doubled to 225 million. The increase at the secondary level will be three or four times the 1964 figure. The increased need for vocational education will be seven times as great in 1980 as in 1964. And the need at a higher level of scientific and technological personnel will be three times as great. These estimates have been based on the need for trained personnel if development rates are to be kept at 5.7 per cent a year, probably a very optimistic target. But it is not one which would improve living standards to such a great degree as we have already seen from the population increase estimates.

Perhaps the most tragic aspect of the whole problem of skilled manpower in the new countries is the so-called brain drain. We have only a few solid statistical indicators of just how important it is. But the evidences are all round us. The Indian and Pakistan communities in Britain, for example, represent not only large numbers of highly skilled professionals from the Indo-Pakistan subcontinent. (The British National Health Insurance system could not function without the Indian and Pakistani doctors serving in it.) But tens of thousands of mechanics have also been drawn off to what by British standards are low-paid jobs, but which are attractive enough to bring immigrants from these countries. An Indian friend and economist, Ashoka Mehta, also makes the argument that they are psychologically the most important people in the society to push progress—the aggressive, the flexible, the ambitious.

The U.S. is every year importing almost half of the graduates of Philippine schools of medicine for staffing the growing American hospital and health services. Dozens of other doctors arrive from Asia each year. And the proportion of students who do not return home from university in the U.S. is very high. The Vietnamese colony in France—and, ironically, thousands serving with French aid services in Africa and Madagascar—not only include several prominent scientists, but also thousands of aggressive businessmen and technicians. Canada's hospitals are full of young Chinese doctors from Taiwan.

Australia, notorious in Asia for her historic exclusion of Asian immigrants, nevertheless has liberalized her immigration quotas to permit the admission of professionals and skilled workmen to meet her increasing needs for manpower. Since March 1966 "applications by non-Europeans (mostly Asians) wishing to settle in Australia will be considered individually on their merits, subject to general suitability, capacity to integrate and *their having useful skills and qualifications* (my italics)." In eighteen months ending September 1967, almost 2,500 have been granted permanent residence prior to their becoming eligible for citizenship status. These included doctors, "highly qualified persons," engineers, university professors, scientists, and others. The Australian government formally requires the young Asians who study there to return to their homelands for at least three years and work there, but even this is voided under certain conditions.

Thus, the frightening prospect: Asian populations are skyrocketing. Food prospects are dim. Educational programs to provide leadership to meet these problems are not under way in anything like the force necessary to begin to meet the problem. And an existing elite is increasingly demoralized by the prospects of the coming catastrophe.

What, then, will be the U.S relationship to this continuing crisis in Asia? What will be the U.S. role in this snowballing list of problems and complexities?

11 ✤

No Escape from Commitment

WE begin with a myth. It is the fiction of what American relations have been with Asia: The generally accepted idea that there has been little and relatively insignificant contact, or at most that it has been a one-way street of our impact on Asia.

True enough we are a European society. Our minorities of Negroes from Africa, Asians from the East, have played only a marginal role in forming our culture. But the texture of American history has always been laced with the threads of our involvement in Asia. The New World was, after all, discovered by our European ancestors looking for Asia. There is hardly a facet of American life which has not been vitally affected by the influence of our contact with the East.

Chester Bowles (an isolationist pre-World War II, by the way) has recalled that his alma mater, Yale, was founded with capital generated from cargoes carried from India and the East to Britain. Many a tight little New England town (and family) built its stability over a nest egg made from the China trade. Elias Haskett Derby of Salem, Massachusetts, perhaps America's first millionaire, died in 1799 leaving the largest fortune in the country, much of it earned in the India trade.

The trade in cotton textiles—sold by both Englishmen and New Englanders—and the export of raw cotton to the East was an important reason for the buildup of the cotton-slave-plantation economy in our South in the nineteenth century. And it could well be argued that this cotton trade with the Orient helped impor-

252

tantly to bring on the great catastrophe of the Civil War in 1860.

"Manifest Destiny," the dream of a continental nation stretching from the Atlantic to the Pacific, began early and always looked west—and on to the East. It is no accident that our "isolationists" of the last four decades have so often been "interventionists" when it came to Asia.

Seward was able to convince a reluctant Congress in 1867 that he should purchase Alaska from the Russians because his agents (along with a few healthy bribes to lawmakers) argued that the Pacific Basin would become the scene of world events in the future. When we built the railways to unite our two shores, we used Chinese coolie labor. Japanese immigrants and Punjabis from India played a key role in the vast agricultural development of California. Indian and British engineers came to advise Americans on the first big irrigation works in the West in the early 1900s.

As early as 1903 Teddy Roosevelt already was worried about a major war with Japan because of the bitter anti-Asian racism in the West. A good part of the fortune of Franklin Delano Roosevelt was based on his maternal ancestors' trade adventures in China, including opium.

And although we fought World War II for the principles of humanitarianism anchored in our European heritage, it was our foreign policy in East Asia which brought us into that war over tremendous domestic opposition.

U.S. power has played a key role in the Pacific almost from the founding of the Republic. The Japanese came "back into the world" after Commodore Perry's "black ships" forced the end of the isolation in 1853. It might have happened, anyway, a decade or so later. Yet the timing was crucial for Japan, and the world, for it gave her the last decades of the nineteenth century to "catch up."

JAPAN

OUT of this past comes one of the Pacific's most important realities of today: Japan is increasingly a major factor in world affairs and increasingly a pivot of U.S. policy and hopes for peace and security in the East—and the world.

The phenomenal Japanese economy is pulling the center of gravity of the industrialized world toward the Pacific. By 1970 Japan will be by all counts the third largest national economy in the world—ahead of West Germany, Britain and France, only smaller than the U.S. and the U.S.S.R.

Furthermore, the more optimistic Japanese economists—proved right in the past—believe the per capita income in Japan will double by 1973. There are even predictions that it will go from the present $1,000 a year to $4,000 a year by 1980, which is about the present level of the standard of living in Western Europe.

These predictions are not as immoderate as they would appear at first glance to those who have not followed in detail Japan's remarkable recovery from World War II. The Japanese moved back to prewar levels by 1955. Since then the gross national product has been climbing on an average of 10 per cent annually.

Japan already leads the world in shipbuilding (half the world's total tonnage in 1966). Its automobile industry has passed West Germany for second place. Steel production, long used as the prime indicator of industrialization, is third largest in the world; in 1967 Japanese production equaled West Germany's and Britain's combined.

It is among the world's leaders in a host of other important manufactures. Research in electronics, optics, and chemicals, one of the great tests of modern industrial progress, is competitive to the U.S. and Western Europe. No longer do Japanese industries simply copy.

The U.S. trade magazine *Electronics*, not given to handing out bouquets to foreign manufacturers in the highly competitive field, had this to say in a 1967 "commentary" entitled "Nippon at our Heels":

> There's a lot to be learned from what the Japanese are doing. Although they still build on others' basic technology, mostly American, [author's note: Something that might be said for U.S. industries' use of British and German scientific breakthroughs in the past thirty years in radar, jet propulsion, plastics, chemistry, etcetera, and even nuclear science] they tend to add unique twists to processing and design and are particularly ingenious in finding new applications.

Living standards today are already at about Italy's level. The diet is improving rapidly. Japanese homes have more television than any except those of the United States. Japan's problems are already our problems: Smogbound, crowded cities, snarled urban communications, growing social problems of "the generation gap," and technological unemployment coupled with a lack of skilled technicians.

The sinews of trade are binding us ever closer to this industrial power. In the six years from 1959 to 1965, American exports to Japan doubled, making her our No. 2 customer (after Canada, a very special U.S. trading partner and, in fact, virtually part of our own economy). They are expected to more than double again by the mid-seventies.

No American has to be reminded of the growing avalanche of Japanese consumers' goods that has become a part of the American way of life. The U.S. has become Japan's No. 1 customer—at the staggering sum of almost $3 billion in 1967.

Behind this mighty industrial complex in East Asia stands the great potential of Japanese military power. No one of my generation can forget it. The tenacity of the Japanese soldier is legendary (it is interesting to compare it with some of the recent writing about the fanaticism of the Vietnamese Communist fighter).

Japanese military science was remarkable, too, given the supposed inferiority of Japanese technology before World War II. We learned to our dismay that the Zero was more maneuverable than our fighters at the outset of the war, that stories of it being put together with baling wire were a typical product of European chauvinism directed against the "Asiatics."

Despite the Japanese constitution—written largely at American dictation under General Douglas MacArthur's military occupation—which prohibits war and the maintenance of a military force, Japan's "self-defense forces" today total more than 250,000 men. That force could be expanded extremely rapidly. The Japanese have been historically among the best soldiers in the world.

In the current five-year, $9 billion expansion plan, these forces will surpass those of Italy. Even in simple statistical terms the Japanese will have by 1971 a force greater than most of the European allies in the North Atlantic Treaty Organization.

Weighed in the balance must also be the technological capability of the Japanese—in these days of electronic and cybernetic warfare as important as manpower and military tradition.

"Considering the narrow confines within which it must operate, JASDF (Japan Air Self-Defense Forces) has developed into a surprisingly well-equipped and efficient air arm—probably the most powerful in the Far East next to the United States and Soviet air units in the region," *Air Force*, the organ of the U.S. Air Force Association, wrote in December 1967.

Japan's potential military strength includes advanced missile-carrying destroyers armed through her electronics industry, the world's second largest and a pioneer in many types of research.

Japan has an acknowledged atomic potential. She is already turning to nuclear power in an attempt to lower her fuel imports, the largest of any country in the world. By 1975 she will be producing annually probably three tons of plutonium, the basic ingredient of the atomic bomb. (By 1980, it is expected that her nuclear power-generating capacity—based on imported technology—will equal West Germany's and Britain's.) With her already growing technology in the use of American missiles, supplied under the present Japanese-American Mutual Security Treaty, she could develop a delivery system for a bomb in relatively short order.

That presupposes, of course, a political decision. And for the past two decades a militant pacifist mood in Japan, backed by a vocal and well-organized pro-Communist minority, has rejected full-scale rearmament. Yet I do not believe that the twenty-year "concussion," brought on by the defeat of the Japanese military in 1945 and the nuclear holocaust she suffered in the final days of World War II, is a permanent characteristic of the Japanese outlook. Her present passive and immobile role in world affairs is not in the traditions of Japanese history nor the character of her people.

Historians like Sir G. F. Sansom believe that Japan was ready to embark on an essentially imperialistic role when the European conquerors arrived on the scene in East Asia. And there is considerable evidence, for example, that had the Spaniards not arrived in the Philippines when they did, Japanese rulers at the time would have considered a military adventure there.

"It now seems obvious that Japan can no longer indulge solely in the pursuit of her self-interest aims of economic expansion," Michio Royama, a prominent Japanese academic wrote in 1967. "In recent years, increasing pressures from within and without have been brought to bear upon Japanese political leaders, as well as the thinking public, urging Japan to take up a greater role in Asia. As discussions of the problems of Japan's national security and her role in Asia grow among political, journalistic, and academic circles, some people see this as a healthy and welcome sign of normalization, while others worry about it as a revival of militarism and imperialism. Both viewpoints have validity."

> . . . The various images of Japan—as the wealthiest industrial power in Asia, as the power that in the past committed a grave act of aggression in Asia and arrogantly aspired for the leadership of the Greater East Asia Co-Prosperity Sphere, and as the power that prospers under the American military protection— are not adapted to form a cohesive whole. They produce suspicions in the minds of Asians, and anxiety in the minds of Japanese, while they create dissatisfaction in the minds of Americans.
>
> . . . If Japan must succeed in convincing her fellow Asian nations that she is not party to an American conspiracy, she must reconcile her interests with American policy in this sphere. How far can she assert her own independent view? To what extent can she co-operate with the United States, Taiwan [Nationalist China], South Korea, Thailand, or, for that matter, Australia and New Zealand, while at the same time trying to pose as *non*-anti-Communist? These are "political" problems, which seem to have been raised as a result of Japan's pursuit of an ostensibly "economic" policy.

Already, in the fall of 1967, Prime Minister Sato dared to speak —despite the opposition of the left wing in Japanese politics representing some third of the nation's voters—of Japan's need to see to her own defenses. He asked the Japanese to be "realistic," to see the significance of Okinawa, now in American hands, for

257

the defense of the region. And he hinted that a bargain might be struck with the Americans in which the island, a major cause of political agitation in Japan, might "revert" to Japanese control as had been promised in the World War II Peace Treaty, if Japan would assume some of the U.S. defense burden in the region.

The issue will arise in dramatic force in 1970 when the present U.S.-Japan treaty comes up for possible abrogation after one year's notice.

When Japan assumes her place—a position forced upon her by her own industrial and economic strength—in the balance of world power, she is likely to take up also a more independent foreign policy position. And that stance is to be a permanent concern of the U.S. in the coming decades.

For those who have doubts about Japan's abilities to pursue her own self-interest, it is important to note the process of importing foreign—principally American—technology and raising the productivity of Japan's industry since World War II. At a moment when Western Europe is increasingly concerned with the economic power arising from the superior U.S. technology, which even French chauvinists and industrialists admit they cannot do without, Japan has developed a pattern of transfer which has protected ownership of her industrial complex.

In fact, American equity investment has fallen proportionately in Japanese industry during the period of great expansion since the end of the Korean War. However much free-trade and free-capital flow apostles may regret the Japanese restrictive practices, the fact is that the Japanese have found a way to have their cake and eat it too: They have imported a maximum of essential American technology with a minimum of direct U.S. business control.

An Achilles' heel of the giant Japanese economy and the present structure of the state is her almost total dependence on imported raw materials. That dependence will grow rather than lessen in the coming decade as the whole size of the economy expands. For example, by 1985 Japanese fuel dependence on crude oil will grow from 58 per cent in 1965 to 75 per cent, despite an increase in nuclear power and increased home-produced coal and natural gas. That will mean that dependence on overseas raw materials for the total energy supply will increase from 66 per cent in 1965 to as much as 89 per cent in 1985. Japan now imports 85 per cent of its iron ore; that will rise to 90 per cent. Copper imports will rise from 45 per cent in 1955 to 80 per cent by 1975. Almost self-sufficient in wood pulp in 1966, Japan will have to import 58 per cent by 1975.

The oil will have to come from the Middle East and Southeast Asia, moving through areas which are already troubled, extremely vulnerable to political instability. Japan will be almost totally dependent on these supply lines. And, in fact, we may well see in our times a modified version of "the lifeline of the British Empire" which stretched across South Asia in the nineteenth century, this time linked from West to East to Japan.

Central to Japan's role in world affairs will be—as it has been throughout her history—her relationship with China. Someday (it is a pity that the great master Freud himself did not attempt it) someone will apply psychoanalytical methods to the problem of the relations of the Japanese and the Chinese. I can contribute only a ten-cent diagnosis by pointing to the obvious love-hate between a people who have borrowed much of the external trappings of their culture—including a major portion of their language—from another.

In fact, such is the reverence of the Japanese for the traditional values of the Chinese that you can make a case for what an old Chinese scholar once told me in Taiwan: The old classic values of China, dynamited so assiduously by the Communists, can only be found in Japan today. Yet the Japanese have an archetype sense of inferiority to the Chinese.

During a substantial residence in Japan, I carried on one little experiment of my own. I had a dilettante interest in Chinese calligraphy—the writing of the ideographs used in Chinese (and Japanese). These were, of course, developed in China and carried to Japan at a period before the Japanese, themselves, had developed a method of writing.

Whatever modifications the Japanese have made, then, have not changed the fundamental character of the Chinese script. On the other hand, Japanese art forms have a basic value of their own. They are of such artistic force that they were a major factor in shaping Western painting toward the end of the last cen-

259

tury through their influence on the French Impressionists. Thus, it is clear that while it may be a different style, a different aesthetic value from classic Chinese calligraphy, Japanese calligraphy (using the basic Chinese characters) has its own heritage and flair. Yet in years of asking Japanese whenever the subject came up, I never found one—not even one chauvinist—who would say that Japanese calligraphy was even an equal of, much less better than, Chinese.

JAPAN'S RELATIONSHIP TO CHINA

Or take another example: During the so-called Great Leap Forward beginning in 1958, the Chinese Communists tried to push their people into an unheard-of sprint of industrial and agricultural growth. It was a time of madness—whether induced purposefully by Mao Tse-tung to break with the overwhelming Chinese past that forever threatens to dilute any attempt at radical modification, or because party fanaticism got the upper hand over technology. (A sample of the mood during this period was the statement that the law of diminishing returns was "a Western bourgeois concept" without relevance in People's China.)

I was reporting for an American business weekly at that time in Japan and Hong Kong. My exposure to the hard statistics of manufacturing and agricultural growth in my own country and elsewhere in Asia, including Japan, made me extremely dubious that Peking's statistics were valid. They were being accepted by many people, generally those expert on China but not acquainted with such figures in other countries. This acceptance was due in part to the fact that until that time the Communist regime in China had been almost maddeningly legalistic and correct, if you were careful to note exactly what they were saying in their propaganda.

In an effort to arrive at some hard judgments, I went the rounds of the Japanese industrial companies. Many of the large firms had had some role in the development of Manchuria in the 1930s and 1940s under Japanese military occupation. And it was obvious that the Manchurian complex was still the heart of any Chinese industrialization program.

In addition, hundreds of Japanese technicians had not been repatriated from Manchuria following the defeat of 1945. They had stayed, or had been held on, at their former jobs, first by the Russians who occupied Manchuria in the last days of the war or later by the Chinese Communists. In several cases, I spoke directly to these people who had returned after the end of the Korean War in 1953.

I would pull out the latest figures on production in China—sometimes broken down in terms of a particular industry in Manchuria—from the reports of Chinese propaganda agencies. The initial reaction of the Japanese technicians was almost always the same: If the Chinese say they are doing it, they must be. Astonished, over and over again, I repeated the same process with the same result.

I would start with Communist figures. We would analyze the potential base on which the Chinese had worked. In most cases, the Chinese were only running out the plans for expansion and production worked out by the Japanese managers earlier.

Then we would test the possibility and the probability of the Chinese reaching the goals listed in the propaganda reports. Repeatedly, we came up with the same results—it was not possible.

All of this was confirmed later on when the whole bubble of the Great Leap burst, and the Chinese, themselves, admitted the total fiction of the statistics. Yet, the only reason I could deduce for why my Japanese contacts were willing initially to accept the reports was a kind of basic awe for the Chinese.

I think it takes nothing from my argument, of course, to say that the Japanese often have an equally strong tendency to denigrate the Chinese. They often, for example, refer—at least the ordinary Japanese does—to the Chinese' "dirty habits." It is a theme I know well from Southeast Asia, where even if Thai or Javanese or Burman can find no other debit to set beside the Overseas Chinese' superior drive and ambition, he points—and quite rightly—to the less importance the Chinese attaches to personal cleanliness than do the Brahminized cultures of South Asia.

THE FUTURE

The possibility of a Japan-Communist China alliance appears on the surface illogical. Japan is, after all, an industrial power. China, whether she be Communist or non-Communist, will continue to be, in the foreseeable future, an essentially underdeveloped country. The gap in living standards is widening between the two countries—just as it is widening between the industrialized and the underdeveloped regions all over the world.

Japan's interests lie in the growing partnership with the U.S. and the rest of the industrialized world. It is there where she can sell her products and, ironically, buy much of her raw materials more cheaply. (In 1967 she bought $900 million in agricultural products and raw materials from the U.S.)

But logic does not always govern the affairs of nations as it does not always determine the lives of individuals.

A famous Japanese woman writer, a brave anti-totalitarian who was beaten and imprisoned by the infamous *kempeitai* ("thought police") for her opposition to the militarists and the Pacific War, told me a few years ago, "I don't know what it is. But I feel the pull of Communist China on us is just like the inevitable pull of the events toward war before 1937. It is like standing on a beach with the tide eroding the sand under your feet."

I believe that a failure of the U.S. to maintain her commitment in Asia—both military and nonmilitary—would increase that erosion. And it could put the enormously powerful industrial might of Japan into the hands of a new Oriental alliance bent on war and world conquest. If that seems far fetched, read the warning of the late 1930s that went unheeded by so many in this country and which cost us more than 100,000 dead in the Pacific between 1941 and 1945.

Royama, who is relatively sanguine about the threat to Japan from Communist China and who seems to believe that the best role for Japan and for the major powers is one of her continued "neutrality," does point up the drama of her future difficulties.

Discussing the possibilities of Chinese Communist "nuclear blackmail" against Japan once Peking has developed an atomic military potential, he says:

> . . . China will have an excellent opportunity to try Japanese morale when she reaches a stage at which she has to conduct a

series of I.C.B.M. [intercontinental ballistics missile] tests. She will naturally choose the Pacific Ocean as a testing ground, because the Chinese land mass is not large enough for such a test. This will be a severe trial for the political and psychological stability of Japan, because it is more than likely that the test will coincide with a political row about "the year 1970."

CHINA

IF the U.S. relationship to this highly industrialized, powerful, and—I believe in present terms—volatile Japan, must be the major concern of American policy-makers in the coming decades, China itself will be only slightly less important.

History has proved over and over again—in our times tiny Israel against the huge numbers of Arabs nominally united around and against her—that power does not reside alone in numbers. Yet perhaps the Marxists do have a point in their theory that a quantitative change, if it is big enough, becomes qualitative.

China today is a country of probably some 780 million people. We can only guess at this figure, much less estimate where it will go in the coming years. But it is probably safe to say that it cannot be expanding at less than 3 per cent a year. By 1985 China could well reach a population of one billion.

We know from the bitter experiences of birth-control attempts in other areas of Asia and Africa to which we have access that whatever the Chinese leadership attempts, it will have no great immediate success at stemming this tide.

We can hope for, we can perhaps expect, major breakthroughs in the next ten years in new methods of contraception, but they will come in the Western-Japan industrialized world with its resources of technology. And there is now little hope that whatever is developed will quickly get through the natural barriers and the ideological fences that the Chinese Communists themselves have thrown up to bar the projection of this technology into their vast geographical areas.

These numbers will pose enormous problems for any Chinese leadership as they already do. I can only believe that Mao Tse-tung rationalizes with his comments to foreign visitors that China, because of these numbers, is the only power that could survive an atomic war. It may be true that China, because of the vast numbers of her population, would still have millions alive after atomic bombardment. But what would be the nature of a country with her major cities and industries wiped out? Numbers only are not a criterion for warfare in our time.

Yet China's manpower resources are without parallel—one-quarter of the human race—and must be thrown into any equation.

By 1965 Communist China had already proved again the strange paradox of our times: She could not feed herself during the fifteen years since the Communists took over and again established in the country one central authority. (China imported some 6.3 million tons of wheat during crop year 1965-66—3.5 per cent of her own food grain production. These figures do not, of course, reflect more than a marginal attempt to meet over-all food needs, but only the minimum caloric problem. And it is significant that the figure has been growing over the past five years.)

But by using her resources in a peculiar fashion we have come to see repeated time and time again in the twentieth century, China was able to build a threatening military machine—including an atomic bomb and a standing army of three million men. Just as the Russian newspapers complain of tremendous shortages at the same time they boast of the newest space probes, the Chinese regime has been able to pursue a similar system of priorities on a more ruthless and primitive scale.

President John F. Kennedy enunciated the problem that China will pose for the foreseeable future in a press conference of August 1, 1963, just before his assassination: "I would regard that combination (a huge population and a bellicose foreign policy) if it is still in existence in the 1970s, of weak countries around it, seven hundred million people, a Stalinist internal regime, and nuclear power, and a government determined on war as a means of bringing about its ultimate success, as potentially a more dangerous situation than any we faced since the end of the Second World War. . . ."

Four years later in the summer of 1967, the U.S. Congress Joint Committee on Atomic Energy laid down the "scientific" basis of the problem we would have to meet in hearings on the Chinese nuclear potential. The committee's report, only part of which was released publicly, concluded:

> Perhaps most significant for the United States is the fact that a low order of magnitude attack could possibly be launched by the Chinese Communists against the United States by the early 1970s. At present we do not have an effective antiballistic missile system which could repel such a suicidal (for the Chinese) but nevertheless possible strike.

And this was followed by Secretary McNamara's announcement on September 18 that the U.S. was to undertake a "thin" antiballistic missile defense of the U.S. against bombardment, from the Chinese and not the Russians.

Whether indeed this was the principal reason for the new round in the armaments buildup in the U.S. arsenal—some have seen the Pentagon's thesis of a Chinese threat as primarily a suberfuge in the continuing maneuvering to reach some sort of permanent nuclear arms settlement with the Russians—it is clear that such a Chinese threat is real to many of those people concerned with problems of our national security.

SOUTHEAST ASIA

INTIMATELY connected with both the problems of Japan's growing power, its relationship to China, and the Chinese threat to American security itself, is Southeast Asia. In the arc from Hong Kong to Calcutta live some 300 million people. They represent the greatest power vacuum in Asia—twelve relatively small (excluding Indonesia) countries (including East Pakistan) just emerging on the world scene after centuries of dominance by the European colonial powers.

Most, by the standards of China, India, or Japan, are underpopulated. Before World War II and the subsequent dislocations of the Japanese occupation, nationalist upheavals, and the inability of their post-independence regimes to maintain security and progress, they were the rice bowl of Asia.

Burma, Indochina, and Thailand exported a total of 6.5 million tons of rice in 1939. Despite increases in their own populations and only a minimum of stability, with new agricultural methods, the region is conservatively capable of exporting 20 million tons of food grains annually today without the introduction of new seed varieties, fertilizer, insecticides, and additional irrigation.

In addition, the region is rich in other raw materials—rubber, tin, petroleum, vegetable oils, fibers—essential to expanding economies of nations either seeking to raise their standards of living or to build war machines. Japan, riding its postwar rehabilitation and boom, has a crucial need for markets in these areas. In 1966 nearly 12 per cent of her exports of chemicals, manufactured goods, machinery and transport equipment were sold in Southeast Asia. And the Southeast Asians supplied Japan with almost 15 per cent of her raw materials, a figure that could increase dramatically if stability returns to the area.

Since 1950, a cornerstone of U.S. policy in Asia has been to deny these raw materials to Communist China on the kind of colonial terms that the Russians used to exploit Eastern Europe from 1945 to 1956. (I use 1956 because of the Gomulka revolt inside the Communist party in Poland, which began to reverse the terms of trade which had until that time been rigged to favor the Russian partner in its dealings with the East Europe Communist states.)

The problem is complicated by the existence in Southeast Asia of the huge Overseas Chinese minority. In all the countries in the area, the Chinese have a virtual stranglehold on retail trade. And should Chinese Communist military power become dominant in the area, many observers believe that Peking's ability to consolidate its economic control could follow as a matter of course through this use of the Overseas Chinese infrastructure.

Through immigration of Chinese, "milking" the area through exploitive terms of trade (much as the European colonial powers did during their control), through the use of the region's vast raw materials and food, control of southeast Asia would enhance the ability of any Chinese totalitarian regime to meet its problems at home. And it could thereby weaken those forces in China which, hopefully, one day would return China to its traditional path of solving its economic problems at home, a China which would play a leading role in peaceful collaboration with the international effort in all the underdeveloped countries to find paths of progress and development.

There is certainly the argument that a Chinese rule of Southeast Asia would encounter the same kind of resistance that any colonial regime might expect from the growing nationalist sentiment in the area. There is, for example, the more than 2,000-year-long history of Vietnamese resistance to Chinese rule.

But there is also ample evidence in the history of the area that a ruthless conqueror might still be able to maintain control. Even nationalism—as I have tried to show—is only skin deep or, to continue the metaphor, a rash which breaks out here and there in most of these new states. And a sophisticated Chinese state would be more than a match for it, reinforced by its military power—if the U.S. shield were removed. After all, let it be added: Vietnamese history is largely the account of *unsuccessful* attempts to beat off Chinese domination and/or suzerainty. Total Vietnamese independence from China in its long history before the nineteenth-century French conquest was only a matter of a few decades.

One of the supports often offered to back the argument that Southeast Asian nationalisms would defeat the Chinese is the experience in East Europe (more rightly called Central Europe) in the twenty years since the end of World War II. There, too, weak (in military and political terms) new states were the victims of a new imperialism from the Soviet Union. But, so the argument runs, nationalism plus the Soviet Union's own problems have been sufficient to break the hammerlock of Russian control. These states (it is sometimes argued too cynically, considering the suffering that existed under Stalinism and still goes on in much of Central Europe) are slowly but surely making their way toward independence in the prosecution of their own destinies.

Accepting this argument on its face value for its relevance to Asia, there are two great differences: Most of the East European states are countries which historically have had cultures as old and rich as Russia's, economies that in many ways were more sophisticated; for example, the Germanized Czechs for centuries had a standard of living higher than that in what is now the Soviet Union. Southeast Asia has, on the other hand, a set of "moonlight" cultures. These were cultures which, before the coming of the European colonialists, were dominated by ideological concepts from either China or India. And their living standards, while possibly higher since abundant food and tropical climates make a subsistence livelihood easy, are worked out in relatively less sophisticated economies than China's.

But I believe there is a much more compelling reason for not accepting this historical parallel. Whatever freedom has come to East Europe in the past decade since the East Berlin revolt and the subsequent struggles in the breaking free of Soviet control in Belgrade, Budapest, Warsaw, Bucharest, and Prague has come about in part because of the real and psychological pressures of a resurgent Western Europe on the other flank. The success of the Marshall Plan and the great prosperity of Western Europe, the defensive power of the NATO alliance (and remember that the Hungarian rebels *thought* the West Europeans and the Americans would come to their aid in 1956) played an enormous role in "springing" the East Europeans.

Unfortunately for Asia, only Japan—isolated by the peculiarities of her own culture from the rest of the continent—provides any such alternative to Chinese power in Asia. India, although its civilization is basic to most of South Asia, is not only a sleeping giant. Her performance during the past twenty years has given a negative image to the rest of South Asia.

In 1948 Charles Tambu, one of the first representatives of the Indonesian Republic, then still unrecognized in the West, told me, "We know that we are ripe in Southeast Asia to be the colonial dependents of the Indians or the Chinese. We want neither. And we are going to do everything we can to keep out of either one of their clutches—including playing them off against each other."

That statement today in Southeast Asia would not even bring a hollow laugh. No one in Southeast Asia today looks to India for leadership, either politically or economically. Indian poverty is notorious—even among those countries whose religions are derived from India and whose every day-to-day cultural identity is largely shaped by Hindu concepts. The Indian fiasco of 1962 when she was at Communist China's mercy has confirmed this contempt. It has been reinforced by the curious habit of Indian representatives—from V. K. Krishna Menon at the Bandung Conference in 1955 to the present day—to attempt to "lord it over" other South Asians.

INDIA

THIS leads me to our fourth East Asian element—India, itself.

It is the inevitable comparison between aggressive, disciplined, organized China and passive, dispirited, and badly organized India that leads many Asian hands to ignore India—either as a threat to Asian peace and security or to the possibility of its playing a positive role. Again a huge population, but in comparison to China a potentially richer country with enormous, easily exploitable raw materials.

Americans interested and knowledgeable in Asian affairs—in part because of the general Sinophilic character of our bureaucracy and Asian experts—generally see India as an American concern in only moral or negative geopolitical terms. A few, like Ambassador Chester Bowles, believe India is an alternative to Chinese power, to the Chinese example of dynamism under a totalitarian system. But they are rare.

I hold still another thesis: It is true, as most observers are quick to point out, that India's role in Asia has been passive. Her history is a tale of invasions from the north, of layers on layers of new overlords who come, rule, are defeated by the climate and the heritage. Whatever role she has had in the all-Asian scene has been largely by acculturation.

I would like to suggest another possibility, however vague, but one which I believe we must keep in mind. Years ago when I was a child in North Carolina, an old friend, the writer Lillian Smith, and I were discussing Wendell L. Willkie. Despite his "internationalism," many of us in the South could remember only one thing—that he had been the lawyer for the giant utility corporations. And in our area, on the edge of the Tennessee Valley Authority with its life and death struggle in the 1930s with the huge utility combines, this was synonymous with evil. Miss Smith said

269

something I have always remembered: An individual's nature rarely changes. But it does sometimes happen under great pressure. She meant that Willkie's newfound humanitarianism was real, brought on by an enormous new set of intellectual stimuli when he was nominated for President.

National character, too, doesn't often change fundamentally. It accounts in great part for the continuity of history. But under tremendous pressures a nation's personality sometimes does change. The Mongolians, after rampaging through the whole of the Eurasian mainland, settled down to become peaceful horse breeders on the steppes of central Asia. (The Russians stopped paying tribute to the Mongols only in 1480.) Or the Swedes, who conquered most of northern Europe in the seventeenth century, became the modern epitome of pacifism and stability. (We know little about the reverse process—what brought on the huge migratory waves of the barbarian hordes from central Asia that broke up the Roman Empire, for example—because a conquering people's fall is usually better documented than its rise.)

The Indian civilization could be on the verge, in historic terms, of such a change. Population explosion could force the Indians out of their traditional preoccupation with passive philosophical attitudes. Or, as one Indian friend puts it, "If you live in Kerala [a state on the southwest coast of India] where the population has increased by 25 per cent in the last few years, it is awfully hard to maintain traditional values. I don't care what kind of philosophical attitudes you have—two people just can't stand on the same piece of ground!"

When I first went out to Asia during and just after World War II, it was extremely fashionable and accepted in most circles where China was known best, to predict the new Communist leadership would never consolidate their position. "No one can rule China," "Chinese family life will defeat the Communists," "China is too big," it was said.

In the long run, these people may be proved right. But, meanwhile, in our generation a unified, militarily powerful China must be at least considered a strong possibility. Despite the events of the Cultural Revolution, that possibility remains. And we know— now—how fragile such power structures can be, yet go on from conquest to conquest; e.g., Hitler's Germany or Stalin's Russia.

India, under the hammer blows of population explosion, humiliation at the hands of outside forces, demoralization of her elite, and even partial application of imported new technology, could also change. And India, at least theoretically, under totalitarian leadership has enormous raw materials and human resources. Not only does she have abundant raw materials for steel, probably oil, radioactive minerals, potential for vast agricultural yield increases; but she has a military tradition. The soldier in Indian history has never been the pariah in India that was his assigned place in traditional Chinese Confucian culture; in fact, he is the hero-god of all Indian literature.

Already overtaxed by the problems of the area, I do not suggest the possibility of such a threat to the security of other nations be taken as a primary concern of U.S. policy. I am only suggesting that the power potential of India cannot be ignored.

AUSTRALIA-NEW ZEALAND

THE problem of Australia-New Zealand defense also looms up out of the future. On two counts, the cultural affinity between our societies and the great industrial potential—compared to its population—of Australasia will be something no American policymakers can ignore. The Australians-New Zealanders are a people sharing our most cherished heritage of representative government, our language, our ideals. And the Australian gross national product of $22 billion tops most of her Asian neighbors.

To put it in its most brutal form, the fourteen million people in the Australasian area are a hostage to our Asian policies. One could envisage a cataclysmic crisis in which the Australians and the New Zealanders would simply be evacuated to North America (as the Algerian Europeans were to France in 1962). But a far more likely sequence of events is a further strengthening of the already extremely close military cooperation that began with the Japanese threat to Australasia in World War II and produced in 1951 the Australian-New Zealand-U.S. (ANZUS) military alliance pledging the Americans to their defense.

But it is not only the Australasians who look to America for leadership and guidance. All of the non-Communist regimes in Asia today depend on the U.S. and its nuclear shield as the basis of their policies.

C. Rajagopalachari, the grand old man of Indian politics and an influential member of the group around Gandhi that won independence, put it this way in his weekly *Swarajya* in January 1967:

> The age of Western domination of Asia is over. . . . An age of partnership has begun, building up a balance of power containing economic, political and military components against the long-range threats confronting non-Communist Asia. The government of India's attitude towards the Vietnam struggle and the U.S.A.'s part in it should change into a clearer and wiser pattern. No unsportsmanlike tripping from behind should be indulged in against a friendly power which for reasons issuing out of a wide objective of world peace, is fighting *our* [author's italics] battle—accepting the responsibilities attached to power.
>
> The *People's Daily*'s appeal in the name of Mao Tse-tung for armed disorders all over the world—to "learn warfare through warfare"—and the fifth Chinese [atomic] test explosion of last week are loud warnings. The hope of preserving democracy in India depends on an effective balance of power built up in Asia on the basis of a partnership with the U.S.A. . . .

Americans at home do not always appreciate the strength of such sentiments in critical public statements about our policy, or lack of statements in our support, from Asians in one crisis or another. But private conversations with old friends in all the chancelleries of Asia present a different picture. On a visit to India in the summer of 1967, for example, a senior Indian diplomat, smiling ruefully, volunteered to open the conversation with the following: "You know, you will find a good deal more support for your stand on Vietnam in this ministry than our public statements would indicate."

There is a good deal of truth to the answer I once got from a Pakistani leader asking why he and others in his country applied a double standard to the behavior of the U.S. and the Communist powers in Asia. He said, rather naively I thought, the criticism of the Americans was "in the family," and that one is always more frank and direct with relatives than with strangers. Or to put it another way: In most local codes of law in Asia, the wealthier participant in an automobile accident is expected to carry a greater part of the burden of the cost, whoever is actually responsible. Why? Because he obviously can afford to pay. In the task of containing aggression in Asia, the U.S. is "rich man" to the Asian nationalists.

One of the most bitter critics in the non-Communist Asian world of U.S. policy has put the basic issue bluntly. Prince Norodom Sihanouk, chief of state of Cambodia, wrote in 1965:

> I have never had the slightest illusion about the fate that awaits me at the hands of the Communists, as well as that which is reserved for my government, after having removed from our region the influence, and especially the presence, of the "free world," and the USA in particular.
>
> . . . I concede again that after the disappearance of the USA from our region and the victory of the Communist camp, I myself and the People's Socialist Community that I have created will inevitably disappear from the scene.

ARE WE MR. FIX-IT?

THAT I believe, in part, is the answer to the question: Are we—in the United States—the world's policeman, Mr. Fix-it? Perhaps not, but a good part of the world expects us to play that role.

I am not an "Asia-firster." I am convinced that modern transport and communications make the world really whole; American security and U.S. foreign policy must conceive of the globe as its arena for policy-making. It is largely irrelevant to talk about "far-away" places in which the U.S. is "bogged down." My generation remembers all too well British Prime Minister Neville Chamberlain's famous words when he returned to London in 1938 with "peace for our time" after selling out the interests of the democracies to Hitler. He spoke of the Central European crisis as a quarrel in a "faraway country between people of whom we know nothing." World War II was to break out only a year later over essentially the same problems.

"A great many things—historic, political, ethnic, cultural, sentimental—affect national interests, including a residue of past technologies like the methods of ocean transport that durably linked Great Britain, Spain, France, Portugal, and the Netherlands to some of the remotest parts of the world," writes Albert Wohlstetter in an article on "Illusions of Distance."

> But future technologies will affect interests, too, and on the whole in a direction that makes the new isolationism pure nostalgia. . . .
>
> High pay-load jets will cover distances still more quickly and cheaply, but may increase the queues. Supersonic jets will be economic only on long trips. Their principal result will be to bring the remote places closer. It has been pointed out that if sonic booms prevent supersonic aircraft from flying over land, New York will once again, as in the time before the building of the transcontinental railroad, be closer to Europe than to Los Angeles. Passenger traffic in the Pacific should increase still more strikingly. Travel time from Los Angeles to Tokyo may be cut by nearly two-thirds. It will perhaps take forty minutes more than to get from Los Angeles to New York.

We have had a striking demonstration of the new technology with the closing of the Suez Canal because of the Israeli-Egyptian struggle in mid-1967. Japan almost immediately started shipping some goods to West Germany by sea to Seattle, overland by rail to New York, and then by sea to Hamburg. And the route was only twenty-eight days as compared with forty-four days through Suez! The Japanese have found that for certain high-value, low-density items, such as electronic parts, the bill was cheaper—and the route is likely to remain a permanent one.

On the cultural front, the great tourist migration to the East from the U.S. has only begun. The U.S. gold drain notwithstanding, the age of the secretaries' two-week visits to Japan, Hong Kong, and Southeast Asia has yet to start. Three out of four American tourists in 1966 went to Europe. As the total continues to grow, and the "veterans" begin to look elsewhere and modes of transport to the East cheapen and quicken, Asia appears more and more likely as a destination.

Already in the summer of 1968 there were 101 weekly flights from North America to Asia. And tourist industry officials were

274

predicting that within a few years there would be a 700 per cent increase over 1967's two million visitors to Asia. This mass cultural impact is likely to expand the present "hippie Orientalism" to a broader influence on U.S. life.

SOVIET UNION

It is in the context of the world scene that I would try to make another point: For the foreseeable future, the Soviet Union with its vast resources is the principal potential source of power that can threaten U.S. security. Perhaps the optimists are correct; perhaps the Soviets are inexorably launched on a road of internal liberalization and external accommodation with the U.S. Yet I question whether that decision has been made, at least if a decision with no turning back has been effected. Ultimately the Russians will have to face a dilemma of whether they are prepared to live under a system of liberalization and its demands for a rising standard of living, or continue their competition with the vastly more productive U.S. for world leadership. Despite Khrushchev's threats of the early '60s to "bury" us, the Soviet Union has fallen behind in the effort of both countries to increase their rates of growth.

I am not sure that the decision—or the vast long set of decisions—is certain to be for the latter choice. For, in fact, has Russian history during the past three hundred years not been one of Russia exerting her force in Europe ("the world" in those centuries) far beyond her resources at the expense of producing the good life for her people? The tsars sat in the councils of Europe only because their peasantry—until 1917—was willing to subsist under living standards below those of the rest of Europe. Will the young Russian intellectual of today be prepared to give up the Soviet role as a nuclear-armed superpower deciding the fate of many countries in the world as the price of liberality and rising living standards at home?

Russia, too, is an Asian, a Pacific power. In fact, the continental thrust which culminated in her arrival on the Sea of Japan was completed only shortly after the U.S. acquisition of California (Vladivostok was settled only in the 1850s). The Soviets, too, must

275

be concerned with Chinese power, with the possibility of a Japan-Communist China rapprochement, with the future of India.

American failures or successes in meeting its commitment in Asia as the most powerful member of the Pacific community of nations are bound to have a reflection in Moscow policy. Could not American failures, then, strengthen those elements in the Russian power complex who want to continue their bid for world power at whatever cost at home?

These are the reasons why I believe American commitment in Asia is unavoidable.

What form that commitment will take will be determined by U.S. resolve, by the efficiency of its policies, and by totally unpredictable elements and events. But it is hard to see, as I have tried to show, how, given the present conditions in the vast continent, the U.S. commitment will not grow in magnitude and complexity in the coming decades.

What, then, is that American role? And what should it be?

12 *

The American As a Revolutionary

WE paced up and down the long mall that stretches through "The Diplomatic Enclave" and in front of the U.S. Embassy in New Delhi. It was spring 1962; one of those long, hot, dry nights when everything about you seems to be strung on tightly-drawn rubber bands, the physical and emotional tension that builds up in northern India before the orgasm-like breaking of the rains.

My companion was one of India's best-known political leaders, a man who, like myself, used to call himself a democratic socialist. But that night he put into words what we both had known and had been unwilling to face for a long time: His program, his party's program, the program of the Indian independence movement of the 1930s, was totally irrelevant now. Never had I had to console one of my Asian friends with less hope, less faith in the future.

Our talk lasted for hours. But the essence came early: "We have failed," he said. "The whole thing hasn't worked. We are being overwhelmed by poverty and the population explosion.

"The only thing that I can hope for now is a tremendous technological development—something so vast that it can't even be guessed at now.

"And, of course, it will have to come from the West, from your laboratories, from your universities."

This expression of faith in American intellectual leadership is the most dramatic example of such trust I know. But to a lesser degree, I believe that it is universal throughout non-Communist Asia.

It arises not only out of the sense of failure and frustration of much of Asia's non-Communist leadership today. But it is also an expression of the enormous stock of confidence which Asians put in the American.

In part, it is still that "reservoir of good will" and respect for the United States of which Wendell Willkie spoke in the 1940s. Communist propaganda notwithstanding, and constant and bitter criticism by Asians on all aspects of American life aside, the average Asian intellectual has great admiration for his concept of the U.S.—part dream, part reality.

It's expressed a thousand different ways, not in grand political gestures or the communiqués of foreign ministers, but in the everyday actions of Asians. Over and over again in Asia, leadership or decisions have been thrust on me personally by Asians—more often than not in situations where my command of information and techniques was, to say the least, limited.

In 1966, I was visiting the Indian state of Bihar during a famine. At the suggestion of an American priest, a long-time resident of the area, I went off to investigate a communal kitchen which his workers had organized only a few days before in a village not far from Patna, the state capital. He explained that he, himself, had not yet been there, that the mission he headed and which was administering emergency relief as an agent of the Indian and U.S. governments, had been called on to help and had set up a communal kitchen.

I went along, accompanying a young Indian woman worker and her helper. When we reached the village, we found a far-too-common Indian phenomenon. The distribution of food had become enmeshed in the problem of caste. The village was in an uproar over where the kitchen was to be relocated and who was to parcel out the cooked food. It had been put in the untouchable quarter of the village because there was a small house and courtyard that could be locked up. The caste members of the village wanted it placed in their sector of the group of huts, the traditional center of the village under a huge banyan tree.

No sooner were we in the village than dozens of villagers surrounded the jeep and walked after me, tugging at my sleeves as I tried to see what was going on. They wanted me to decide the dispute. I, of course, tried to avoid involvement, realizing that I knew nothing of the local situation and the problem. But all of them insisted that I must give them a decision, and even the young mission worker (though a Christian, an outcaste) begged me with her eyes to help solve the desperate dilemma which had brought feeding to a standstill.

I only escaped the whole situation by insisting that I had to leave, and by telling them that I would tell the bloc officer—the representative of the Indian government in the area—about the problem. I did see him. And he listened patiently to me, putting me ahead of a small mob of people trying to get his help on a number of problems. I had little hope that he would or could do anything to sort out the problem. But I had the feeling then, as I have had so many times in equally critical decisions like it, that he accepted my evaluation of the situation as an outsider, a "neutral," and an American who could be expected to try to be fair.

This faith in the American exists despite a widespread knowledge of our failings. It would be impossible to exaggerate how much publicity American faults get in Asia. Most Asian non-Communist leadership reads American periodicals. *Time* and *Newsweek*, denounced by almost every Asian intellectual at the drop of a hat, are nevertheless must and constant reading. The freewheeling discussion of American problems for an American audience that goes on in our mass publications, as well as many of the smaller magazines, is common knowledge for members of the elite. In fact, one finds them more often than not at least superficially aware of current problems in the U.S. and relatively less aware of those of their own countries—and always more aware of the U.S. than of their neighbors.

It is remarkable, all things considered, how seldom the subject of American racism comes up in conversations—even with acknowledged Communist sympathizers. I asked C. Rajagopalachari once why he thought this was true. His answer was the same as that given me by so many other Asians through the years: Most educated Asians are very much cognizant of their own particular brands of racism, its irreconcilable character. Color

279

prejudice, for example, is not only widespread throughout all Asia, but in many instances is as virulent as in the U.S.

The "whiteness" of skin is synonymous with feminine beauty in Japan and Vietnam. Indian caste levels, as is well known, almost parallel skin colors. Women peasants in Southeast Asia go to almost any lengths to cover their faces at work in the fields in order to avoid becoming darker.

Most Asian intellectuals, even those who take a Communist line in arguments, use American publications, books, periodicals, statistics, and opinions as the major props of their criticisms of U.S. policy and American life. The most bitter critics of the vulgar aspects of what is called Americanization of Asian societies are often its most ardent practitioners. A good example is the novelist known in the West as Han Su Yin. Her novels and articles bear little resemblance to any Chinese forms she would appear to admire, but are a splendid example of popular American mass culture (and one might add, in their profitability).

SPIRITUALITY AND MATERIALISM

On one of my earliest trips to Asia, I remember discussing with a famous Indian editor, now deceased, the question of so-called Asian "spirituality" versus Western materialism. He was an economist. And although he had been trained in Western studies, he was of a traditionalist South Indian Brahmin family. Hindu rites and food prohibitions were practiced in the household, a huge old Calcutta mansion of many floors surrounding a court where the joint family system of several generations living together still held sway. Yet he denied the whole concept of the Western cultists who see in the East a concentration on the higher values, on "spiritual" values of life, while the Westerner grovels in his quest for things. His proof? The Western credit system. Capitalism and the whole modern economic society of the West, he argued, was based on credit. There is nothing like it in the pre-industrial societies of Asia. And what is credit based on? he asked. It is basically trust of individuals in other individuals. What could be a greater evidence of "spiritual" values than that, he concluded.

An American in Asia soon finds that, willy-nilly, he is considered a walking representative of his technological society. I find the role extremely difficult, since I am almost totally unmechanical and without a basic education in science. For example, I remember once a political conversation with a very sophisticated South Asian which was interrupted when I took out a lighter to smoke a cigarette. It was a common butane gas lighter. My host, an aging Indian traditionalist, insisted on dropping politics and discussing for three or four minutes what kind of device it was, how it worked, how much it cost, where it was bought, how it could be replenished. He seemed somehow miffed that my mechanical skills and information only went as far as knowing how to light it and refill it, that I was uninterested and could not explain in some detail how it worked.

Of course, even the most mechanically unskilled American brings into the Asian environment talents which his Asian intellectual counterpart may not have. Driving an automobile, for example, which is integral to an American's education, is not common to Asians of the same relative status and abilities.

In part, of course, this arises out of the whole system in which Asians in authority do not handle—nor have they ever in their ascent of the ladder of bureaucracy handled—many of the mechanical jobs that are common for an American. When one of the new agricultural colleges was organized a few years ago in India, modeled after our land-grant schools in the U.S., there was enormous discussion about whether or not filing cabinets would be used and kept in the professors' offices. The ordinary Indian (Pakistani, Burmese, or Indonesian) procedure is that files are kept in a central filing room and ushers are used to carry them back and forth in a futile exercise that takes enormous time.

I cannot remember speaking with an Asian executive who had a typewriter at his desk in his office. And I am sure that it is a rare governmental official or company official who can type. (The problem is exceedingly difficult in Japan, of course, where the language requires a Rube Goldberg invention that uses several thousand Chinese characters, plus two phonetic alphabets, for the simplest kind of communication.)

This widespread Asian confidence in the American as a representative of a society of higher values—at least in pursuit of higher levels of equality and justice—and the equally widely diffused confidence in American technology produces a crucial, if difficult to substantiate, phenomenon in relations between the East and the United States:

Every American in Asia moves about in an aura of revolution. His presence in any society in the East—and I include Japan here —is the introduction of a totally alien influence, "a man from outer space," who literally exudes new concepts and new vitality.

Largely passive, cynical, rarely questioning the concepts of government below the highest levels of his society, the Asian, at whatever level of sophistication he makes contact with the Americans, is bowled over by the American.

His own self-professed radicals have a tremendous impact, obviously. But much of what they say and do can be discounted (when they do not have the reins of power, as in China) by the fact that they are part and parcel of their own society. An Indian never forgets for one moment the caste or linguistic or regional affiliation of a Communist leader. An Indonesian is never unaware that a PKI leader is first and foremost a Javanese aristocrat. A Lao is never unmindful of the fact that Pathet Lao leaders are either *metisse* Vietnamese or Chinese.

The American, on the other hand, has no fixed place in the incredibly complex hierarchy of these societies. For better or for worse, the American today represents the intrusion of the Western world—the modern world of technology and movement—on the largely stagnant societies of Asia.

Panikkar, writing some years ago, tried to summarize what would be the long-term effects of the period of 450 years of Western dominance in Asia which he saw coming to an end with the events leading to political freedom after World War II. With a few more years' perspective on events, it is interesting to see what he listed as an Asian nationalist, even chauvinist, historian and political thinker.

His list: The impact of Western law, its accent on equality. The introduction of modern political organization, particularly republicanism which he foresaw as an end to the tradition—and perhaps more important, the mystique—of Asian despotism. The formation of a middle class in the cities with its new values. The creation of (or I would now amend it to read the *attempt* to create) nation-states. The introduction of science. The literary revolution, especially the introduction of a literature for the mass. The end of the isolation of Asian cultures from the mainstream of world events. The cross-fertilization of the arts; the effect of the Asians on European art and the end of "Eurocentrism" in such fields as archaeology.

That was a summary in 1954. But today it is still a good list.

Yet to all this must be added the special qualities of the American. For while he has picked up the banners of Western influence in Asia, his modifications of the European spirit and its technology are critical in the long-term effects of the elements Panikkar has listed.

The very naiveté of the American, his extreme activism, his faith in progress, his belief in solutions to all problems, his concern (however modified and hypocritical) is crucial. Were he not naive, did he not believe in the inevitability of progress, he would long ago have thrown up his hands and turned passive, as much of Asia's leadership traditionally has. Were he not a scion of radical Hebraic Protestant tradition of concern, he would long ago have turned cynical and content to see the Communist use traditional modes of Asian despotism to try to build a new order.

AMERICAN IDEALISM

AMERICAN idealism, whether directly applied to Asian colonial peoples or not, has always been an important factor in Asian revolutionary movements. It was to play a tremendous role in the movement for decolonialization. "Throughout the world, like the voice of a prophet, has gone the word of Woodrow Wilson strengthening the weak and giving courage to the struggling. And the Chinese have listened and they too have heard . . ." said a students' pamphlet written in 1918, part of the movement to reverse China's nineteenth-century capitulation to European and Japanese power. And the May Fourth Movement (1919), which brought the Chinese intellectual into the struggle for national renewal, was to a considerable extent the reaction to the failure of the Versailles Peace Conference to meet the promises of that arch-idealist, Wilson, announced on America's entry into World War I.

The Americans still provide much of that idealistic drive in Asia. In 1965, I called on my friend Ram Lohia, the left-wing Indian socialist leader, after a visit he had made to the United States where he had been briefly arrested for participating in a civil rights demonstration in the American South. Instead of finding him bitter or disappointed by that experience, his eyes lit up when I brought up the whole matter. "Think of it," he said, "think of what you are trying to do: To wipe out racism and the color bar in your society. I don't know how much chance you have. It has never been done. No one has ever done it. It will be terribly difficult, if not impossible. But what a thing you will have done if you can do it!"

All this leads to a single and transcendental fact: The American is the chief revolutionary force in Asia today, perhaps the only revolutionary in the sense that he *tries* to turn his back on Asian history and plows ahead toward new forms.

Yet the reader may well ask here: How can I maintain that the American represents the only revolutionary force in Asia when the confrontation between forces suggests that the Communists are the most powerful proponents of change? Is it not the Communists, he might ask, who are leading the onslaught on the *status quo*? Have the Communists not already changed radically old societies—notably China—into something new and decisive for the future of Asia?

My answer is no. I am prepared to concede that the very semantics of the problem are germane. That is, if I say I preach revolution, I may to a considerable extent have a revolutionary effect, even though my actions do not in fact carry out a revolutionary program. To the extent that the Communists propagandize—and very effectively—that they are approaching the problems of Asia with new intellectual tools and new talents, they may contribute to a revolution.

But I believe that here, too, it is necessary to abandon "theological" discussions and come to grips with real issues. From what I have written earlier, I believe it is clear that most of Asia today has a set of primary problems for which there must be answers if there is to be a change for the better which most revolutionaries there preach. And I believe those are very concrete problems:

Population control.
Food.
Education.
Industrialization.
Relative political stability.

To what extent do the Communists have answers to these problems? And to what extent do *we* have answers to these problems? That is the real question at issue.

CHINA'S PROBLEMS

I HAVE treated China only in the most cursory fashion. This is, in part, because I have not myself had personal experience in that country, so largely cut off from the West since 1949.

Much that has been written about Communist China is the most simple-minded propaganda. I think now of a book of photographs and text written by a young, self-proclaimed Scandinavian radical, presented as a case study of a Chinese village through the radical events of the past thirty years. There is only one fault: The village he has written of is one of the Potemkin settlements which has been presented to and written about by hundreds of sympathetic visitors to Communist China since the regime began its long and arduous campaign of convincing Westerners of its great strides forward. It has about as much relevance to China's problems as were a visitor to write about the trials and tribulations of Levittown, Long Island, to explain what has been happening in the Bedford-Stuyvesant black ghetto of Brooklyn, New York City, during the past twenty years.

The Peking regime has not come to terms with any of China's basic problems. It has fluctuated violently on birth control and any attempt to control population. Official propaganda has included everything from swallowing tadpoles as a method of contraception to Mao's famous remark to foreign visitors that China was the only country that could sustain atomic warfare and still continue to exist because of its millions.

THE FUTURE

During the 1950s, the Chinese Communists put little emphasis on any program for population control—and, in fact, as orthodox Marxists, Malthusian theories of population outdistancing resources were unacceptable. Now some of the modern birth control methodology has been introduced into the country. But the problem remains much that of the rest of Asia: How, and with what speed, will it be possible to break through cultural and technical problems of distribution to reach the overwhelming majority of the Chinese who live in the villages? Peking has put its greatest emphasis on winning the young people in the country to a program of delayed marriage and a small family.

Here is how the noted demographers, Irene B. Taeuber and Leo A. Orleans, have summed up China's prospects of population control under Communism:

> Perhaps the dynamics of the Communist system itself have already transformed youth so deeply that acceptance of delayed marriage and the family of one or two children present few problems. This may be true for the youths of the cities. It is not likely to be true for the youths living in the rural areas remote from great metropolitan centers. Paradoxical as it may seem, the success of programs to secure the postponement of marriage and the limitation of childbearing among the oncoming generations of the Communist-born and the Communist-reared will provide an objective measure of the extent to which the People's Republic of China has achieved those fundamental transformations of person and personality that are its goals.

The use of the youth groups, *drawn from outside the Communist party*, in Mao's attempt to gain the upper hand in the Communist party struggle during the Great Cultural Revolution beginning in 1965 could be used as evidence to prove that the Communists are achieving some success here. But there was equally great evidence during those events reaching the outside world that what was essentially happening was an attempt toward stabilization after the events of the last twenty years. At least one element in the controversy between Mao and the Communist party leadership was an attempt by the bureaucracy of the party and government to end the radical departures toward new policies.

286

If Mao sees the permanent problem of how to keep a huge and traditionalist country, steeped in five thousand years of history, from falling back into the patterns of its history, the opponents of Mao see the danger in a constant fulmination in the country which prevents bureaucracy from going ahead with the mundane tasks necessary to implement any policy, including such a detailed and demanding job as population control.

Repeatedly, we have seen—in the Soviet Union, in eastern Europe, and elsewhere—that even a totalitarian regime's methods cannot win a young generation presumably totally under its control. True enough, the methods used in China in the past twenty years have been even more thorough and ruthless. But Chinese tradition, also, has a rigidity that has rarely been equaled in other societies. And integral to that tradition has been the family, the very basis of Chinese life. I think it would be a very brave observer who would predict the success of a Chinese Communist program based on population control which would use as its main rationale the winning away of the younger generation from the traditions of the Chinese family.

Yet it almost goes without saying that population control is essential to any progress in China. Failure of the Chinese Communists to limit their population increase will be catastrophic. If births and deaths continue at the level estimated in 1957, population could reach more than a billion by 1980.

Can China feed these growing numbers with Marxist-Leninist formulated agricultural policies? I believe there is little evidence to show that they will, or—more important to my argument—that they can so long as they hold to policies arising out of their dogma.

Firstly, there is an important difference between the problems of Chinese agriculture and most of the other underdeveloped areas. The Chinese farmer is a better farmer, given his resources, than those in most other backward countries. Unlike most of the farming in South Asia, Chinese production methods have exploited to a far greater extent the resources available to the peasant. The organized use of "night soil"—human waste—as fertilizer is thousands of years old in China; it is virtually unknown in most of South Asia. China's huge irrigation systems are hundreds of years old and were some of the most elaborate human construction projects long before the opening of the technological age in the West. China has virtually no virgin lands, despite her enormous size, that could be brought under profitable exploitation—short of an industrialization of agriculture. That Chinese efforts along these lines have fallen short of her needs is evidenced by her large imports of grain over the past decade. In 1960-64, the Communists spent over $400 million annually of their carefully guarded foreign exchange for these imports, possibly half of their total foreign exchange earnings.

What are needed, of course, are vast new expenditures of capital into new seed varieties, research, fertilizer, and new water resources. And despite a general misunderstanding to the contrary, a Communist society, too, must distribute resources out of a fixed total. So long as Peking is intent on expending vast sums of money for maintaining a gigantic war machine—including the enormous amounts of capital put into an atomic weapons program—that much less will be available for agricultural development.

AGRICULTURAL FAILURES

J. LOSSING BUCK, the foremost Western agricultural-economist expert on China, writes:

> The public has been misled by the boasts of the Chinese Communists and by their foodgrain production statistics for 1949-58 which began with too low a figure in 1949 and then increased every year until they reported the greatly exaggerated amount in 1959.
>
> . . . The Chinese Communists, in their statistical effort to make production agree with their ideology, have claimed a significantly smaller average production for 1949-58 than for the pre-Communist periods of 1929-33 and 1931-37.
>
> The total population estimate for 1929-33 based on the *Land Utilization in China* farm survey of farm population density per square mile of cultivated land is 592 million which includes the population of Manchuria, Sikang, and Singkiang, compared with the Communist claim of 597 million year's-end population for 1949-58. The commonly accepted population figure in the early 1930s was 400 to 500 million.

The *Land Utilization in China* data on per capita consumption of foodgrains for a total population of 592 million in 1929-33 indicates that 262 kilograms of unprocessed grain per capita were available annually and that for the Communist period of 1949-58 for a year-end population of 597 million, 231 kilograms were available. In terms of calories per capita from all foods for the entire population *LU* data indicate that 2,410 calories were available, including net imports; the Communist data indicate that 2,017 calories per capita were available, excluding net exports, or 83.7 per cent of 2,410 calories. These calories represent availability, not actual intake, which would be less because of losses and possibly a less efficient metabolism for such a highly vegetarian diet.

. . . The apparent severe downward trend in Communist production [editor's note: During the Great Leap Forward] that began in 1958 has led to extreme hunger and malnutrition, and possibly some starvation. This collapse in Communist food production may be ascribed to the following: the reorganization of the farm production unit into large Agricultural Producers' Cooperatives and later into Communes; to the absence of sufficient incentives; to wrong directives from Peking on what and how to plant; and in 1960-61, partly to natural calamities.

Buck's study was completed in 1964. But it appears likely that conditions in Chinese agriculture may have improved by a retreat by the Communists from the more radical measures of change in land tenure; they have returned, for example, considerable land to private plots to the peasantry. Yet the excesses of the new Cultural Revolution beginning in 1965 are bound to have again disturbed employment on the land and distribution of food.

In the field of education, too, there appears little that the Chinese Communists have to offer that is an answer to the needs of Asia. China's foremost problem for mass instruction, the difficulty of the language, has been attacked only nominally by the Communists. They have adopted a simplification of characters—much of which was done in Japan fifty years ago. They have proposed and accepted as dictum an eventual romanization of the written national dialect, against enormous opposition among both "progressive" and traditional Chinese scholars who see it as a "loss of the past." Yet beyond writing the names of a few party publications in the new style beneath the mastheads of the party and government publications, little else appears to have been done.

The use of the school children for political in-fighting during the Cultural Revolution, plus the abuse of teachers and professors, has again undermined the educational system, rocked as it was by the period of *Let a Hundred Flowers Bloom* (1956-57). Hundreds of thousands of school children were not attending class during 1965, 1966, and 1967, while they participated as Red Guards in demonstrations in support of Mao. The program to spread modernism and prevent the "bourgeoisation" of students of higher learning by sending them back to the villages has ruined the careers of hundreds of thousands of future technicians of the country.

Undoubtedly enrollment of children in schools has dramatically increased since the regime was consolidated in 1950. But whether education, which has striven to put the accent on Communist loyalty, rather than on academic or technical competence, has actually increased the ability of the educated classes to deal with the enormous problems of the country is extremely doubtful.

You get an idea of where Chinese education has gone under the Communists and the Mao-ist eruption called "The Cultural Revolution" from this description written from Peking by David Oancia, in April 1968:

> . . . columns of school children guided by their teachers and often by soldiers, march up to huge billboards portraying Chairman Mao in military garb. They open their red books and, led by their teacher or by a soldier, select appropriate quotations and read them reverently while they bow to the portrait.
>
> This is part of the effort to rebuild the educational system along still unspecified "revolutionary" lines. The schools, with their statues or portraits of Mr. Mao, still bear the scars of the earlier period of turmoil. Windows that have been shattered and furniture that has been smashed still await replacement. In some schools, the students are using wooden packing cases and thin plastic to cover holes.

If industrialization is the great need of the Asian scene, there, too, I do not believe the Chinese Communists have given evidence of successes that could form the pattern for Asia.

Sorting out propaganda from reality is difficult. But the China watchers are generally agreed that the frenetic attempt to overcome difficulties by throwing a new mystical element into industrial and agricultural development during The Great Leap Forward (1956-59) was not only a disaster. It created such chaos that Chinese production did not regain its levels of the mid-1950s until 1965. In other words, an attempt to introduce a new method of advancement based on Mao's interpretation of Marxism-Leninism lost China another decade while the population continued to mount.

The breakdown in China's relations with the Russians has cut China off from important sources of planning and aid. True enough, the Chinese have turned to Western European manufacturers for the import of some capital equipment—and, in part, for imported technology. But the tremendously important, if difficult to quantify, intellectual interchange between the industrially developed world and the underdeveloped countries (whether they call themselves Communist or not) has virtually been cut off. China has few young engineers, scientists, or managerial talent learning new techniques abroad. Only a few Western or Japanese industrial technicians or managers go to Communist China to see, comment, and work and advise.

I do not underestimate the Chinese genius. But I believe it is a valid assumption that without this transfer of technological information, the Chinese will move at a much slower pace than would otherwise be possible. And in China, as elsewhere in the underdeveloped world, time is of the essence in outdistancing the population growth and maintaining enough stability for progress.

CULTURAL REVOLUTION

THE Cultural Revolution, which for more than two years induced chaos into much of Chinese life, has destroyed the last illusion in most non-Communist Asian observers' minds about the nature and stability of the regime. Many Asians, even non-Communists, aware of the enormity of China's problems paralleling their own, had in recent years taken some comfort in the fact that the Communists had at least provided China with relatively competent, stable leadership. There were none of the tortures of the failure of governmental institutions modeled after parliamentarianism in the West. There was strong, central control. Chinese self-respect, at least, had been salvaged from a century and a half of mortification.

Now that claim, too, is rapidly fading. As I write in mid-1968, there are hints that the Cultural Revolution may be drawing to an end, that China may be temporarily stabilizing her internal political situation with a new, careful balance in the leadership. But it is evident that the hope of a stable political order is considerably diminished, if it is there at all.

If the ferocity of the Cultural Revolution was possible once, it is probable that it is possible again. Although it has had its peculiarities, the Chinese regime has demonstrated that it, too, has not found a way for a Communist state to transfer power to a new generation. And, in fact, there is no evidence at all that the question of succession to Mao's leadership has been settled. There is even some evidence that the Chinese political scene is regressing to the historic pattern of China at the breakdown of a dynasty in which army warlords assumed regional control in an untidy and unstable order until a new dominant figure emerged.

Many of the arguments I have made here apply to the lesser Communist states in Asia. Before the Vietnamese war escalated to a major and all-consuming preoccupation of the Hanoi Communist regime, there was ample evidence there, too, that basic problems had not been solved. And, in fact, one of the reasons why Hanoi had no choice but to back an attempt to overthrow the regime in Saigon was the need for the resources of South Vietnam to stabilize its power. North Korea, despite its advantages of a smaller population and industrial raw materials, with the beginnings of an industrial complex dating back to the Japanese pre-World War II occupation, has not forged ahead. South Korea, with all its difficulties, was by the mid-1960s providing an example of a more dynamic society.

In sum, what I am saying is this: The problems of Asia are on such a vast scale that no amount of holding up Mao Tse-tung's little red book of quotations in front of them will produce solutions. The attempt to find solutions will have to come out of the

widest possible acceptance of ideas and their interchange. And
that, at least in principle, is what the Americans are "selling" in
Asia. It is the opposite of the dogmatic attitude implicit in the
Communist philosophy which begins with the preaching of a determinist doctrine and degenerates into a simple manipulation of
power for power's sake.

The American, a product of a relatively "open society," then is
the revolutionary who can change the destiny of Asia.

Yet a revolutionary is only as effective as he is armed. If my
American revolutionary is to accomplish his purposes in Asia, he
will have to have more than the psychological and philosophical
background for it that I have described at the beginning of this
chapter. He has to have tools. And a third complement to his
equipment will have to be method as well as tools.

In view of the enormity of the problems of Asia, what tools does
the American have? And how can he use them effectively?

REVOLUTION OF THE LEFT HAND

THERE are two distinct aspects of the revolutionary activity of American influence in Asia. We have what I would call the
Revolution of the Left Hand. It is what the American does by
simply being there—the effect of his carrying into the Asian environment the essences of the American scene.

Imagine, if you will, the impact of a situation I saw in Qui Nhon
in 1967—not much more than a village in Vietnam turned into
a deep-water port for the purposes of prosecuting the war there.
(It was, incidentally, only one of five ports built by the Americans,
in addition to increasing the pier capacity of Saigon by more than
100 per cent which, until 1965, was the only ocean port south of
the seventeenth parallel.)

South Korean troops, able to buy at the incredibly well-stocked
American post exchanges, were purchasing television sets. They
resold these into the local black market. They were bought by
Vietnamese, suddenly wealthy by their own standards from the
payments received for working for the American military establishment. Some of the Vietnamese who bought them were simple
workmen, even *pousse-pousse* (the Vietnamese version of the bi-

cycle rickshaw) drivers. And they were watching the local tele-casting of filmed American network shows. I have no idea what a Vietnamese watching "I Love Lucy" made of the whole thing; but it is likely that such cultural novelties had much more to do with attitudes and reactions to his changing life than all the official American and Vietnamese government (and Communist!) prop-aganda to which he was subjected.

Or I remember chatting one steaming evening in 1957 with a group of young Indonesians in the port city of Medan in Sumatra. We stood outside a local cinema. The half-dozen kids were all dressed in black leather jackets, looking a little like overcooked lobsters in the heat. They enthused over a Hollywood film they had just seen, then tore away on noisy Japanese-made motorbikes in the best traditions of Southern California juveniles. They are only part of the youth of the elite everywhere in Asia who model their lives, insofar as they can, on what they hear about the young in the U.S.

I don't think it is possible to analyze what the effect of this left-handed revolution, quietly being waged unintentionally by the Americans, will be. My suspicion is that in the long run it may turn out to be more influential than what we are deliberately try-ing to do to change ideas and improve living standards in Asia.

We can talk with more concreteness about the right-handed revolution. It is the planned, deliberate, and organized attempts to undertake population control, increase food production, intro-duce the beginnings of the industrialization which is the basis of modern society, improve education, and lend what weight we can toward a political system which can be the framework for ad-vancement.

Our greatest tool is the outstanding technological capabilities of the American society. In both the fields of contraception for population control and increased food productivity, we are on the verge of developments which are almost "science fiction" in their potential impact.

Totally revolutionary biochemical contraception methods are now being investigated to halt population growth. These go be-yond presently commercially marketed "the pill" and the I.U.D., a permanently-inserted contraceptive device. These two methods, along with the more traditional contraceptive devices and sterilization, have only limited application in the underdeveloped countries of Asia.

A "time capsule," a continuous low dose of antifertility compound released from capsules of silicone rubber which can safely be implanted under the skin, has been perfected in the laboratory. Dr. Sheldon J. Segal, of the Population Council, Rockefeller University, in New York, says that the release on a daily basis of this chemical substance has been established without inhibiting ordinary female functions.

A "morning-after pill," which, if taken within a few days of copulation, would inhibit pregnancy, has been successfully used with monkeys. Some work with human volunteers has been tried, but clinical tests have not yet been meaningful.

A "once-a-month pill," with the possibility of a "once-every-six-months" or "once-a-year" modification of the principles involved, is under consideration.

"Long-term injectable" is also being considered. It would replace the daily pill and periodic injections. So far, published reports indicate troublesome problems with unpredictable bleeding and with uncertainty as to the restoration of ovulatory cycles.

But Dr. Segal concludes: "The possibilities for the use of these compounds or related ones to inhibit progesterone production, for example, or in some other fashion to manipulate a key event in reproduction, have just begun to be evident. These are but a few examples drawn from a rapidly growing field of biological science. They are some of the future pathways; undoubtedly there will be others as well."

These developments, of course, may still be a long way from fruition—at least in a method which can be applied on the wide scale necessary to avoid the catastrophic population explosions coming in Asia. But they offer radical hope in what has appeared until now to be a totally black picture.

In food production, hopeful signs are even brighter and clearer. Years of patient and little-publicized development of new seed varieties of grain are beginning to reach fruition.

The Rockefeller Foundation started in Mexico in 1944 an effort to meet the grain deficit of that country. With newly developed, higher producing wheat and corn, it has virtually done so even though the Mexican population has doubled in the twenty-five years since the research and development started. Now much of the methodology—and even some of the varieties developed—are being transferred to the tropical regions of Asia.

At the International Rice Institute at Los Baños in the Philippines, also a Rockefeller-supported institution, new varieties have been produced which, under proper growing conditions, not only add a mere 10, 20 or 30 per cent to yields, but have under ideal conditions more than doubled the crop yield!

Some of these varieties are already influencing production. One estimate is that the preliminary introduction of the varieties from Los Baños throughout Southeast Asia has already increased the gross national product of these countries by $300 million annually.

AN AGRICULTURAL REVOLUTION

LESTER R. BROWN, a U.S. Department of Agriculture agricultural economist and one of the most pessimistic about trends in Asian agriculture throughout the 1950s and early 1960s, says:

> The new food grain varieties are far more than another technological breakthrough—they may be to the agricultural revolution in Asia what the steam engine was to the industrial revolution in Europe. In addition to their influence on production, the new varieties are playing a critical role as a catalyst, causing farmers to break with tradition and reconsider their agricultural practices.

Equally revolutionary on the food front are developments in experimentation in new kinds of protein foods. Brown and others see hope here of repeating for Asia the experience in the U.S. with the need for low caloric food development. In the U.S a whole new technology developed after World War II to produce low-calory foods; as a result the industry now markets annually something like $700 million worth of such products.

Until now, the need for protein in the diet had been seen satisfied largely through the expensive and difficult production of livestock. But American science is now developing protein sub-

stitutes for meat and milk from soybeans or other protein vegetable products. The Japanese have been able to produce some of
these foods from petroleum—opening up vast new possibilities.

The introduction of amino acids into conventional foods, for
example, can boost the protein content enormously. The addition
of four pounds of lysine, costing $4, to a ton of wheat raises the
final product to the level of casein, the protein in milk. The Indians, encouraged by the U.S. government, have begun a program to introduce this item into bread. The introduction of such
chemical ingredients into traditional products or the introduction
of new varieties with higher protein yield could overcome the
economic problem and the perhaps even more taxing problem of
adjusting the eating habits of large Asian populations to otherwise
strange foods.

Other even more far-reaching technological innovations are
now beyond the speculative state. Take the possibility of salt
water conversion—turning seawater or saline pools (like the great
reservoirs of such water on the Indo-Gangetic Plain) into fresh
water to be used as a source of irrigation and drinking water. The
application of atomic and solar energy to distillation processes
has only begun to be researched on anything like the scale necessary to come up with breakthroughs. If such developments
could be found in the next decade, large areas of Asia considered
until now uninhabitable, as well as arid reaches of much of the
continent, could be put under production to take care of the
expanding population. Collaboration between Israeli scientists,
who have done some fundamental research in water conserva-
tion because of their desperate need, and the U.S. is already
under way. This calls for the building of a million-watt nuclear
reactor and desalination plant with an annual capacity of 125
million cubic feet of water.

These, then, are glimpses at the great technological tools—perhaps touching the developments which my Indian friend said
might be so large as to be beyond the layman's imagination—
which might aid the American revolutionary in Asia. But what
about his methods? I have been extremely critical of what has
been done so far. In what directions could we go to achieve the
maximum effect, to avert some of the catastrophic consequences
which have seemed inherent in the over-all situation?

297

13 ∗

The Job

No American policy in Asia will be effective until we accept basic intellectual attitudes which arise out of the logic of the situation there.

I see five concepts that are essential:

We must accept with unmitigated realism the desperate nature of the situation. It does no good to gloss over the bitter realities of the failures in population control, food production, education, industrialization, and stability.

In view of the magnitude of the problems, *our approach must be long term.* We must accept the fact that progress may be slow —in American terms—and that we are talking in timespans of generations, not just years or decades. Whatever we do to achieve short-term successes, our basic planning must aim at correcting situations through efforts which may not bear fruit for much longer periods.

There is a most curious but important paradox: We can begin to exercise our maximum influence for good on the situation if we are aware of just how marginal our effort can be. *Only by understanding how little we can do, can we do our most.* "The name of the game," as the GI's in Vietnam have said, is getting Asians to do what they have to do—with our help.

And, finally, *we must rid ourselves of the kind of "mechanistic" approaches that have dominated much of our thinking in the past two decades.* There are no magic solutions. There are no gimmicks. There are no ready-built "systems." We are dealing with problems that have never been so complex in the history of the human race, and solving them will require the widest possible interchange of ideas in a nonideological framework.

On this basis *we must proceed to attempt to evolve an integrated policy for all of Asia.*

This concept, too, has only limited value. As I have tried to indicate, the whole question of Asia as a single entity is open to question. Yet, while facing up to the reality of the very little that unites these areas to each other, we must formulate policies which will attempt to bring them together for concerted action. For, with careful scrutiny and a flexible approach, solutions and remedies in one area may have application in another.

Our No. 1 priority in Asia—in the long term—must be Japan.

That country, with its growing power and influence, must be the center of our policy whether we want it or not. Negatively, a Japanese industrial complex in the hands of forces inimical to U.S. interests becomes a major threat to American security. Positively, if—despite all the problems I have suggested—Japan can more effectively begin to throw her weight into the balance for economic and social progress in Asia, we have an important new force and a *de facto* partner who can take some of the load from our shoulders.

I believe there is a too facile acceptance in some quarters of U.S. officialdom and academic circles of the concept of Japan as a permanent ally in the struggle. But I do believe that there are vast and important forces in the Japanese society which are working for a partnership with the U.S in maintaining stability and fostering progress in Asia. We must do everything we can to aid them.

JAPANESE PROPOSALS

THE current speculation in Japan about the possibility of a Pacific free-trade area could be the basis for a concrete mechanism for this partnership. What the more adventurous Japanese suggest, in proposing the idea, is the creation of a common market among the developed countries in the Pacific Basin—Japan, the U.S., Canada, Australia, and New Zealand.

It could accomplish two things: It could provide the Japanese and the other partners with rapidly expanding markets on the principle that trade among developed countries moves ahead more rapidly than between developed and underdeveloped states. This hope is grounded in the experience of the trade patterns around the world since the end of World War II.

Perhaps even more important, out of such a grouping of industrial countries could come efforts to mobilize their joint resources for an attack on the problems of underdevelopment in Korea and South Asia. Sharing the burden of capital export to the underdeveloped countries, it could move ahead with an integrated policy. The newly created Asian Development Bank, whose capital was largely subscribed by these same powers, already has set up the kind of clearinghouse that might be needed.

Equally important would be an attempt by such a grouping of "the rich nations" intimately involved with the future of the Pacific area to stabilize the purchase of raw materials from the underdeveloped producers. Two methods of attack are possible: Technological renovation of such industries as rubber, for example, with new strains and mechanized tapping, as well as the promotion of new uses, could assure these countries of a longer duration for their major exports and earners of foreign exchange in world markets. And guaranteed prices through equalization funds for commodity exports of Southeast Asia—on the pattern of national subsidies for agriculture in all the developed countries —could avoid the drastic swings in income which have been almost as disastrous as the long-term falling ratio of raw material prices to manufactured goods.

In Southeast Asia—from Hong Kong to Dacca—there is real hope for programs of regional cooperation. The ten countries of the area share many of the same problems. There are, of course, internal conflicts. But compared to their hostilities and relationships with powers outside the area—the threat of Communist China, hatred of former European colonial states, fear of American domination—these are minimal.

Small but potentially important projects are already under way. The International Rice Center in the Philippines, the Southeast Asia Engineering College (originally set up under the Southeast Asia Treaty Organization) in Thailand, the Southeast Asia Education Ministers' Conference point the way.

The Mekong River development scheme—a huge proposal to control one of the world's largest rivers flowing through China, Laos, Thailand, Cambodia, and Vietnam—could provide the kind of international base for cooperation at a development level. The size of the program is so vast that although preliminary projects are already under way in Laos and may soon begin in Cambodia, it is hard to see how it can go far without at least temporary stability in the region. Yet it is the sort of revolutionary scheme on which sights must be focused if real progress is to be made in Asia.

American policy should put the emphasis on promoting such joint undertakings with generous financing and, particularly, technical assistance wherever that is possible. One major omission which the countries themselves have not begun to solve, and which is paramount, is the improvement of communications through an interchange of personnel, periodicals, study groups, etcetera. I believe this is a role our nonprofit foundations should be playing in Southeast Asia, rather than national programs which have received their relatively meager attention until now. Out of such economic and cultural cooperation could eventually come a political and military consensus. This would be a grouping with more solidity than the now moribund SEATO alliance.

In the Indo-Pakistan subcontinent, I believe that Washington will have to take a new, radical tack: All aid and support must be made contingent on an Indian-Pakistan accommodation.

I am fully aware of the possibilities of such a policy boomeranging. Soviet Russia in India and Communist China in Pakistan have both sought to use the bitter antagonism between the two countries for their own ends. And a strong American initiative to bang heads together will be exploited by both Communist states in these countries. But the alternative to a strong American policy attempting to force a settlement is, I believe, in the long run more hazardous. It is perfectly clear that neither country has military security unless there is a settlement. The short Indo-Pakistan war of 1965 was only the prelude to other and probably greater conflicts if an understanding is not reached. Even if war does not come, so long as vast amounts of potential development funds are diverted into a constantly escalating military buildup, living standards in both countries will continue to fall. This can only produce, in the end, a vicious combination of instability and the constant risk of a catastrophic test at arms between the two countries.

The U.S sponsorship of the Indus Waters Treaty, sugared with a commitment for American funds for its development, shows that it will not be easy to carry out such a program. Although the treaty is being implemented, it has not proved an indirect method of bringing the two countries together as it was conceived.

I believe that we must take a much tougher line. All American aid to both countries should be made contingent on a settlement of the Kashmir dispute and a mutual security pact with limitation of weapons. And Washington must be prepared for more than a bluff. If such a program is not acceptable in New Delhi and Rawalpindi, then we must cut off our economic and military assistance to both parties. If the risk seems great, let me point out that the breakdown of the present power structure in the subcontinent—which appears inevitable under present strains—will make our difficulties in Vietnam pale into insignificance.

Do we have this kind of "leverage"? I believe we do. Over and over again through the years, Asian acquaintances in high places have begged me as an American to understand that we *can* make demands for our contributions to Asian economic progress and political security.

I remember now a conversation in 1962 with one of the most important political figures in South India. He was then a minister in one of the states, but has since gone on to take important posts in the central government's cabinet. He was appalled, as so many observers, American and Indian, have been over the use of American economic aid in that country. He suggested that the U.S make its offers of aid contingent on certain principles; for example, the promotion of a liberal economic system in those countries we aid. He pointed out that the Russians demand and get for the most part controls over their "aid" to India that we have never sought.

Take one outrageous example: The Agency for International Development (AID) schedules only 2 per cent of its budget to help client countries develop programs to arrest population explosion. And although there is more and more acceptance in the underdeveloped countries of Asia of the need for some kind of effective program, it will not get top priority until *we* insist on it.

A few years ago I was traveling in the U.P. in India. And I visited one of the mobile hospital vans that were being used for male sterilization. Yet the huge state had only three such operations going, and even though there were enormous difficulties in convincing rural men to accept sterilization, it was not reaching even those ready to accept it. When I got back to New Delhi, I asked one of my friends in the government why New Delhi did not call on the Americans to supply more of these units, even to ask for them supplementary to the existing aid program. He hemmed and hawed, at first giving me the obviously false argument that foreign exchange was no problem in getting the units into the field. But the real reason was obvious from his conversation: It was still a taboo subject, one that would take a good deal of pressure from both inside and outside India to overcome.

AID AND QUID PRO QUOS

IT will be hard to turn the clock back. There has been so much permissiveness in the way we have handled our munificence. But Asians do expect a *quid pro quo* for help; and, if anything, they are more suspicious of our motives when we extend our help without demanding it.

No better example exists than our shipments of surplus foodstuffs to South Asia during the past twenty years. It is certainly true that we saved millions of people from starvation. We contributed toward stability in the short term. We built up a reputation for charity. But at the same time, by not insisting that the countries who were recipients take measures to emphasize agriculture in their economic planning, we helped erode the whole economic structure. Our surplus food was used in India, Pakistan, and Indonesia to buttress a program that stressed forced, high-cost industrialization. It provided the "cushion" for the totally irresponsible policies of regimes like Soekarno's.

Turning to Communist China, I frankly see no alternatives to our present policy. We must rely on the erosion—which I believe the events of 1965 to 1967 demonstrate is under way—of traditional Chinese values overtaking the Communist regime. And at the same time, we must maintain an opposition to Chinese expansion by force.

Such a passive policy runs counter to that widespread American "activism." Nor is it sure of success. In the short term, it could again mean sacrifices on our part such as took place in the Korean and in the Vietnam wars. Should we fail to hold the line in East Asia against Chinese Communist-inspired attempts to upset the independence of neighboring countries by open aggression or covert subversion, we will slow down the process of change in China itself. Rewarding aggression by inaction to meet Peking's challenge is the surest way to strengthen the present regime.

I cannot accept the thesis propounded so often that Peking's leadership has adopted its present policies because of the isolation enforced on it by the U.S. since 1950. A reading of the history of the late period of the civil war in China indicates that the U.S. was prepared, was moving without formal announcement, to accept the new regime in China. It was the Chinese Communist initiative—for example, the jettisoning of our consulates from north China—which brought on the break. The break was compounded by the Korean War, a war initiated by the Soviets, of course, but carried through to the *detente* by the Peking regime.

But the nature of the Chinese regime has been one of studied, self-imposed isolation so that the fabric of a new revolutionary society could be built without outside influences playing a role. And when Russian policy turned, at least superficially, toward an accommodation with the West, Peking cut herself off from the Communist bloc as well.

Attitudes in China will, of course, depend to a considerable extent on what happens in the rest of Asia. If we can draw Japan into a working, total relationship with the other developed countries of the Pacific Basin, and into a joint program of aid to South

Asia, if we can build a pattern of regional cooperation among the nations of Southeast Asia, if we can begin to effect a reconciliation in the Indo-Pakistan subcontinent, the forces of reason in China will have that much more chance to prevail.

That is a large "if." But we are dealing, I repeat, with a situation which must be viewed in its realistic and grim aspects.

No program for advancement in Asia led by the U.S. can be effective, however, no matter the realism of its intellectual concepts and the soundness of its strategy, if it cannot be implemented by a relatively efficient, functioning bureaucracy.

A total reorganization of the whole bureaucracy administering American foreign policy in Asia is necessary.

The tangle of policy research and formulation agencies is incredible. The State Department's own Policy Planning Board has simply become a place to "kick upstairs" members of the service who, for one reason or another, are no longer wanted or needed in the actual administration of policy. The White House advisers, a perversion of the historic role of "the kitchen cabinet," has grown beyond all reason. Today it is impossible to tell whether the basis of policies is formulated at the State Department or in the Executive Offices of the White House. A simple rejuxtapositioning of advisers back into the Department of State and under the Secretary of State would untangle some of the administrative snarl.

"One can only imagine what the Marine Corps would look like if its structure and personnel practices were modeled after those of the Foreign Service," a long-time Washington-watcher, Nathaniel McKitterick, writes. "The Commandant of the Corps, far from being a member of the Joint Chiefs of Staff, would have only ceremonial duties. The General Officers in charge at headquarters would have come up through the supply services or accounting office with no command experience or even indoctrination at Parris Island or Camp Lejeune. Thirty per cent of all field commands (ambassadorships), including the most prized commands, would be given to political appointees from civilian life, creating great uncertainty about promotions of regular captains and lieutenants. And the line between commissioned officers and non-com (the Foreign Service staff) would have completely broken down. It isn't surprising that the Foreign Service in Washington looks like an *esprit* in search of a *corps*."

The value of the "think tanks"—privately hired research groups —has virtually disappeared. They are no longer independent organizations, impartially surveying American military and political policy. They are, in fact, hired expertise—used simply to back up one part of the administrative organism's arguments against another. If the "think tanks" still have a function at all, perhaps it could best be used by organizing a truly independent agency for the review of national policy which would have its own resources and complete independence, checking out policy and performance in the manner that the General Accounting Office checks on fiscal responsibility.

THE NEED FOR TRAINED MEN

"The Secretary (of State) may sit at the center of this vastness," Professor Richard E. Neustadt told a Senatorial Committee in 1963, "but his office has almost no staff which he can call his own. To weld together such a staff out of these scattered pieces, to imbue it with cohesion and a government-wide outlook, to implant it as a Presidential agent of coordination for the sweep of national security affairs: All this is far from done. I need not tell you why I think the doing may take time. . . .

"The Secretary of State has a dilemma all his own. These (many) roles are mutually reinforcing: His advice gains weight because he represents the whole Department; his public statements and internal orders gain in potency because he is so often at the White House. But these roles are also mutually antagonistic: Fronting for officials strains his credit as an adviser; advising keeps his mind off management; negotiating pre-empts energy and time. No modern Secretary has performed the miracle of playing all these roles at once so skillfully and carefully that he obtains the benefits of all and pays no penalties. Presumably there is no way to do it."

But it seems to me that Neustadt makes his most important point as a *caveat* against putting total emphasis on organization:

"Even with time, even with good use of it, even if we master complex institution-building, we can expect no miracles from policy. Even if the Secretary's office should become a partner with the White House in the Presidency's business while the Secretary's business is protected and enhanced, even then both sorts of business would be botched on numerous occasions. For methods and procedures at their best cannot abolish the deep difficulties of perception, of analysis, of judgment, of persuasion, which confront policy-makers now and in the future."

It is precisely for this reason—knowledge over system—that a complete reorganization of research facilities is a pressing need in the Department of State, perhaps meshed with the Central Intelligence Agency's operations. Collaboration on biographical studies of Asian personalities, for example, an enormously rewarding method of studying current political affairs, is now at the level of amateurs. In part, this is a result of the breakup of a previously joint system between the Department of State and the Central Intelligence Agency during the administration of Roger Hilsman as Assistant Secretary of State for East Asia at the beginning of the Kennedy administration.

You get an idea in what disarray the whole method of research and analysis is by one flagrant example: In the spring of 1968, despite the intensity of the Vietnam crisis and the American commitment there, no real research in depth—such as had been carried on since the early 1940s in several academic and governmental institutions on the Soviet Union and Communist China—was proceeding on North Vietnam and the Vietnamese Communist party. In State, itself, research on North Vietnam was divided into three different sections of the department. There was no adequate continuing biographical study of Hanoi personalities. Training of State, AID, and CIA personnel for the Vietnam program of military and civilian support of the Saigon regime was scattered in half a dozen schools throughout the country. And faculties and instruction material for these courses were gathered in a hit-or-miss fashion. Each of the branches of the armed services had its own "think tanks" employed on various projects involved in the war effort and the pacification program. But there was little coordination except at the highest levels, and there only at the level of policy-making. A half-dozen Americans and Vietnamese in the country with expertise on Vietnamese problems were being used only spasmodically—if at all—to research and suggest American policy alternatives. An example of the waste of resources: One of the most important Vietnamese authorities on North Vietnamese economic and political developments was being used as a translator for the Voice of America, instead of being assigned to research in depth.

Although there has been a great deal of discussion about the use of new information storage and retrieving devices in the field of international relations, they have yet to be put into use. For example, although the suggestion has been made innumerable times, the cybernetic system of recording and making available information on foreign political personalities has not been used anywhere in the whole spectrum of intelligence. An example might have been to program the history of the 40,000 or so Vietnamese political personalities on computers so that information would be available instantaneously when American diplomats were dealing with the constant flux of Communist agents and Saigon political figures.

A REDEFINITION OF ROLES

There must be a redefinition of roles of the various American agencies dealing with foreign policy. If, as has always been assumed, the State Department is to be the overseer of all U.S. policy abroad, then its power to control the other agencies, especially AID, must be enforced. So long as AID is funded directly by Congress and responsible for its expenditures directly to Congress— but not *through* the Department of State—then State's control will be only nominal. In theory, of course, this coordination now takes place at the level of the U.S. ambassador who is the President's representative to the foreign country and who heads all the activities of the various agencies—State, AID, CIA, and the military—in that country. But, in fact, directives from Washington by their own agency chiefs often carry more weight than the ambassador's authority.

The role of the Central Intelligence Agency is perhaps the most controversial of all the government agencies. But I submit that the controversy is in the U.S., not in Asia. Asians assume that all Americans, all Americans in residence in Asia whatever their formal job or profession, belong to the U.S. Establishment. The role of clandestine operations versus official functions is blurred there —not only because it is obviously more difficult to disguise, but also because of the assumption by Asians that intrigue and subterfuge are a part of relations between countries.

CIA failures in Asia—the attempted revolt in Sumatra in 1958 against Soekarno's Indonesian regime, the backing of "strong man" Phoumi Nosouvan in Laos—have left far less of a residue in Asians' minds than most Americans would suspect. Operating in societies where the great mass is inert, where a few individuals and families decide the role of government, some of the CIA miscalculations seem smaller in Asia.

Again, CIA, as the other American organizations in Asia, suffers more from the lack of "hired help." A hardened veteran CIA hand from the "wars" of eastern Europe's sophisticated Communism-anti-Communism brings little with him to Asia. And, with the exception of a few very notable individuals, the organization there has suffered from the same Eurocentrism that has dogged other U.S. operations.

Where is the coordination to take place? The whole problem is extremely complex. For example, if surplus food and agriculture are primary ingredients of any American relationships with India, where does the expertise of the Department of Agriculture on methods of increasing production, the availability of surplus food in the U.S., and general attitudes toward Indian agricultural policy feed into the over-all concept held by the diplomats of relationships between the U.S. and India? At the present moment, there is a hit-or-miss confrontation between these two elements all along the line from the cabinet to the relations between the agricultural attaché (paid by, and a part of, the Department of Agriculture's Foreign Service) and the ambassador.

Whatever the table of organization, no program of coordination will be effective if it is not administered by trained cadres who know their fields. Our own system in the U.S. is throwing in large numbers of technicians who know their particular fields as they exist in the U.S. The difficulty is the lack of expertise in these same fields in the foreign countries with which we are dealing.

Dr. Wharton writes:

> . . . Part of the explanation [for our failures] may lie in the extreme degree of provinciality which characterizes U.S. agricultural colleges and universities. Not only are the students and faculties usually unaware of and unconcerned with problems outside their state, they are even less aware of and concerned with the problems outside the United States. Therefore, adding and strengthening an international dimension for U.S. agricultural colleges and universities will do more than prepare them to contribute to the solution of problems of foreign agricultural development. Perhaps most important it will help to reduce the provinciality and "loco-centricity" of U.S. agriculturists and agricultural scientists at a time when the United States is being forced to play a world role—a world which is predominantly agricultural.

I believe that our training for these tasks can be only minimal, given the variety of problems in the various countries and the severe paucity of information. But it should be possible to fit foreign service officers for these jobs by giving them a broad general knowledge of the countries in which they will work.

A start has been made on this kind of program with the emergence in the post-World War II period of numerous "area study" programs in a large number of American universities. The program got a fillip from the National Defense Education Act of 1958, mostly aimed at subsidizing training in the so-called exotic languages. As I write, Congress has failed to authorize funds for the equally important International Education Act, which would carry this program further.

Yet I believe if the need for trained experts in Asian affairs over the next few decades, in the numbers they are needed, is to be met, this program will have to be expanded and coordinated with government recruiting.

While I have said earlier that most Asian observers are agreed that the Peace Corps is not an important contribution to the meeting of the Asia problems *per se,* it is a beneficial experience for

American youth and a testing ground for personnel candidates for the necessary bureaucracy that must be built by the U.S. abroad.

In time of great need, both domestically and overseas, for a wide appreciation of the domestic and foreign social problems the U.S. faces, I think it would be fitting and proper that a national service requirement be made of all young Americans. By a process of selection, on the basis of their abilities as well as their choices, I think each young American between the ages of eighteen and twenty-one should have to give one year's service to his country as a worker on such domestic projects as Vista, the volunteer program for social work in depressed areas, or overseas in the Peace Corps. Out of this would come a better understanding of American national responsibilities on the part of the majority of our young people reared in an atmosphere of luxury—by the standards of two-thirds of the rest of the world and by the depressed 10 per cent of our own population. And it would incidentally provide a vast new reservoir of talent and set up a selection process for recruiting members of the foreign services.

An essential ingredient of any massive attack on our problems in Asia is a program of closer collaboration with the Asians themselves on a personal level. I have been appalled over and over again at our lack of continuing contact at a personal level with Asians who have somehow been related to the American entity. We have neglected some of our most valuable resources in the struggle for a new Asia.

In early 1968, Prince Sihanouk complained bitterly that the CIA was using the three hundred Cambodian students still in the U.S., despite the 1965 break in formal relations between his country and the U.S. Unhappily, my own estimate is that the "plot" is not true. Not only have we *not* cultivated the thirty thousand foreign students who annually come to this country from abroad, but for the most part they have had to find their own way through the jungle of modern American life. This is particularly difficult for the Asian student, who comes from a totally different environment.

In part, Communist strength in Asia today is the result of the program of the Comintern which, more than forty-five years ago, set up the "School for the Toilers of the East," the Institute of Oriental Languages, and half a dozen other training institutions for agents in the East. The expressed purpose of these institutions was to preach Communist revolution and to organize cadres for the international Communist movement in Asia.

(Ho Chi Minh, then known as Nguyen Ai Quoc, was elected to the presidium of the International Peasants Union, the so-called Krestintern, in 1923. That year there were some 800 students studying the strategy of subversion and revolution in the University of the Toilers of the East, most of them Asians.)

It is easy for an American, with his much broader based society, to neglect the significance of a handful of well-trained and in-doctrinated young people. But had we begun to organize the young Vietnamese educated in this country after World War II into a cohesive force, they might well have provided the leadership for which we searched after the overthrow of Diem in 1963. Instead, the Association of American University Alumni in Vietnam was all but a paper organization. And by 1968, even, a significant number of the Vietnamese students studying in the U.S. were totally antithetical to our program and aims in Vietnam.

Much has been made in the press—particularly in *The New York Times*—over the limited attempts of the Central Intelligence Agency to meet the threat of international Communist subversion through the sponsorship of cultural groups. It is certainly arguable that the financing of these organizations might have been done through another agency of the U.S. government. But the charges have far exceeded the guilt. In fact, it is a curious truth that in several instances groups supported with these funds were instrumental and extremely effective in opposing American policy. (The Latin-American Labor Fund, for example, in part funded by CIA, was one of the chief critics of our 1964 intervention in the Dominican Republic.) Such a program of cultural and social activities is not only consistent with U.S. ideals, but absolutely necessary to a coherent foreign policy in Asia. Other ways than clandestine funds from CIA must be found to finance them.

Yet always we return to the essential problem: No mechanics

will effectively work toward the goals of progress, peace, and stability in Asia until there is a recognition of the enormity of the task and our necessity to take it on. This, given all the contradictory evidence, a small part of which I have tried to present here myself, is in itself an act of faith.

POSTSCRIPT

Articles of Faith

ASIA and its problems will be there in the coming decades, no matter what U.S. policy exists or does not exist to deal with them.

These problems are profound, arising out of Asia's long past. And I have tried to show some of the difficulties in meeting them.

But I have argued that if the future is dark, and that it cannot be otherwise given this heritage, there is hope. And I have argued that hope arises in no small part from the possibility of an effort which the Americans are uniquely equipped to undertake in the modern world.

I have argued that the U.S. has no real alternative than to turn her attention to these problems: They will not go away if we turn our backs on them. And inevitably, I believe, our very own security is involved in their solution. Should we fail to help solve them, in a world of growing interrelation and contracting geography, Asia's problems will destroy us too.

But I believe that there are also profound moral arguments for American concern for the coming catastrophes in Asia.

It has become fashionable in the past twenty years to talk of American "moralism," failures of American policy based on our too pronounced emphasis on moral values in international politics. There is a growing school of learned and lay students of foreign affairs who have argued for a more "realistic" view of our nation's role and its place in human events.

314

I cannot accept this thesis. I believe it is "impractical," to use the terminology of its proponents.

Our very success and our power have to a large part been based on our essentially romantic—if you will—view of our role in the world. The U.S. owes its origins, more than any modern nation, to a new expression of the human endeavor. Regardless of the inconsistencies, the hypocrisies, the very real vested interests and concepts which established the new nation in the Western Hemisphere spawned by European civilization, the concept of the U.S. from the very beginning was of a revolutionary character in world affairs. "The American Dream," with all that phrase connotes, was in its intense emphasis on equality of opportunity a new concept in the development of human society. It still is today in the world of The Bomb, the population explosion, and prospects for famine.

Nowhere did it have more impact than among the peoples of Asia, living as they had in hierarchical societies under despots from time immemorial. As I have tried to explain, I believe that today—despite all our mistakes, despite all the contradictions in our policies, despite all the new problems we export with us to Asia—the U.S. is still the most revolutionary factor in the highly volatile Asian development.

My critics may call this old-fashioned American chauvinism. They may charge that I am simply calling for a new version of "the white man's burden," for a new phrasing of the old *mission civilatrice française*.

There are, of course, similarities. Like the British and the French (and earlier the Dutch and the Portuguese), we are the harbingers of technological change in Asia. Our power is far beyond anything the Asians know or could muster. We dominate the world scene, much as the Europeans did in earlier centuries.

Yet there are basic differences which make our phenomenon something else altogether. We are pledged—however much we may fail to achieve it—to oppose racism, the foundation of the European empires in Asia. We are—with all the faults of the system—a nation governed far more by a larger number of our citizens than ever before in the history of the world. We are—to an extent we cannot yet delineate—the precursors of such a vast array of new technological skills that it is hard to conjure up what the world and the society of man will be like in material things a few decades from now.

We are pledged to an internal decolonialization, an effort to destroy within our own society the cancer of racism, or, if you will, colonialism, which has afflicted Asia for four hundred years. Slaves and/or racism have been accepted in most societies down to our day.

Those militants of the American civil rights movement who argue that we must leave Asian problems to the Asians, that we have our own tasks at home in cleaning up our own race and poverty issues, fail to see that these two issues are linked forever.

Our failure to understand and meet the needs of our Negroes and other minorities and our dispossessed (in relative terms) is part and parcel of our failure to understand the Asians. I doubt that we can make progress with the one without insights into the other. Conversely, I believe that to the extent we are able to meet the challenge of bringing the Asians into the modern world, to that extent we will also be able to integrate our own citizens of color and our underprivileged.

Just as the internal strains on our own society now make tenuous any American commitment in Asia and the world outside the U.S., so the pressure from the unsolved problems of Asia will jeopardize any attempt for us to turn our attention to solving our own internal conflicts.

It would be good, perhaps, if we were able to turn our backs on Asia, on the rest of the world and its problems, and devote all our intellectual resources and our energies to solving our domestic problems. But life does not give a nation—just as it does not give an individual—those kinds of neat, packaged decisions. Life is, after all, for nations as for individuals, the setting of priorities, the sifting of alternatives from rather bad and confusing choices, in this, a far from perfect world.

But, as a member of my family put it to me recently, who gave us the right to play God in Asia? By whose authority have we appointed ourselves the moral arbiters of the world?

I cannot answer the question directly. I can only point out that the choice is no longer there. Our very existence plays a role in the affairs of Asia. Unless you can foresee a total withdrawal of the U.S., a total break of all contact with the Asian continent, we will continue to play a role there even should we back away from political and military exercise of our power. Minor changes in the habits of our citizens—eating food out of more glass jars rather than from tin cans, a discovery in a test tube of a new synthesis for natural rubber, fashions in cocktail party nut consumption—affect profoundly the life of the lowliest peasant in some "far away" Asian country.

So I say that we are already playing a God-like role in the lives of the Asians and there is no possibility of ending it.

Given the range, the variety, the still unknown qualities of the enormous complexity of the Asian problems, it would be foolish, I believe, to talk only in logical terms of their threat and our need to meet them.

Such a vast complexity of fact, theory, and speculation leaves the individual adrift.

Only a fool, I believe, would not admit that his approach, if he has one, must be based on nonrational principles as well as whatever argumentation he makes. That does not call for metaphysics. But it does call for a statement as simple as possible of his articles of faith.

I have tried to do that here. And I would end a summary of my argument with quotations from the *Bhagavad Gita* and from one of the most influential philosophers of modern times, "That Individual," Soren Aabye Kierkegaard:

> When one sees Eternity in things that pass away and Infinity in finite things, then one has pure knowledge. But if one merely sees the diversity of things, with their divisions and limitations, then one has impure knowledge.
>
> And if one selfishly sees a thing as if it were everything, independent of the ONE and the many, then one is in the darkness of ignorance.

> If thou wilt not fight thy battles of life because in selfishness thou art afraid of battle, thy resolution is in vain: nature will compel thee.

Because thou art in the bondage of Karma, of the forces of thine own past life; and that which thou, in thy delusion, with a good will dost not want to do, unwilling thou shalt have to do.

. . . I would say that learning to know dread is an adventure which every man has to affront if he would not go to perdition either by not having known dread or by sinking under it. He therefore who has learned rightly to be in dread has learned the most important thing. . . .

He who is educated by dread is educated by possibility, and only the man who is educated by possibility is educated in accordance with his infinity. Possibility is therefore the heaviest of all categories. . . . When a person, therefore, goes out from the school of possibility, and knows more thoroughly than a child knows the alphabet that he can demand of life absolutely nothing, and that terror, perdition, annihilation, dwell next door to every man, and has learned the profitable lesson that every dread which alarms may the next instant become a fact, he will then interpret reality differently, he will extol reality, and even when it rests upon him heavily he will remember that after all it is far, far lighter than the possibility was.

. . . If you will understand me aright, I should like to say that in making a choice it is not so much a question of choosing the right as of the energy, the earnestness, the pathos with which one chooses. Thereby the personality announces its inner infinity, and thereby, in turn, the personality is consolidated. Therefore, even if man were to choose the wrong, he will nevertheless discover, precisely by reason of the energy with which he chose, that he had chosen the wrong.

BIBLIOGRAPHY

INDEX

BIBLIOGRAPHY ❇

THE effort to give readers unacquainted with Asia a broad-stroke sketch of the vast continent, its problems, and my own opinions inevitably has meant that many complex issues have been only lightly touched if at all. There are numerous reading lists available from the learned societies and the universities on any of the problems of the Asian nations and the continent as a whole. I am listing here, therefore, only books and articles which I have found particularly stimulating. In some cases, their authors have taken views toward problems diametrically opposed from my own. But I have included them since they do form, even negatively, a part of the continuing "dialogue" on problems so vast that there can be no pat "solutions."—S.S.

CHAPTER 1

BENEDICT, RUTH, "The Chrysanthemum and the Sword; Patterns of Japanese Culture" (Boston: Houghton Mifflin, 1946)

EMBREE, JOHN F., "Thailand—A Loosely Structured Social System" (*American Anthropologist*, Vol. 52, No. 2, April-June 1950)

FUCHS, WALTER, "The Chinese Jews of K'aifengfu" (*Tien Hsia Monthly*, Vol. V, No. 1, Nanking, August 1937)

LOTHIAN, A. C., ed., "A Handbook for Travellers in India, Pakistan, Burma and Ceylon," 17th edition (London: John Murray, Publisher, 1955)

BIBLIOGRAPHY

PASCOE, EDWIN H., ed., "The Indo-Gangetic and Brahmaputra Plains," from *A Manual of the Geology of India and Burma*, 3d edition (rev.), Vol. III, Ch. 37 (Calcutta: Government of India Press, 1964)

RAUCAT, THOMAS, "The Honorable Picnic," tr. by Leonard Cline (New York: The Viking Press, 1927)

RIENCOURT, AMAURY DE, "The Soul of India" (New York: Harper & Brothers, 1960)

SCHRIEKE, BERTRAM, "Ruler and Realm in Early Java," *Indonesian Sociological Studies: Selected Writings of Bertram Schrieke*, Part 2 (The Hague: W. Van Hoeve, 1957)

VAN LEUR, JACOB C., "Indonesian Trade and Society: Essays in Asian Social and Economic History," tr. by James S. Holmes and A. van Marle (The Hague: W. Van Hoeve, 1955)

WINICK, CHARLES, "Dictionary of Anthropology" (New York: Philosophical Library, 1956)

CHAPTER 2

FURNIVALL, J. S., "Colonial Policy and Practice" (London: Cambridge Univ. Press, 1948)

——, "The Governance of Modern Burma" (New York: Institute of Pacific Relations, 1958)

ISAACS, HAROLD R., "No Peace for Asia" (Cambridge, Mass.: The M.I.T. Press, 1967)

LEACH, EDMUND, "Minority Groups in Asia," from Wint, Guy, ed., *Asia: A Handbook* (New York: Praeger, 1966)

MUIR, RAMSAY, "The Making of British India, 1756-1858" (London: Longmans, Green, 1915)

SIVAJI, article on, "Encyclopaedia Britannica," Vol. 20, 1966

CHAPTER 3

AYUB KHAN, MOHAMMAD, "Friends Not Masters" (New York: Oxford Univ. Press, 1967)

CHAUDHURI, NIRAD C., "The Autobiography of an Unknown Indian" (New York: Macmillan, 1951)

CHOW TSE-TSUNG, "The May Fourth Movement: Intellectual Revolution in Modern China" (Stanford, Calif.: Stanford Univ. Press, 1967)

DUPREE, LOUIS, "A Presidential Autobiography: The Life and Opinions of Mohammad Ayub Khan" (*American Universities Field Staff, Reports Service*, South Asia Series, Vol. XI, No. 1, Pakistan: Dec. 1967)

FEITH, HERBERT, "Decline of Constitutional Democracy in Indonesia" (Ithaca, New York: Cornell Univ. Press, 1962)

GANDHI, MOHANDAS K., "Gandhi's Autobiography: 'The Story of My Experiments with Truth,'" tr. by Mahadev Desai (Washington: Public Affairs Press, 1954)

322

GROSLIER, BERNARD, and ARTHAUD, JACQUES, "Angkor, Art and Civilization," tr. by Eric E. Smith (London: Thames and Hudson, 1957)

HU SHIH, "Autobiography" (Shanghai: East Asia Publishing Co., 1933)

LIN YU-TANG, "Moment in Peking: A Novel of Contemporary Chinese Life" (New York: The John Day Co., 1939)

MINTZ, JEANNE S., "Mohammed, Marx, and Marhaen; The Roots of Indonesian Socialism" (New York: Praeger, 1965)

MOON, PENDEREL, "Strangers in India" (London: Faber & Faber, 1944)

NORMAN, E. HERBERT, "Japan's Emergence as a Modern State: Political and Economic Problems of the Meiji Period" (New York: Institute of Pacific Relations, 1940)

RHODES, ALEXANDRE DE, "Rhodes of Viet Nam: The Travels and Missions of Father Alexander de Rhodes in China and Other Kingdoms of the Orient," tr. by Solange Hertz (Westminster, Maryland: The Newman Press, 1966)

SJAHRIR, SOETAN, "Out of Exile," tr., with an introd., by Charles Wolf, Jr. (New York: J. Day Co., 1949)

VITTACHI, TARZIE, "The Brown Sahib" (London: A. Deutsch, 1962)

YUNG WING, "My Life in China and America" (New York: Henry Holt, 1909)

CHAPTER 4

CENTRAL STATISTICAL ORGANIZATION, DEPT. OF STATISTICS, CABINET SECRETARIAT, GOVERNMENT OF INDIA, *Monthly Abstract of Statistics,* Vol. 20, No. 9, September 1967

HANNA, WILLARD, "From Jail to Jail: The Saga of Tan Malaka, An Analysis of the Qualities Necessary for Indonesian Political Leadership" (*American Universities Field Staff Reports,* Southeast Asia Series, Vol. 7, No. 2, April 1959)

HATTA, MOHAMMED, "Verspreide Geschriften" (Djakarta: C. P. J. Van der Peet, 1952)

HOW, JULIE LEIN-YING, "The Development of Ch'en Tu-hsiu's Thought, 1915-38" (unpublished Master's thesis, Columbia University Library, New York, April 1944)

ISAACS, HAROLD R., "The Tragedy of the Chinese Revolution" (New York: Atheneum, 1966)

MAO TSE-TUNG, "Where Do Correct Ideas Come From?" (Peking: Foreign Language Press, 1966)

MC LANE, CHARLES B., "Soviet Strategies in Southeast Asia: An Exploration of Eastern Policy under Lenin and Stalin" (Princeton, New Jersey: Princeton Univ. Press, 1966)

NOMAD, MAX, "Capitalism Without Capitalists" (*Scribner's Magazine,* June 1934)

———, "Rebels and Renegades" (New York: Macmillan, 1932)

NOMURA, KOICHI, "Mao's Thought and the Chinese Revolution" (*The Developing Economies,* Vol. V, No. 1, March 1967, The Institute of Asian Economic Affairs, Tokyo)

ROY, M. N., "If I Were Stalin" (*Independent India,* Vol. X, No. 28, July 21, 1946)

STRONG, ANNA LOUISE, "The Thought of Mao Tse-tung" (*Amerasia,* New York, June 1947)

BIBLIOGRAPHY

TRAGER, FRANK N., ed., "Marxism in Southeast Asia" (Stanford, Calif.: Stanford Univ. Press, 1959)

WITTFOGEL, KARL A., "A Stronger Oriental Despotism" (*The China Quarterly,* Jan.–March 1960)

———, "Oriental Despotism; A Comparative Study of Total Power" (New Haven: Yale Univ. Press, 1957)

———, "The Chinese Red Guards and the 'Lin Piao Line'" (*Free Trade Union News,* New York, February 1967)

———, "The Russian and the Chinese Revolutions: A Socio-Historical Comparison" (London: The London Institute of World Affairs, 1961)

CHAPTER 5

BEICHMAN, ARNOLD, "The 'Other State Department'" (*Interplay,* July-August 1967)

COLE, ALLAN B., ed., "Conflict in Indo-China and International Repercussions: A Documentary History, 1945-1955" (Ithaca, New York: Cornell Univ. Press, 1956, The Fletcher School of Law and Diplomacy, Tufts University, and the Southeast Asia Program, Cornell University)

COXILL, H. WAKELIN, and GRUBB, KENNETH, eds., "World Christian Handbook, 1968" (London: The Survey Application Trust, Lutterworth Press, 1967)

"Directory of Protestant Church-Related Hospitals Outside Europe and North America" (New York: Missionary Research Library, 1963)

GARSIDE, BETTIS A., "One Increasing Purpose: The Life of Henry Winters Luce," with an introd. by Henry P. Van Dusen (New York: Fleming H. Revell Co., 1948)

JACKSON, HENRY M., ed., "The Secretary of State and the Ambassador" (New York: Praeger, 1964)

LEDERER, WALTHER, and CUTLER, FREDERICK, "International Investments of the United States in 1966," from Office of Business Economics, U.S. Dept. of Commerce, *Survey of Current Business,* Vol. 47, No. 9, September 1967

MILLOT, RENÉ-PIERRE, "Missions in the World Today," tr. by J. Holland Smith (New York: Hawthorn Books, 1961)

MORIKAWA, JITSUO, "The Oneness of Man and Universality of the Gospel" [Press Release] (Atlantic City, New Jersey: National Council of Churches, Dec. 11, 1961)

ORR, CLARA E., ed., "Directory of Christian Colleges in Asia, Africa, the Middle East, the Pacific, Latin America and the Caribbean" (New York: Missionary Research Library, 1961)

CHAPTER 6

BOUSCAREN, ANTHONY T., "The Last of the Mandarins: Diem of Vietnam" (Pittsburgh: Duquesne Univ. Press, 1965)

BRACKMAN, ARNOLD C., "Southeast Asia's Second Front: The Power Struggle in the Malay Archipelago" (New York: Praeger, 1966)

CHIANG JUNG-CHING, "Ho Chi-min and China" [Chinese language] (*Con Currence,* Vol. I, No. 2, Sept. 1967, Wah Mai Trading Co., New York)

"Excerpts from Remarks Made by Dean Acheson at the National Press Club in Washington, January 12, 1950, on Far Eastern Policies," in Trefousse, H. L., ed., *The Cold War: A Book of Documents* (New York: G. P. Putnam's Sons, 1965)

FISCHER, RUTH, "Ho Chi Minh: Disciplined Communist" (*Foreign Affairs,* October 1954)

GREENE, GRAHAM, "The Quiet American" (London: Heinemann, 1956)

HENDERSON, WILLIAM, and FISHEL, WESLEY R., "The Foreign Policy of Ngo Dinh Diem" (*Vietnam Perspectives,* Vol. I, No. 1, August 1966)

SANDERS, SOL W., "Crisis in Indo-China" (*The New Leader,* Vol. XXXVIII, No. 12, March 21, 1955, New York)

——, "Viet Nam Has a Third Force" (*The New Republic,* pp. 14-15, July 30, 1951)

——, "Vietnam's Gains Spur Red Terror" (*Business Week,* pp. 56-8 +, July 18, 1959)

CHAPTER 7

ABEGGLEN, JAMES G., "The Japanese Factory, Aspects of Its Social Organization," printed by the Free Press (Glencoe, Ill.: The Center for International Studies, Massachusetts Institute of Technology, 1958)

CHAPTER 8

CHIANG KAI-SHEK, "China's Destiny" (New York: Roy Publishers, 1947)

EUDIN, XENIA J., and NORTH, ROBERT C., "Soviet Russia and the East, 1920-1927: A Documentary Survey" (Stanford: Stanford Univ. Press, 1957)

HLA MYINT, U., "The Economics of the Developing Countries" (New York: Praeger, 1964)

REY, LUCIEN, "Dossier of the Indonesian Drama" (*New Left Review,* No. 36, March-April 1966)

"The Silent Slaughter; The Role of the U.S. in the Indonesian Massacre" [Pamphlet] (New York: Youth Against War and Fascism, 1966)

SUN YAT-SEN, "San Min Chu I," tr. by Frank W. Price (Shanghai: Commercial Press Ltd., 1929)

TARUC, LUIS, "He Who Rides the Tiger: The Story of an Asian Guerrilla Leader" (New York: Praeger, 1967)

TRUONG BUU LAM, "Patterns of Vietnamese Response to Foreign Interventions: 1858-1900," printed by The Cellar Book Shop (Detroit: Monograph No. 11, Southeast Asia Studies, Yale University, 1967)

BIBLIOGRAPHY

ZINKIN, MAURICE, "Development for Free Asia" (New York: Oxford Univ. Press, 1963)

CHAPTER 9

GORDON, MANYA, "Workers Before and After Lenin" (New York: Dutton, 1941)
MEIER, GERALD M., "Leading Issues in Development Economics" (New York: Oxford Univ. Press, 1964)
NAIR, KUSUM, "Blossoms in the Dust; The Human Factor in Indian Development," foreword by Gunnar Myrdal (New York: Praeger, 1962)
PINCUS, JOHN, "Trade, Aid and Development: The Rich and Poor Nations" (New York: Council on Foreign Relations, McGraw-Hill, 1967)
SANSOM, G. B., "The Western World and Japan" (New York: Knopf, 1950)
WHARTON, CLIFTON R., JR., "Economic Research on Rural Development in Southeast Asia" (Southeast Asia Development Advisory Group, 1966)

CHAPTER 10

"Asian Agricultural Survey," Vol. 1: Regional Report, Asian Development Bank, (Manila, 1968)
"An Asian Model of Educational Development: Perspectives for 1965-80" (Paris: UNESCO, 1966)
BERELSON, BERNARD, ed., "Family Planning and Population Programs" (Chicago: Univ. of Chicago Press, 1965)
BERG, ALAN D., "Malnutrition and National Development" (*Foreign Affairs*, October 1967)
BUREAU OF THE CENSUS, DEPT. OF COMMERCE, "United States Exports of Domestic and Foreign Merchandise, Country of Destination by Subgroup; Report No. FT 420," 1945-1950 (Washington: U.S. Govt. Printing Office, 1946-1951)
CHANDRASEKHAR, S., ed., "Asia's Population Problems" (New York: Praeger, 1967)
————, "India's New Population Policy," [Speech] Feb. 10, 1968, Tirupati, Andhra Pradesh, India
COALE, ANSLEY J., and HOOVER, EDGAR M., "Population Growth and Economic Development in Low-Income Countries: A Case Study of India's Prospects" (Princeton, New Jersey: Princeton Univ. Press, 1958)
DAVIS, KINGSLEY, "Population Policy: Will Current Programs Succeed?" (*Science*, Vol. 158, Nov. 1967)
DOMINION BUREAU OF STATISTICS, DEPT. OF TRADE AND COMMERCE, "Trade of Canada," 1945-1950 (Ottawa: D.B.S. also publisher, 1946-1951)
ECONOMIC COMMISSION FOR ASIA AND THE FAR EAST, UNITED NATIONS, "Economic Survey of Asia and the Far East," *Economic Bulletin for Asia and the Far East*, Vol. XVI, No. 4, Bangkok, 1966
FREEMAN, ORVILLE L., "Malthus, Marx and the North American Breadbasket" (*Foreign Affairs*, Vol. 45, July 1967)
HANKINSON, R. K. B., et al., eds., "Proceedings of the Eighth International Con-

ference of the International Planned Parenthood Federation, Santiago, Chile, 9-15 April 1967" (Hertford, England: International Planned Parenthood Federation, 1967)

HU SHIH, "Civilization of the East and West," in Beard, Charles A., ed., *Whither Mankind* (New York: Longmans, Green, 1928)

PADDOCK, WILLIAM and PAUL, "Famine—1975!; America's Decision: Who Will Survive?" (Boston: Little, Brown, 1967)

SCRIMSHAW, NEVIN S., "Infant Malnutrition and Adult Learning" (*Saturday Review*, March 16, 1968)

"The State of Food and Agriculture 1967" (Rome: Food and Agriculture Organization of the United Nations, 1967)

STATISTICAL OFFICE OF THE UNITED NATIONS, Dept. of Economic and Social Affairs, "Statistical Papers," Series D, "Commodity Trade Statistics" Vols. I, No. 10; II-XI, No. 4; XII, Nos. 1-15, 1-20 (1951-1962), Part II, "Exports" (New York: United Nations, 1952-1963)

———, "World Trade Annual," 1963-1967, printed by Walker and Co. (New York: United Nations, 1964-1968)

UNITED NATIONS ECONOMIC AND SOCIAL COUNCIL, "Development and Utilization of Human Resources in Developing Countries, Report to the Secretary-General" (New York: United Nations, May 8, 1967)

VANDENBOSCH, AMRY, "The Dutch East Indies, Its Government, Problems and Politics" (Berkeley, Calif.: Univ. of Calif. Press, 1941)

WHARTON, CLIFTON R., JR., "Revolutionizing University Education: Observations on Southeast Asia" (*International Development Review*, Vol. 8, No. 1, March 1966)

"World Survey of Education," Vol. IV: "Higher Education" (Paris: UNESCO, 1966)

CHAPTER 11

"Administrative Policy Speech by Prime Minister Eisaku Sato, Opening of the 58th Session of the National Diet," Jan. 27, 1968

AXELBANK, ALBERT, "Japan's 'Non-Military' Buildup" (*The Reporter*, Vol. 34, No. 1, Jan. 13, 1966)

BAGBY, PHILIP, "Culture and History: Prolegomena to the Comparative Study of Civilizations" (Berkeley, Calif.: Univ. of Calif. Press, 1963)

BINGHAM, HIRAM, "Elihu Yale, The American Nabob of Queen Square" (New York: Dodd, Mead & Co., 1939)

BOWLES, CHESTER, "A 'Marshall Plan' for Asia," *The Conscience of a Liberal: Selected Writings and Speeches* (New York: Harper & Row, 1962)

BUREAU OF INTERNATIONAL COMMERCE, U.S. DEPT. OF COMMERCE, "U.S. Foreign Trade 1966 and 1967 (preliminary)" (*Overseas Business Reports*, No. 68-5, Feb. 1968)

CHAMBERLAIN, NEVILLE, "In Search of Peace" (New York: G. P. Putnam's Sons, 1939)

CHRISTY, ARTHUR E., ed., "The Asian Legacy and American Life" (New York: The John Day Co., 1942)

BIBLIOGRAPHY

CHURCHILL, ALLEN, "The Roosevelts: American Aristocrats" (New York: Harper & Row, 1965)

DENNETT, TYLER, "Americans in Eastern Asia" (New York: Macmillan, 1922)

"Economic Survey of Asia and the Pacific" (*The New York Times*, Jan. 19, 1968)

ELEGANT, ROBERT S., "Crucial Arc of Countries on Periphery of China Favors U.S. in Vietnam" (*Los Angeles Times*, Nov. 19, 1967)

"Future Course of Defense Is Sato's Biggest Problem" (*The Japan Economic Journal*, Tokyo, Jan. 2, 1968)

GALINSKY, VICTOR and PAUL, "The Japanese Civilian Nuclear Program" (Rand Corporation, Aug. 1967)

HAYES, CARLTON J. H., and MOON, PARKER THOMAS, "Assimilation of the Mongols," p. 663 of *Ancient and Medieval History* (New York: Macmillan, 1955)

HOOK, SIDNEY, "A Pragmatic Critique of the Historico-Genetic Method," pp. 156-174, *Essays in Honor of John Dewey on the Occasion of His Seventieth Birthday, October 20, 1929* (New York: Henry Holt, 1929)

HUGHES, H. STUART, "History As Art and As Science: Twin Vistas on the Past" (New York: Harper & Row, 1964)

HULLEY, CLARENCE C., "Alaska, Past and Present" (Portland, Ore.: Binfords & Mort, 1958)

JOINT COMMITTEE ON ATOMIC ENERGY, CONGRESS OF THE UNITED STATES (90th, 1st Session), "Impact of Chinese Communist Nuclear Weapons Progress on U.S. National Security" (Washington, D.C.: U.S. Government Printing Office, July 1967)

KASSOF, ALLEN, ed., "Prospects for Soviet Society" (New York: Council on Foreign Relations, 1968)

LARSON, ARTHUR, "Last Chance on Nuclear Nonproliferation?" (*Saturday Review*, Oct. 7, 1967)

LOCKHEIMER, F. ROY, "A Note on Japan" (*American Universities Field Staff Reports*, East Asia Series, Vol. XIV, No. 5 (Japan)

"The Long Way Around" (*Business Week*, July 22, 1967)

MC CAGUE, JAMES, "Moguls and Iron Men, the Story of the First Transcontinental Railroad" (New York: Harper & Row, 1964)

MC NEILL, WILLIAM H., "A World History" (London: Oxford Univ. Press, 1967)

"Nippon at Our Heels" [Commentary] (*Electronics*)

"The President's News Conference, August 1, 1963," *Public Papers of the Presidents of the United States, John F. Kennedy, Jan. 1st to Nov. 22, 1963* (Washington, D.C.: U.S. Government Printing Office, 1964)

PRICE, ROBERT L., "International Trade of Communist China, 1950-65," *An Economic Profile of Mainland China*, Vol. 2, Part IV (Washington, D.C.: Joint Economic Committee, Congress of the United States, 90th Congress, 1st Session, Feb. 1967)

"Problems Concerning Natural Resources in Future" (Tokyo: Ministry of International Trade and Industry, Nov. 1967)

RAJAGOPALACHARI, C. (*Swarajya*, Jan. 16, 1967)

RANDALL, JOHN HERMAN, JR., "Nature and Historical Experience: Essays in Naturalism and in the Theory of History" (New York: Columbia Univ. Press, 1962)

ROYAMA, MICHIO, "The Asian Balance of Power: A Japanese View" (*Adelphi Papers*, The Institute for Strategic Studies, London, No. 42, Nov. 1967)

SCHECTER, JERROLD L., "Japan's New Bid for Leadership" (*The Reporter*, Vol. 36, No. 10, May 18, 1967)

"The Secret Behind the Steel Industry's Growth, A Round-Table Discussion" (*Asian Scene*, Tokyo, Jan. 1968)

SHERWOOD, MORGAN B., "Alaska and Its History" (Seattle: Univ. of Washington Press, 1967)

SHIMOMURA, OSAMU, "Japan's Economy in Ten Years" [Resumé] (Washington, D.C.: U.S.-Japan Trade Council, Report No. 64, July 13, 1967)

STATISTICAL OFFICE OF THE UNITED NATIONS, 1963-1967 editions also listed III-2 (369) for food exports, "1966 World Trade Annual" (New York: United Nations, 1967)

WEINSTEIN, MARTIN E., "Japanese Air Self-Defense Forces—Restrained, but Powerful" (*Air Force*, Dec. 1967)

"Welfare Society through Economic Growth," White Paper on the Japanese Economy (Tokyo: Liberal-Democratic Party, 1967)

WICKIZER, V. D., and BENNETT, M. K., "The Rice Economy of Monsoon Asia" (Stanford: Stanford Univ. Press, 1941)

WOHLSTETTER, ALBERT, "Illusions of Distance" (*Foreign Affairs*, January 1968)

CHAPTER 12

"Asia-Pacific Economic Sphere: A Step toward Realization" (*Asia Scene*, Tokyo, March 1968)

BROWN, LESTER R., "New Directions in World Agriculture," speech given at the Second International Conference on War on Hunger, Washington, D.C., February 20, 1968

BUCK, J. LOSSING, "Food and Agriculture in Communist China" (New York: Praeger, 1966)

FREEMAN, ORVILLE L., Secretary of Agriculture, Address given at the Second International Conference on War on Hunger, Washington, D.C., February 20, 1968

LYONS, EUGENE, "Worker's Paradise Lost, Fifty Years of Soviet Communism: A Balance Sheet" (New York: Paperback Library, 1967)

MC KITTERICK, NATHANIEL, "Diplomatic Logjam" (*The New Republic*, March 27, 1965)

OANCIA, DAVID, "Maoism Changes the Face of China" (*The New York Times*, April 28, 1968)

PANIKKAR, K. M., "Asia and Western Dominance: A Survey of the Vasco Da Gama Epoch of Asian History, 1498-1945" (London: G. Allen & Unwin, 1959)

"Report of the Committee on Foreign Affairs Personnel (Herter Committee)" (Washington: Carnegie Endowment, 1962)

SEGAL, SHELDON J., "Biological Aspects of Fertility Regulation" (unpublished as of June 1, 1968, Rockefeller University, N.Y.C.)

TREVOR-ROPER, HUGH, "The Philby Affair; Espionage, Treason, and Secret Service" (*Encounter*, London, April 1968)

"U.S.-Israel Desalination Agreement" (New York: Israel Information Service, October 1964)

BIBLIOGRAPHY

WHARTON, CLIFTON R., JR., "Southeast Asian Agriculture: A Critical Dimension of U.S. Foreign Policy," paper for Conference: "U.S. Defense Policy: Containing Communism?" (Boston: World Affairs Council of Boston and Boston Latin School, January 1967)

POSTSCRIPT

BARRETT, WILLIAM, "Irrational Man: A Study in Existential Philosophy" (Garden City, N.Y.: Doubleday, 1962)

330

INDEX

Acheson, Dean, 147
Afghanistan, 6
Africa, African, 4, 6-7, 21-22, 67, 93, 96, 216, 230, 251-52, 263
Agency for International Development (AID), 103, 105, 125-26, 128, 177, 303, 307-08
Agra, 111, 130, 227
Agricultural Producers' Cooperatives, 289
Air Force, 256
Alasha, 253
Alexander of Macedon, 39, 52
Algeria, Algerian, 183, 271
Allahabad, 23
All-India Congress movement, *see* Congress movement
All-India Radio, 53
Ambon, 7
Amerasia, 98
America, American, *see* U.S.
American Association for the Advancement of Science, 238
American Club, 50
Angkor, 37, 69

Annam, Annamese, vii, 34
Arab, Arabs, 4, 69, 121, 263
Armenian, 198
Ashoka, 39
Asia and Western Dominance, 70
Asian Development Bank, 300
Assam, 6, 207
Association of American University Alumni, 312
Atlantic, the, 4
Attlee, Clement, 169
Australasia, Australasians, 271
Australia, Australians, 4, 92, 161, 171, 244, 251, 257, 271-73, 300
Australian-New Zealand-U.S. military alliance (ANZUS), 271
Ayub Khan, 23
Ayudthia, 26

Baber, 52
Baghdad, 214
Bahasa, 55, 249
Bali, Balinese, 12, 44, 55, 81
Ballia, 206

INDEX

Baluch Rifles, 52

Bandung, 91-92, 230; Conference, 269; Technical Institute, 247

Bangkok, 19, 26, 46, 72-73, 89, 105, 111-12, 122, 179, 182, 214

Bao Dai, Emperor, 150-52, 172

Batavia, *see* Djakarta

Battambang, 38

Beichman, Arnold, 129

Beirut, 5

Belgium, 31

Benares, 53, 111

Bengal, Bengalis, 6, 9, 36, 77, 93-95, 129, 130, 214

Berlin Allied Control Council, 196

Bhagavad Gita, 40, 317

Bible, the, 23, 40, 69

Bihar, 221-22, 232, 240, 278

Binh Xuyen, 152

Bismarck, Otto, Fürst von, 74

Blitar, 81

Blum, Robert, 115

Bolivia, 133

Bombay, 10, 23, 40-41, 45, 76, 188, 235; University, 248

Borneo, 3, 6, 31, 33, 43, 94, 142, 221; *see also* Kilmantan

Boroboedoer, 59

Bowles, Chester, 112, 252, 269

Boxer Rebellion, 87

Brackman, Arnold, 140-42

Brahmaputra River, 6

Brahmin, Brahmins, 22, 24, 67, 104, 172, 197, 280

Brazil, 210

Britain, British, *see* England, English

British Broadcasting Company, 138

British East India Company, 83

British Indian Empire, 51, 94

British National Health Insurance, 250

British Royal Air Force, 3

Brown, Lester R., 296

Brown Sahib, The, 57

Buck, J. Lossing, 288-89

Buddha, Buddhism, 21, 26, 37-40, 112, 119, 157-61, 163

Bunker, Ellsworth, 140

Burchett, Wilfred, 161

Burma, Burmese, 26, 34-35, 46, 88-89, 91, 95, 179-80, 188-89, 197-98, 208, 217, 226, 232, 261, 265, 281

Business Week, 154

Cai Dai, 152

Calcutta, 4-5, 10, 23-25, 49, 58, 77, 84, 93-95, 120, 129, 188, 198, 222-23, 265, 280

Cambodia, Cambodian, 5, 26, 35, 37-38, 90, 148, 157, 159, 195, 232, 273, 301, 311

Cambridge University, 67

Canada, Canadian, 117, 241, 244, 251, 255, 300

Catholics, Catholicism, *see* Roman Catholic

Celebes Island, 31-32, 43-44

Central Intelligence Agency (CIA), 104, 110, 125, 151, 153, 232, 307-09, 311-12

Ceylon, 159, 208, 234, 242

Cham, 37-38

Chamberlain, Neville, 273

Champa, 37

Chancellor, John, 137

Chang I-p'ing, 51

Chang Kuo-tao, 78

Chao Phya River, 37

Chavan, Y. B., 41

Ch'en Tu-hsui, 97

Cherrapunji, 6

Chiang Kai-shek, 87, 154

China, Chinese, 4-10, 12-14, 16, 18, 20-21, 23-26, 29-30, 33, 35, 38, 42-43, 45-46, 49-51, 54, 60-62, 65, 68-70, 78-79, 84, 86-99, 119-20, 122, 125-26, 129, 134, 145, 147-48, 150-51, 155-56, 160, 170, 173, 182-85, 195, 198, 209, 211, 213-14, 219, 222, 232, 245, 251-53, 257, 259-72, 276, 280-92, 300-01, 304, 307; *see also* Overseas Chinese

Chins, 46

Cholon, 163

Chow Tse-tsung, 51

Christian, Christianity, 21, 23, 32, 40,

44, 69, 119-21, 158, 166, 179, 188, 197, 279

Christian Science Monitor, 150

Cochin China, 34, 51, 178; *see also* South Vietnam

Collins, J. Lawton, 153

Columbia University, 28, 163

Comintern, 79, 95, 97, 143, 312

Communist, Communism, vii, 5, 18, 20, 23, 33-34, 39, 42-44, 54, 60, 63, 68, 71-99, 114-15, 117, 119-20, 122-23, 129, 135-36, 138, 140, 142-54, 156-59, 161-63, 167, 169-70, 172-74, 176, 179, 181-85, 190-91, 195, 198-201, 208, 218-19, 226-27, 229, 232, 255-56, 259-66, 268, 270, 272-73, 276, 278-80, 282-88, 290-94, 300-01, 304, 307-09, 311-12

Confucian, 9, 18, 21, 26, 137, 158, 200, 271

Confucius, 62

Congress movement, 29, 39-40, 66, 93, 96, 208, 229

Cornell University, 185

Cuba, Cubans, 133-34

Cultural Revolution, 95, 270, 286, 289-93

Czeck, Czecks, 86, 267

Dacca, 129, 300

Daily Express, 57

Dai Viet, 160

Dam, Richard, 221

Da Nang, 106

Dange, 95

Davis, Kingsley, 238-39

Dayaks, 31

De Gaulle, Charles, 4, 115

de la Torre, Raul Haya, 118

Delhi, 45, 58, 104, 187-88; University, 182

Den Pasar, 130

Derby, Elias Haskett, 252

De Rhodes, Alexandre, 54

Dewey, John, 19

Diem, *see* Ngo Dinh Diem

Diem Bien Phu, 151

Djakarta, 18, 31, 44, 55, 81, 84, 92,

139-41, 146, 194, 230, 249; University, 232

Djogjakarta, 55, 249

Doc Phu Su, 178

Dominican Republic, 312

Donne, John, 10

Dulles, John Foster, 147

Dutch, *see* Holland

Dutch Labor Party, 82

Dutch New Guinea, 31, 82, 138-42

East Indies, 30

Egypt, Egyptian, 235, 274

Eisenhower, Dwight D., 64

Electronics, 254

Engels, 74-75, 85

England, English, 6, 13-14, 20, 25, 29, 31-34, 39-40, 42-43, 45, 48-53, 55, 57-58, 67, 73, 75, 81-82, 86, 90-92, 95, 108, 115-17, 119, 133, 136, 138, 142, 148-49, 155, 158, 169-70, 173, 185, 188, 190, 192, 196, 198, 200, 210-11, 213-14, 219, 221, 227, 234-36, 247-50, 252-54, 256, 259, 273-74, 315

Eta, 172

Eurasian, Eurasians, 55, 270

Eurocentrism, 283, 309

Europe, Europeans, 4-5, 7-8, 12-13, 15, 17, 20-22, 25, 27, 29, 31-33, 35, 39, 49-52, 55, 59-60, 62-63, 68-70, 75-76, 78, 81, 83-86, 88-89, 92, 94, 96-98, 105, 113-15, 117, 121, 125-26, 132, 136, 142, 151-52, 197, 210, 213, 225-27, 230-31, 233-34, 237, 247, 252-53, 255-56, 266-68, 270-71, 273-75, 283, 287, 291, 300, 309, 315

Famine—1975!, 245-46

Filipinos, 20, 32

Fishel, Wesley R., 156

Five Year Plan, 217-18, 221; *see also* Second Five-Year Plan

Formosa, *see* Taiwan

France, French, 13, 20, 31, 34-35, 37-38, 49, 51, 54-56, 60-61, 69, 72-73, 78, 86, 113-15, 132, 136, 143-44, 149-58, 162, 171, 178, 196, 198, 200,

France, French (*Cont.*), 221, 227, 232, 248-49, 251, 254, 258, 260, 267, 271, 274, 315
Francis Xavier, 7
Freeman, Orville, 245-46
French Indochina, vii, 150, 178; War, 54, 132, 152
Freud, Sigmund, 259

Galbraith, John Kenneth, 111, 166, 182-84
Gandhi, Mohandas, 21, 39, 66-69, 95, 170, 224, 236, 272
Geneva Conference, 152
Germany, German, 8, 15, 30, 54, 63-64, 76, 86, 148, 179, 220-21, 225-26, 229, 254, 256, 267, 271, 274
Gilgit, 52
Goa, Goan, 10, 197
Gomulka, Wladyslaw, 266
Gordon, Manya, 217
Great Britain, *see* England
Great Leap Forward, 260-61, 289, 291
Greene, Graham, 132-33
Gujerat University, 225
Gujerati, 53, 66-67, 235

Haka, 172
Han culture, 9
Hanoi, 18, 20, 34, 49, 54, 56, 60, 73-74, 113-14, 132, 147, 149-52, 156-58, 160-61, 163, 199, 292, 307
Han Su Yin, 280
Harvard University, 163, 171
Hawaii, 111
Heath, Donald, 115
Henderson, William, 156
Hilsman, Roger, 307
Himalayas, Himalayan, 6, 8, 52, 84, 183
Hinayana, 151
Hindi, 53
Hindi-Urdu, 53
Hindu, Hinduism, 9, 19, 21-23, 26, 39, 44, 49, 53, 58, 67, 77-78, 86, 93, 173, 183, 190, 197, 199, 208, 219-20, 229, 233, 268, 280
Hindu Kush, 51
Hiroshima, 72

History of the Awakening Ego in the Modern Era, 64
Hitler, Adolf, 95, 148, 227, 271, 273
Hitoshibashi University, 182
Hla Myint, 189
Hoa Hao, 152
Ho Chi Minh, vii, 143-44, 149-50, 153, 167, 172, 312
Hokkaido, 104
Holland, Dutch, 7, 17, 20, 29-31, 49-50, 55, 59, 62, 68, 76, 80-84, 86, 88, 92, 95, 136, 138-40, 142, 144, 158, 191, 198, 214, 230-32, 247-48, 315
Hong Kong, 4, 33, 84, 87, 150, 228, 260, 265, 274, 300
Hook, Sidney, 142
Howard, Roy, 155
Hsieh Chen-ping, 79
Hue, 159, 172
Hyderabad, 23

Ikeda, Prime Minister, 184
India, Indians, vii, 4, 6-10, 17, 20-24, 28-30, 33-42, 45-46, 48-50, 52-53, 58, 62, 66-67, 69-70, 75-77, 80, 83-84, 93-97, 99, 103-06, 109, 111, 116-18, 120, 126-30, 165-66, 168-71, 173, 182-84, 187-88, 192-97, 205-08, 212, 214, 216-17, 219-27, 229-30, 232-33, 235-37, 240-44, 246-48, 250, 253, 265, 268-72, 276, 282, 297, 301-03, 309
Indochina, vii-viii, 34, 37, 49, 72, 94, 114-15, 142-43, 146, 150-51, 184, 219, 265
Indonesia, Indonesian, vii-viii, 4, 7, 12, 16-18, 20, 25-26, 30-33, 43-44, 49-50, 54-55, 59-60, 68, 75-77, 80-86, 88-89, 91-93, 95, 97, 138-42, 144, 151, 154, 198-99, 208, 210, 215, 219, 221, 226, 230-32, 235, 237, 240-41, 247-49, 265, 268, 281-82, 294, 303, 309; *see also* P.K.I.
Indo-Pakistan subcontinent, 5, 36, 46, 51, 197, 219, 235, 250, 301, 305; war, 67, 237, 302
Indus Waters Treaty, 302
Institute of Oriental Languages, 312

International Education Act, 310
International Peasants Union, 312
Irrawaddy River, 46
Islam, Islamic, 22, 58-59, 76, 86, 138, 199, 237
Israel Israeli, 9, 232, 274, 297
Italy, Italian, 6, 13, 166, 255

Jan Sangh, 183
Japan, Japanese, 6-7, 9-21, 23-26, 28, 30, 33, 44, 50, 60-66, 80, 84, 87, 106, 116-19, 122, 124, 126, 135-36, 146, 148, 150, 154-55, 160, 162, 181, 184, 191-92, 194, 210, 215-16, 228, 231-32, 234, 236, 244, 253-63, 265-66, 268, 274, 276, 280-83, 289, 291-92, 294, 297, 299-304
Japanese Air Self-Defense Forces (JASDF), 256
Japanese-American Mutual Security Treaty, 256
Japan's Emergence as a Modern State, 61
Java, Javanese, 7, 16-18, 20, 26, 31-32, 43-44, 46, 50, 55, 59, 76-77, 81-83, 85-86, 90-91, 195, 199, 208, 214, 221, 230-31, 235-36, 261, 282
Jesuit, Jesuits, 7, 54, 58, 69
Jesus Christ, 69, 121
Jews, Jewish, 9, 22-23, 76, 118, 121, 137, 148
Johnson, Lyndon Baines, 111, 237, 245
Julius Caesar, 69
Jung, Carl, 26

Kachin, Kachins, 46, 172, 179
Kaffir, Kaffirs, 23, 42
Kaistes, 9
Karachi, 5, 23
Karakorams, 4
Karens, 46, 179
Karma, 318
Kashmir, Kashmiri, 67, 183-84, 302
Kennedy, John Fitzgerald, 34, 111, 114, 140, 160-61, 171, 237, 264, 307
Kennedy, Mrs. John Fitzgerald, 52
Kennedy, Robert Francis, 140

Kerala, Keralites, 22, 105, 121, 197, 221, 249, 270
Keynesian, 65, 209
Khan, President Ayub, 237
Khmer, Khrone, 38
Khrushchev, Nikita, 22, 195, 275
Kierkegaard, Soren Aabye, 317
Kiev, 5
Kilimantan, 31; *see also* Borneo
Knierim, George, 126-27
Korea, Korean, 21, 60, 124, 147, 154, 161-62, 181, 194-95, 300; *see also* North Korea, South Korea
Korean War, 113, 147, 153, 162, 258, 261, 304
Kuala Lumpur, 33, 42
Kusum Nair, 206
Kyoto, 64, 130
Kyushu, 65

Ladakh, 4
Lahore, 56, 219
Land Utilization in China, 288-89
Lange, Oskar, 170
Lansdale, Edward, 153
Laos, 5, 33-35, 37, 46, 72, 74, 89, 110, 153, 155, 161, 179, 282, 301, 309
Latin America, Latin American, 117, 134, 145, 214-16, 233, 312
League Against Imperialism, 76
Lee Kwan Yew, 32-33, 42, 90
Leimena, Dr. Johannes, 7
Lenin, Leninist, 75, 77-78, 85, 88, 98, 118, 287, 291
Leopold II, 218
Liu Shao-chi, 79, 98-99
Lodge, Henry Cabot, 137, 162-63
London School of Economics, 211-12
Luang Prabang, 35
Lubis, Mochtar, 85
Luce, Henry Winters, 119
Lucknow, 23

MacArthur, Douglas, 181, 255
Macaulay, Thomas Babington, 40, 249
Madagascar, 251
Madras, 5, 48

INDEX

Mahabharata, 21, 59
Mahalanobis, P. C., 169-70, 222
Maharastrian, 41
Mai Van Bo, 172
Malay, Malays, 7, 17, 25, 30-33, 38, 42, 50, 94-95, 141, 249
Malaysia, 5, 33, 42-43, 73, 90, 142, 191, 209, 228
Manchuria, 5, 260-61, 288
"Manifest Destiny," 253
Mao Tse-tung, Maoism, 79, 95-99, 260, 263, 272, 290-92
Marathas, 40-41
Marshall Plan, 125, 127, 152, 268
Marxist, Marxian, 61, 65, 70, 74-78, 85, 88, 98, 195, 209, 211, 218, 263, 286-87, 291
Maryknoll Fathers, 150
May Fourth Movement, 51, 78, 283
McCarthy, Joseph, 151, 184
McKitterick, Nathaniel, 305
McNamara, Robert, 265
Medan, 44, 294
Mehta, Ashoka, 250
Meiji, 61-62, 64
Mekhong River, 34-35, 46, 179, 301; Delta, 153, 157, 162-63, 167
Menangkabau, Menangkabauer, 31, 85-86, 172
Menon, Krishna, 84, 183, 269
Mexico, Mexican, 6-7, 86, 165, 295-96
Minahasa, 31
Moghul, 9, 40, 52
Mohammed, Mohammedans, 22-23
Mohammed Ali Jinnah, 67
Mohammed Hatta, 76, 89
Mohenjo-Daro, 6
Moluccas, 44
Mongolia, Mongolians, 6, 270
Moon, Penderel, 149
Moral Rearmament Movement, 28-29
Morikawa, Rev. Jitsuo, 121
Moslem, 9, 17, 22-23, 31-32, 35-39, 42, 44, 46, 56, 67-68, 92, 116, 120, 136, 220, 233, 238
Myrdahl, Dr. Gunnar, 170

Nagas, 28-29, 46

Nagasaki, 72
Nanking, 51
National Council of Churches, 121
National Defense Education Act, 310
National Press Club, 147
Ne Win, General, 89, 91
Nehru, Jawaharlal, 39-40, 46, 53, 58, 66-69, 83, 94, 97, 151, 166, 169-70, 182-83, 212, 220, 222, 229
Nepal, 5, 242
Netherlands, see Holland
Netherlands-Indonesia Union, 139
Neustadt, Richard E., 306-07
New Delhi, 10, 45-46, 49, 52, 56, 77, 80, 93, 96-97, 103-04, 111, 127, 151, 184, 188, 192-94, 219-20, 222, 224, 242-43, 277, 302-03
New Economics, 65
New Guinea, 59, 85, 139-40, 144
New Leader, The, 169
New Left Review, 185
New Republic, The, 151
Newsweek, 279
New York Times, The, 312
New Zealand, 4, 257, 271-73
Ngo Dinh Can, 159
Ngo Dinh Diem, 133-35, 149-63, 172, 178, 200, 211, 312
Ngo Dinh Nhu, Madame, 74
Nolting, Frederick E., Jr., 163
Nomad, Max, 74
Norman, E. Herbert, 61
North Atlantic Treaty Alliance (NATO), 255, 268
North Korea, North Korean, 94, 122, 146, 148, 292
North Vietnam, North Vietnamese, 16, 34-35, 78, 94, 123, 133, 147-48, 153, 158-60, 164, 175, 184, 198, 307-08
Notestein, Frank W., 234-35

Oancia, David, 290
Office of Strategic Services (OSS), 72
Offshore Islands, 90, 147
Okinawa, 122, 257
Opium Wars, 42-62, 213
Orleans, Leo A., 286

Overseas Chinese, 26, 32, 37, 42-43, 46, 51, 75, 88-92, 94, 138, 266
Oxford University, 53

Pacific, the, 31, 50, 113, 210, 253-54, 262-63, 274-76, 299-300, 304
Paddock, Paul and William, 245
Pakistan, Pakistani, 6, 20, 22-23, 35-37, 39, 46, 51-52, 56, 67, 77, 115-16, 128-30, 136, 169, 182-84, 208, 221, 224, 226-27, 233, 235-37, 240-42, 248, 250, 265, 281, 301, 303
Panay, 122
Panikkar, K. M., 62, 70, 282-83
Papuan, 139
Parsi, 235
Pathans, 6
Pathet Lao, 74, 282
Patna, 278
Peace Corps, 103, 128, 310-11
Peking, 5, 18, 51, 75, 77, 89-94, 96, 98, 119, 142, 145, 199, 208, 232, 260, 262, 266, 285-86, 288-90, 304
Penana, 43
People's Action Party, 32
People's China, 260
People's Daily, 272
People's Republic, 286
People's Socialist Community, 273
Perry, Commodore Matthew, 253
Peru, 118
Phan Huy Quat, Dr., 178
Philippines, 32, 88, 95, 121, 208, 250, 257, 296, 301
Phnom Penh, 26, 38, 172
Phoumi Nosouvan, 309
Pincus, John, 216
P.K.I. (Indonesian Communist Party), 85, 282
Poland, Polish, 170, 266
Polo, Marco, 69
Portugal, Portuguese, 7, 54, 158, 197, 274, 315; East Indian, 10
Potemkin, Grigori, 285
Prebisch, Raúl, 214
Prince Norodom Sihanouk, 26, 38, 148, 232, 273, 311

Prince Philip, 52
Protestant, Protestantism, 69, 103, 120-21, 159, 283
Pueblo, 122-23
Punjab, Punjabis, 6, 22, 56, 58, 80, 115-16, 222, 253
Pyongyang, 18, 122

Quang Ngai, 146, 174, 200
Qui Nhon, 293
Quiet American, The, 132
Quoc Dan Dang, 146

Rabindranath Tagore, 9, 36, 67
Rajagopalachari, C., 272, 279
Ramayana, 21
Ram Mohan Roy, 62
Ram oh dar Lohia, 173, 229-30, 284
Rangoon, 46, 91, 179, 198
Rawalpindi, 302
Reischauer, Edward C., 184
Rhee, Syngman, 161
Riouw Islands, 31
Rockefeller Foundation, 116, 295
Rockefeller, J. D., 218
Roman Catholic, 121, 132, 138, 150, 157-59, 161
Roosevelt, Franklin Delano, 253
Roosevelt, Theodore, 253
Roy, M. N., 75, 97
Royama, Michio, 257, 262
Rusk, Dean, 110
Russia, Russian, 4-5, 21, 53, 70, 74-75, 83, 85, 95-97, 184, 216-19, 221, 243, 253, 261, 264-68, 270-71, 291, 301-02, 304, 307; *see also* Soviet Union
Russian Revolution, 75, 78, 97, 219
Russo-Japanese War, 64

Sabah, 3
Sacks, Milton, 195
Saigon, Saigonese, vii, 37, 49, 53, 56, 105-06, 113-15, 132-33, 135, 137, 145-47, 149, 151-53, 155-64, 166-67, 172-73, 175-77, 199, 249, 307-08

337

INDEX

Sanskrit, 8, 36, 40, 53
Sansom, Sir G. B., 213, 256
Sarawak, 94
Sato, Prime Minister, 257
Schacht, Hjalmar, 227
Science, 238
Second Five-Year Plan, 169-70, 212
Segal, Sheldon J., 295
Seoul, 162
Seward, William H., 253
Shakespeare, William, 40, 248
Shanghai, 49, 148
Shans, 34-35, 46
Shenoy, B. R., 225
Shiva Sena, 41
Shivaj, Maharaj, 40-41
Shrivijaiya empire, 26, 77
Siem Riep, 130
Sihanouk, *see* Prince Sihanouk
Sikang, 288
Sikhs, 80
Singapore, 4-5, 20, 25, 31-33, 42, 50, 90-91, 191, 209, 228, 250
Singkiang, 288
Sister Theresa, 120
Siteman, Steve, vii-viii
Sjahrir, Soetan, 59-60, 68, 85, 144, 146, 191-92
Smith, Lillian, 269-70
Smith-Mundt Fellowship, 168
Soebandrio, Minister, 68, 139
Soeharto, General, 18, 249
Soekarno, President, 4, 7, 18, 26, 44, 60, 68, 76-77, 81-82, 84-85, 91-92, 139-42, 185, 231-32, 247, 304, 309
Soerabaja, 50
Souphanouvong, 72, 74; Madame, 73-74
South Korea, South Koreans, 146-47, 155, 181, 229, 236, 239, 257, 292-93
South Vietnam, South Vietnamese, 37-38, 53, 56, 114, 133-34, 148, 152-55, 158, 161, 163-64, 167, 172, 175-78, 292; *see also* Cochin China
Southeast Asia Engineering College, 301
Southeast Asia Treaty Organization (SEATO), 301

Soviet Union, Soviet, 22-23, 33, 52, 74, 79, 86, 88, 98-99, 133, 141, 144, 169, 205, 223-24, 227, 254, 256, 275-76, 287; *see also* Russia
Spain, Spanish, 54, 158, 256, 274
Spock, Dr. Benjamin, 19
Stalin, Stalinist, 77-78, 95, 97, 144, 147, 217-18, 264, 267, 271
State Trading Corporation of India, 83-84
States' Reorganization Commission, 40-41
Strong, Anna Louise, 98-99
Suez Canal, 33, 104, 274
Sultan of Solo, 81-82
Sumatra, Sumatrans, 20, 31-32, 43-44, 59, 294, 309
Sun Yat-sen, 29-30, 88
Suripno, 199
Swarajya, 272

Taeuber, Irene B., 286
Taiwan, 5, 87, 147, 154-55, 208, 222, 228-29, 234, 236, 251, 257, 259; Straits, 90
Takeo Naoi, 63
Tambu, Charles, 25, 268
Tan Malaka, 75, 97
Tan San, Nhout, 137
Tengu Abdul Rahman, 42
Thailand, Thai, 18-20, 26, 35, 37-38, 43, 46, 55-56, 72-73, 88-89, 94, 122, 154, 159, 179, 181, 190-92, 209, 228, 239-40, 257, 261, 265, 301
Thant, U, 140
Thich Tri Quang, 159
Thimayya, Kodendera S., 49
Thomas, Norman, vii
Thompson, Jim, 72-73
T'ieh-min, 51
Time, 279; Time, Inc., 119
Tokyo, vii, 4-5, 11-12, 14, 25, 62, 86, 105, 118-19, 148, 182, 184, 192, 274
Tolstoy, Leo, 218
Tomonaga, Dr., 64
Tonking, 34, 198; *see also* North Vietnam
Trivandrum, 105

Trotskyist, 144, 152
Truong Chinh, 54

U.N., vii, 5, 129, 140-41, 205; Economic and Social Council (ECOSOC), 250
University of Chicago, 170
University of the Toilers of the East, 312
Upanishads, 40
Urdu, 77
U.S., 9-16, 18, 20, 23, 25, 28, 33-35, 45, 50, 53, 56, 59, 63, 68, 70-76, 81-82, 86, 90-91, 93, 98-99, 103-201, 211, 218-19, 221-22, 225-28, 230-32, 234, 237, 241-47, 250-58, 260, 262-63, 265-69, 271-317; Air Force, 140; Air Force Association, 256; Civil Aeronautics Administration, 105; Department of Agriculture, 246, 296, 309; Department of Defense, 219; Foreign Agricultural Service, 105; Foreign Service, 109, 112, 128, 130, 305-06; Information Agency, 105, 110-11, 128, 138; Information Service, 145-46, 248; State Department, 125-26, 150, 153, 164, 184, 305-08
U.S.S.R., *see* Russia, Soviet Union
Uttar Pradesh, 45, 205-06

Venezuela, 179
Vientiane, 34, 179
Viet Cong, 146, 163, 166
Viet Minh, 54, 60, 72-73, 143, 150
Vietnam, Vietnamese, vii-viii, 4, 18, 20-21, 26, 30, 35, 37-38, 46, 53-56, 60, 72-74, 78, 88, 91, 95, 105-06, 113-15, 132-33, 135, 137, 142-46, 149-62, 164, 166-67, 172, 174-76, 178-80, 184, 198-201, 211, 249, 251, 267, 272, 280, 282, 292-94, 298, 301-02, 307-08, 312; *see also* North Vietnam, South Vietnam
Vietnam War, 113, 122, 198, 239, 304
Vista, 310
Vittachi, Tarzie, 56-57
Vo Nguyen Giap, 78
Voice of America, 137-38, 151, 308

Ward, Barbara, 10
Weber, Max, 70
Western Ghats, 41
Wharton, Clifton R., Jr., 168, 211, 310
Willkie, Wendell L., 269-70, 278
Wilson, Woodrow, 283-84
Wittfogel, Karl, 70
Wohlstetter, Albert, 274
World Bank, 225
World War I, 49, 215, 284
World War II, vii, 25, 28-29, 48-50, 52, 55, 58, 60, 63, 66, 72, 80, 86, 95, 97, 112-13, 122-24, 128, 132, 140, 143, 170-71, 181-82, 191, 205, 208, 210, 214-16, 221, 230-31, 235, 237, 243-44, 252-56, 258, 264-65, 267, 270-71, 273, 282, 292, 296, 300, 310, 312

Yale University, 252
Yun Kang, 119

Zinkin, Maurice, 190-91